TABLOID NATION

TABLOID NATION

THE BIRTH OF THE DAILY MIRROR TO THE DEATH OF THE TABLOID

By Chris Horrie

André Deutsch

First published in 2003 by
André Deutsch Ltd
an imprint of the
Carlton Publishing Group
20 Mortimer Street
London W1T 3JW

A catalogue record for this book is available from the British Library

ISBN 0 233 00012 7

The publishers would like to thank the following sources for their kind
permission to reproduce the pictures in this book:

Page 1: Lord Northcliffe - Hulton Archive/Getty images;
Hannen Swaffer - E.O.Hoppe/CORBIS
Page 2: The Daily Mirror front page 1918 - Mirrorpix
Page 3: Ruth Snyder; Harry Guy Bartholomew - Topham (both)
Page 4: The Price of Oil cartoon - Philip Zec/Mirrorpix;
Soldier cartoon - Philip Zec/Mirrorpix
Page 5: Hugh Cudlipp - Hewitt/Hulton-Deutsch Collection/CORBIS
Page 6: Cecil Harmsworth King; Harold Wilson - Topham (both)
Page 7: David Montgomery; Larry Lamb - Uppa/Topham (both)
Page 8: Piers Morgan - Peter MacDiarmid/Rex Features;
Richard Desmond - Peter Jordan/PA Photos

Every effort has been made to acknowledge correctly and contact the source
and/or copyright holder of each picture, and André Deutsch Ltd apologises
for any unintentional errors or omissions which will be corrected in future
editions of this book.

Typeset by E-Type, Liverpool
Printed in Great Britain
by Mackays

Chris Horrie is a former staff reporter, writer and editor for News on Sunday, The Sunday Correspondent *and the* BBC *and, in addition, diarist for the* Independent on Sunday *and* The Observer. *He has freelanced extensively for a number of national daily and Sunday newspapers and many magazines in the UK and USA. He has also worked as a television researcher, reporter and producer and is a frequent radio commentator and broadcaster. He is the author or co-author of ten books. He is married and lives in London.*

Also by Chris Horrie

Disaster! – The Rise and Fall of the News on Sunday
Stick It Up Your Punter – The Rise and Fall of The Sun
L!ve TV: Telly Brats and Topless Darts
Fuzzy Monsters – Fear and Loathing at the BBC
Citizen Greg – The Story of Greg Dyke and How He Captured the BBC
Sick as a Parrot – The Inside Story of Football Business
Premiership – Lifting the Lid on a National Obsession
British Monarchy Plc
What is Islam?

To Lotte, Tom and Clare …
Wait until the readers of the Daily Punctilio see this!

TABLOID NATION

"Like the music halls, they are a sort of saturnalia, a harmless rebellion against virtue. They express only one tendency in the human mind, but a tendency which is always there and will find its own outlet, like water.

"On the whole, human beings want to be good, but not too good, and not quite all the time."

George Orwell, "The Art of Donald McGill" – genius of the saucy seaside postcards, *Horizon* magazine, 1941.

CONTENTS

PART FOUR: TABLOID NATION

ACKNOWLEDGEMENTS

During my research for this book I sought to interview all the living editors of the *Daily Mirror*. All of those still alive who held the office before the paper was taken over by David Montgomery in 1992 spoke to me, some at great length and all completely "on the record". The current editor, Piers Morgan, refused to grant an interview, saying through his PR office that the *Mirror* was producing its own "official" history in the near future and that everything he had to say would be said to the author of that work. Likewise, after, it has to be said, a fairly staggering display of incompetence, the *Mirror's* corporate press office refused me any access to the paper's official archives (though they expressed confusion over whether such records were even kept). The refusal was on the grounds that "we prefer to work with the author we have chosen". So in this futile way the *Mirror* group tried to confound my innocent efforts. Futile because much of the important historical documentary information about the *Mirror* is available at Cardiff University as part of the massive collection of Hugh Cudlipp's papers kept there. Likewise the British Library's newspaper collection at Colindale and the St Bride's Institute Printing Library just off Fleet Street contained not only complete series of the *Daily Mirror* since 1903, but much other documentation and many rare and ancient books dealing with the *Mirror* and its personalities. I also made use of the modern records centre at Birmingham University, which contains fascinating original source material of the British fascist leader Oswald Mosley, including correspondence with *Mirror* owner Lord Rothermere in the 1930s and with Cecil King in the 1960s. My thanks go to the staff of these libraries, especially Alison Charles and her team at Cardiff who put up with me during my marathon sessions and who were extremely professional and unfailingly helpful.

My main thanks go to current and former *Mirror* employees, at all levels of the paper, some with distinguished careers stretching back to before the Second World War, who provided the bulk of the information for the book. All those currently employed by the *Mirror* would speak only on a non-attributable basis, as some feared they might be committing a sackable offence by speaking without permission. But those who can be named include the former *Mirror* editors Tony Miles, Mike Molloy, Richard Stott and Roy Greenslade. Ronald Bedford, Alex Jarratt and Douglas Howell also provided a great deal of help. In addition, I have drawn upon research and interviews I conducted for a book about the Mirror Group's interests that I published three years ago. At the time, the interview subjects gave me a great deal more background about the fate of the *Mirror* Group in the early and middle 1990s than I was able to use when writing simply about L!ve TV. So I wish to thank again Bill Haggerty, who spoke to me for the best part of a day about the *Mirror* under Robert Maxwell and about the arrival and impact of David Montgomery on the paper. I also want to thank members of the staff and student body at the University of Westminster and especially Richard Adamson, Rachel Platt and John Tulloch who read the manuscript and provided many useful comments. I am also of course grateful to my agent, Robert Kirby, at Peters Fraser and Dunlop and Miranda Filbee, my publisher at André Deutsch. Last of all my thanks, as ever, go to the ever-patient Clare and the increasingly impatient Lotte and Tom who put up with the horrors of living with an author trying to put a book together on a mad and engrossing subject while on a very tight deadline.

FOREWORD

No British newspaper has attracted such love, loathing and outright myth-making lies as the *Daily Mirror*. And no newspaper has been so protean in its transformations. Chris Horrie's book lovingly documents it all.

British tabloids are endlessly fascinating – by far the most interesting thing about the British press. Their interest lies in their turbulence, the vigour of their language, the violence of their campaigns and vendettas, their artful aping of popular speech and the rough music by which they celebrate and then mock celebrities in a patois that is profoundly subversive of authority. Media critics differ about the significance of this last tendency. Some argue that tabloid subversion is a sham, that papers offer no genuine social vision and no alternative to the power structures that they mock. Others argue that the tabloid style itself erodes all authority by its buttonholing, matey, I'm as good as you mode of address, which, however modulated by sentimentality or servility, always asserts its right to mock the mighty. Where would the royals be without the tabloids? The answer is – a good deal more secure. The lack of reverence for the great, the rough carnival atmosphere, the puncturing of the pompous – surely these are a peculiarly British part of public life, and badly needed, given the strength of the opposing tendencies.

Do newspapers have souls? One of the most debilitating aspects of debates on the press is the tendency to lump different newspapers together – and the most notable example is the tabloids. What this does is to deny the importance of organisational culture and the work of individual journalists. And history. Crudely put, the argument runs thus – because *The Sun*, the *Daily Mirror* and the wretched *Daily Star* are all small papers packed with sledgehammer headlines, big photographs, soap celebrities, human interest stories and sport and pursue the same readers and the same advertising, they all amount to the same thing. They obey the same economic laws. They're not newspapers, but consumerist magazines. They abdicate the arena of political debate – known to media critics as the public sphere – to heavyweight broadsheets such as *The Times* and *The Guardian*. Thus the media scholar Dick Rooney writes in 2000:

"There can be no doubt that the *Mirror* and the *Sun* have abandoned the public sphere. Editors, owners, and other practitioners can no longer sustain the argument that the titles are anything other than vehicles for non-serious material". (Dick Rooney. "Thirty Years of Competition" in C. Sparks and J. Tulloch (eds). *Tabloid Tales*. Maryland: Rowman and Littlefield 2000)

What the events of the last three years tell us about this is that 1) the public sphere is more complicated than that 2) it's perfectly possible to have extremely serious material cheek by jowl with lightweight trivia and 3) history works in mysterious ways. If the public sphere exists as an arena for national if not rational debate it does so as a field of possibility held in place by a competing mass media forced to respond to events. Some events are too big to ignore or trivialise. But the response to events is profoundly influenced by previous experience – in the case of an individual by memory, in the case of a society or organisation by what it believes its history to be. For, despite the mad proprietors and drunken hacks, the *Daily Mirror* also has a glorious (and yes, frequently over-hyped) history of campaigning radical journalism. Every so often, it recovers its voice. The *Daily Mirror's* sustained campaign against the US/UK during the war on Iraq is such an example. It went on for weeks. It went on for pages. It cost the paper 200,000 in circulation from readers who didn't want to be browbeaten. It was magnificently right.

As the war began the *Mirror's* front page bore the headline:

UNlawful
UNethical
UNstoppable

with a picture of the desert at dawn, with a tank entering stage left. When I showed the page to an audience in India, a few days after publication, they cheered.

The magic of Chris Horrie's book is that, in between the vainglories of Northcliffe, Bartholomew, King, Cudlipp, Maxwell and Montgomery, that history speaks. A paper that has accommodated the work of some of Britain's finest radical journalists, including John Pilger and Paul Foot, is revealed in unsentimental and compelling detail. Long may it continue.

John Tulloch
Chair, Department of Journalism and Mass Communication
University of Westminster

PART ONE:
Those Horrible Harmsworths

1 THE CHIEF'S MAD FROLIC

November, 1903, Fleet Street, London.

Alfred Harmsworth, the future Lord Northcliffe, the "Napoleon of Fleet Street" and the richest and most powerful man in British journalism, is sitting behind the mammoth leather and mahogany desk in the middle of his gigantic and fabulously ornate office. The room takes up the greater part of a whole floor of Carmelite House, headquarters of the *Daily Mail*, the *London Evening News* and several specialist magazines.

Before him at a respectful distance stands Hamilton Fyfe, editor of the pub and brewery trade paper the *Morning Advertiser*. There is silence. Alfred is evidently pained and finding it difficult to talk. For a few minutes he makes distracted small talk about Fyfe's paper the *Advertiser*.

Alfred then raises his head, stares hard at Fyfe and says: "How would you like to come to work on one of my papers?"

Fyfe, who is on the brink of being fired by the *Advertiser* and is desperate for a job, suppresses an impulse to jump across the desk and hug him. But he controls himself and, playing hard to get, replies: "Well, that depends on what arrangements can be made".

Northcliffe shrugs, sighs deeply and looks embarrassed and then nervously names the *Daily Mirror* – recently and disastrously launched as "the first daily newspaper in the world produced for and by gentlewomen".

He tells Fyfe that the paper had been "an unmitigated disaster" – the first setback in twenty years of unprecedented financial and publishing success. With a yet more pained expression Alfred says the *Mirror* has become "the laughing stock of Fleet Street".

"It won't do as a paper for women. The *Daily Mirror* has taught me two things," Alfred continues, wiping sweat from his furrowed brow with a massive silk handkerchief. "Women can't write and don't want to read. But we've got to do something with it. I should like to see what you can do." Fyfe took the editorship without hesitation. His first job was to get rid of the small army of female journalists hired from fashion magazines, literary publishing houses and the women's page of the *Daily Mail*.

"The change was made abruptly over a weekend," Alfred's cousin Geoffrey Harmsworth later reported. "On Friday night, the editor's room was like a woman's boudoir. By Monday morning the scene was transformed. Gone were the dainty wall mirrors, chintz curtains and Queen Anne chairs. Masculinity had taken over and filled the room with pipe smoke and cynical laughter."

Fyfe did not enjoy the process of sacking Mary Howarth, the woman chosen by Northcliffe to be the *Daily Mirror's* first editor and, in fact, the first woman editor of a daily newspaper in modern times. But at least she had the option of returning to the *Daily Mail*, also owned by Northcliffe, where she had been a fashion writer. For many of the others it was the end of the line.

"The poor things were squawking like chickens," he later wrote. "They begged to be allowed to stay. They left little presents on my desk. They waylaid me tearfully in the corridors.

"It was a horrid experience... like drowning kittens."

★★★

Alfred Harmsworth, the creator of the original *Daily Mirror*, was born in comfortable circumstances at Chapelizod near Dublin in 1865. He was the oldest child of a moderately successful barrister who liked the bottle and a forceful, highly intelligent mother, Geraldine, whom he worshipped. Alfred wrote to her almost every day, even in later life, and took her advice on every important decision he ever made in his life. He named the *Daily Mirror's* editorial offices Geraldine House and her image dominated his office in Carmelite House, headquarters of his first and most successful newspaper, the *Daily Mail*.

Alfred was educated at a minor public school in St John's Wood, London. He was hopeless at his studies, but was athletic and liked following modern crazes such as lawn tennis and cycling. He left school early and started work on an illustrated magazine for boys. He then progressed to the position of reporter on *The Illustrated London News*, a successful weekly picture magazine. In 1886, aged 21, Alfred was appointed to the editorship of the mass circulation *Bicycling News*. But he hated working for others and was soon planning to launch his own titles. Alfred's big break came when he stole some paper and used *Bicycling News* presses to print *Answers to Correspondents On Every Subject Under the Sun* – or *Answers* for short – his very first magazine.

Answers was an unabashed copy of *Tit-Bits,* which was the best selling weekly magazine of the time. The formula was the cheap and cheerful one of throwing together a mishmash of "amazing facts", a sort of scrapbook of bizarre happenings and madcap antics from around the world. The advertising strap-line on the front page of *Answers* promised the magazine would be "Interesting! Extraordinary! Amusing!" and the first edition contained such gems as "What the Queen Eats", "Narrow Escapes from Being Buried Alive", "How to Cure Freckles" and "Why Jews Don't Ride Bicycles".

The circulation of *Answers* began to grow, boosted by what turned out to be Alfred's most commercially valuable skill – the knack of thinking up clever and essentially un-winnable cash-prize competitions and give-aways, apparently offering the readers something for nothing. One of the first was an offer of £200-worth of free "life insurance" which would be paid to the family of anyone who happened to be killed in a railway accident *and* had a signed a signed copy of *Answers* about their person.

The break-through insurance gimmick was followed up by a prize competition offering "£1 a week for life" to any reader who could guess the exact value of all the gold in the Bank of England on a given date in the near future. The odds on getting the figure right were astronomical. But entry was free, postage was cheap, the prize was tempting and it was fun to do. The competition attracted 700,000 entries and sent circulation through the roof.[1]

Alfred's first daily national newspaper venture was the *Daily Mail*, researched, tested on thousands of potential buyers and planned for months before its launch in May 1896. The *Mail* was a big newspaper by the standards of the times – it had eight broadsheet pages and sold for a halfpenny. Alfred promoted it under the slogan "a penny paper for a halfpenny". Another advertising strap-line described the *Mail* as "the busy man's newspaper". The rule on the *Mail* was that no article should be more than 250 words in length. Alfred wrote to the staff of the paper, telling them that they were writing for an entirely new type of newspaper audience. State-funded Board Schools were for the first time "turning out hundreds of thousands of boys and girls annually who can read," he enthused. The *Daily Mail* was to capture them as an audience, just as *Answers* had. "They do not care for the ordinary penny newspaper," Alfred explained. "They have no interest in society, but want anything which is interesting and sufficiently simple." On the first day of publication it sold 397,215 copies – far more than expected or needed to make a profit. When the sales figures came in at the end of the first week Alfred turned to his brother and business partner Harold and said: "we've struck a gold-mine".[2]

Alfred made himself editor-in-chief of the *Daily Mail* and was thereafter known to all as "The Chief". But the day-to-day editing was by done by Kennedy "KJ" Jones, a hard-working and hard-drinking Glaswegian bully, feared by the staff in the *Mail*'s Carmelite House offices just off Fleet Street. Jones had learned his trade in New York, working for William Randolph Hearst's *Journal,* and was thus a veteran of the City's ruthless "yellow press" circulation wars.[3]

KJ had an unsentimental approach to news and in his dealing with humanity generally. Hamilton Fyfe, the man appointed to "drown the kittens" and save the *Mirror*, summed him up as being "an intelligent but coarse man with no charm of manner or expression". He once greeted a reporter returning to work after a major stomach operation by saying: "I knew you'd be all right. You never had any guts to begin with." He was also famous for having described the Dreyfus Affair – a French political scandal involving the framing of a Jewish army officer by anti-semitic generals – as "The biggest newspaper story since the crucifixion of Jesus Christ".

The Chief had introduced a women's section into the *Daily Mail* – the first of its kind in a national daily – filled with fashion, decorating and cookery features previously only available in the expensive, sixpenny, weekly women's magazines. The "women's pages" of the *Daily Mail* were so successful that in 1903 Alfred decided to cash in with a new daily half-penny paper aimed solely at women. The name chosen for this first ever women-only daily morning paper was to be the *Daily Mirror.*

KJ was put in overall charge of the project, which was promoted with money-no-object enthusiasm. The launch cost £100,000, with even more money lavished on assembling the paper's main gimmick – an all-female staff, described in the pre-launch advertising as "a large staff of cultivated, able and experienced women". Huge ads were taken out in the *Mail* itself reminding "sir" to buy a copy of the *Daily Mirror* for the wife at home. "No newspaper," Alfred later wrote, "was ever started with such a boom. I advertised it everywhere. If there was anyone in the United Kingdom not aware that the *Daily Mirror* was to be started he must have been deaf, dumb, blind or all three."

The launch of the *Mirror* was not smooth. Production jobs remained in the hands of men. In 1903, no upper-crust, "cultivated" woman of the sort promised in the advertising would have been thought capable of enduring the filthy, oily presses or the factory-like composing room where molten lead was poured into moulds and then hammered into shape to make the pages. KJ complained that the women fainted under the strain of meeting deadlines and had to be revived with a continuous supply of Champagne. His assistant compared the whole operation to a French farce with "women on the brink of hysteria rushing in and out all the time". The male composing-room staff, meanwhile, did not like working "under the appraising eye of elegant women in low-cut evening gowns who had just returned from the theatre to supervise the assembling of their works of art in the mechanical department".

The first-ever edition of the *Daily Mirror* was put to bed on time on the evening of Sunday, November 2, 1903. The Chief recalled in his diary visiting the composing room where he found KJ "in full swing" bringing the paper out. The first copies of the 20-page paper came off the press at 9.50pm in the evening bearing the next morning's dateline. "It looks a promising child, but time will tell if we are on a winner or not,"The Chief wrote in his diary, adding: "machines going until the afternoon; total 276,000."

The new *Daily Mirror* had all the hallmarks of one of Alfred Harmsworth's newspapers. It appealed to suburban snobbery and was filled with competitions and giveaway offers – the most enticing being a coupon for a free, commemorative, gilt and enamel Pompadour hand-mirror. The front page followed the style of *The Times* and other up-market papers and was covered in adverts. In the *Daily Mirror's* case they were for department-store dresses, cheap furs and perfume, corsets and Tiffany jewellery. The first edition's leading article was written by The Chief himself and promised that the paper would combine feminine preoccupations such as "the stitching of a flounce" and "the arranging of flowers for the dinner table" with political news such as "changes in Imperial Defence and the disposition of Armed Forces in the Far East", for example – and it would all be done in a way which would not cause "mental paroxysm".

But, despite the optimism of launch-night, there was doubt and disappointment over the quality of the paper. The otherwise indulgent Chief had berated his female staff for showing off by using foreign or obscure words like "soupçon" and "yclept" (meaning "named"). The main story in the first issue was the amazing news that the King was planning to drive a motorcar between Buckingham Palace and Windsor castle to go to lunch. There was a "news" story about Claridge's being a little overcrowded at lunchtime the previous day, and there were weather forecasts from Harrogate, Biarritz and Cairo (but not Huddersfield, Birmingham or Cardiff).

The longest article was a piece of uncharitable snobbery called "Other people's uncomfortable houses". It consisted of an anonymous woman railing against the trend toward tipping butlers, waiters and chauffeurs and complaining about the quality of hospitality she had received while traipsing around the "draughty and badly furnished" homes of her best friends. And editor Howarth made the error of calling the paper's regular column of gossip from Paris "Our French letter".

After the first day, sales of the *Daily Mirror* began to drop off dramatically. After eight weeks the paper was selling less than 25,000 copies. The paper was so lavishly staffed it was losing £3,000 a week, eating up almost all the profits from the *Daily Mail* and threatening to sink the entire Harmsworth-family publishing empire unless something was done about it.

Alfred later said he could not understand how he talked himself into "so mad a frolic as a paper for ladies".

2 THE POPE OF FLEET STREET

"**F**reedom of the Press in Britain," Hannen Swaffer told his biographer Tom Driberg in 1928 "is the freedom to print such of the proprietor's prejudices as the advertisers don't object to."

He was speaking from bitter experience. More than any other man it was Swaffer who had rescued the *Daily Mirror* from its disastrous launch as a ladies' paper, transforming it into Britain's first "picture paper" and pushing regular sales from 25,000 to just under a million in a few years. And more than any other man, Swaffer knew what it was like to clash with Alfred Harmsworth – The Chief – raised to the House of Lords as Lord Northcliffe, the press baron who owned it.

Swaffer was an extraordinary figure: a terrible, violent drunk who in later life campaigned for teetotalism, a composer of racist music-hall songs who backed the left wing of the Labour Party throughout his life. Swaffer was also fantastically scruffy – looking like the Wilfred Bramble character in *Steptoe and Son*, never seen without a cigarette dangling from his lower lip and avalanches of fag ash streaking down his shirtfront. Northcliffe, making one of his regal visits to the *Mirror's* factory-like offices, spotted Swaffer dishevelled and drunk as usual and told him to go out and buy a new pair of trousers at once.[4]

Hannen Swaffer was one of the first journalists to be hired by Hamilton Fyfe when in 1904 he re-launched the paper as a "picture paper", calling it *The Illustrated Daily Mirror*. Swaffer took the key position of picture or "art" editor, in charge of the photos and the look of the paper. The April 2, 1904 edition – the first brought out under the title of the *Illustrated Mirror* – featured pictures of King Edward VII, his wife and his children, Henry, Albert and Mary. The respectful poses and lumbering captions gave the paper a positive, wholesome – not to say grovelling – feel. Circulation trebled to over 71,000 overnight. The profitable love affair between the tabloid press and the Royals was born.[5]

Fyfe and Swaffer followed up this triumph with *Hello!*-style picture front pages and inside spreads featuring the lesser royals, society types, actresses and sportsmen, supplemented by photographic beauty contests, bonny babies and much-loved cats, dogs and horses. The paper combined sycophancy towards the rich and famous with campaigns highlighting child poverty in the slums. Fyfe caused a stir with an impassioned and tear-jerking editorial denouncing "Britain" for tolerating poverty and slum conditions in London, the Imperial capital, "a city where the death of a child through malnutrition can be thought of as normal".[6]

The *Mirror*'s new-found social conscience was mostly cant, however. Fyfe said in his memoirs that the paper was designed "not to supply serious information" but to provide customers with something to look at on their journey to work, "to entertain them, occupy their minds pleas- antly, prevent them from thinking." Pictures, he said, were easier on the eye than words: "Everything in the *Daily Mirror* was calculated to be easy of absorption by the most ordinary intelligence." Circulation reached 140,000 within a month of the re-launch. On the first anniversary the paper (now once again simply titled the *Daily Mirror*) was selling 290,000.

The paper forged ahead again in 1907 when Fyfe left the paper to be replaced by Alexander Kenealy who, like KJ, was headhunted by Northcliffe from William Randolph Hearst's New York *Journal*. Kenealy was in charge of the words and Swaffer dealt with the pictures. Swaffer used to look through hundreds of photos every day – supplied by the cottage industry in photographic agencies that had been spawned by the old, weekly, sixpenny picture papers like the *Illustrated London News* and was now boosted by the huge sums Swaffer was willing to pay for the right sort of pictures, generally those featuring accidents, disasters, crime, royalty or sporting heroics.

The pace was furious. Thousands of amateur snaps were sent to the paper; piles of mailbags were emptied all over the floor. Acid from the engraving rooms – presided over by Swaffer's assistant Harry Guy "Bart" Bartholomew – rotted the sewers in Fleet Street, resulting in a huge bill for repairs. The *Mirror* building's electrical system was still rudimentary and Swaffer and Bartholomew's experiments aimed at speeding up the block-making process – frequently carried out when they were both worse for wear from booze – caused the fuse box to exploded with an un- nerving frequency, leaving Swaffer, Bart and others working by candle-light.

Hamilton Fyfe's worthy campaigns about social conditions were quickly dispensed with. Swaffer started a "crusade", not about the housing conditions of the London poor and other intractable social problems, but a much more winnable and photogenic one – to improve the conditions suffered by pit ponies. Eventually, a reporter was sent to buy a pony, which the paper could therefore rescue from its "horrible fate of being born, living and dying without once seeing sunlight". Northcliffe agreed to finance the escapade on condition that the pony was shown at the *Daily Mail* Ideal Home Exhibition. It was and – as a bonus – the Lord Mayoress of London offered to buy the pony and look after it.

Swaffer's approach to photography was revolutionary. Until that point, photographs had been thought of as a simple substitute for illustration. Cameras were bulky machines and exposure meant that subjects had to remain completely still. Swaffer worked with Harry Guy Bartholomew and other technical experts to make cameras more portable and to treat film so that it needed less exposure time. Swaffer wanted action shots and he encouraged his photographers to get into dangerous situations. A team of *Mirror* photographers became the first humans to climb inside the smoking mouth of Mount Vesuvius; another of Swaffer's photographic daredevils became the first man, apart from the crew, to fly on board a Zeppelin airship. Other picture-led triumphs included a pictorial memorial edition produced to honour General Booth, the founder of the Salvation Army – the first edition of the *Mirror* to sell over a million copies. And there were pictures of the funeral of the Emperor of Japan and the coronation of the King of Siam – fabulously exotic creatures to the mass audience in 1900s Britain.[7]

Kenealy likewise specialised in stunts – the sort of "make your own news" approach he had learned from Hearst in New York. These ranged from the po-faced and serious – such as the decision to send a reporter to experience and write about the horrors of travelling with immigrants in steerage class from Liverpool to New York – to the merely attention-grabbing. He put a beehive on the roof of Carmelite House to prove that it was possible to make honey even in the middle of London. When this was proved to be the case 50,000 "*Daily Mirror* bees" were coated in white flour so they could be identified. The hunt to find a "*Daily Mirror* bee" became a craze in the summer of 1909. Many stunts sprang from readers' letters to the paper. The *Mirror* offered £5 for "useful suggestions" on how the paper should be improved. Two hundred and fifty prizes were given away – but all the ideas were useless. One included perfuming the pages with a different fragrance every day. Another was that individual articles should be perforated so they could be torn out and read separately.[8]

The paper's greatest scoop in these early years was the bold step of printing exclusive deathbed pictures of the body of King Edward VII, the playboy son of Queen Victoria. Swaffer and Kenealy had been in The Falstaff, the office pub at the time, a few days after the King's funeral on May 14, 1910, when they overheard two reporters from the *Daily Express* yapping about a set of final pictures of the King, taken at the moment of his death. They were wondering whether to write a story about the fact that the pictures had been taken. Swaffer worked out that, if the pictures existed, they must have been taken by William Downey, the official court photographer since the time of Queen Victoria. He turned to Kenealy and demanded: "Give me a hundred pounds in cash". An hour later, he had the pictures in the office.

The most dramatic shot – a close-up of the dead king's head resting on a pillow, looking skeletal but peaceful – was printed poster-size on the *Mirror*'s front page with Swaffer's caption hinting at the late King's infidelity: "White Roses. The Queen Mother's last tribute of love laid beside her dead husband." The paper sold out the minute it arrived on the news stands. Extra editions were rushed out, but there was no way of satisfying demand. Within hours copies of the halfpenny paper were changing hands at black-market prices – as much a shilling. The morning after the King's funeral the picture was run again. This time the *Mirror* was ready and kept its three lines of presses running night and day, supplying what was then a world record newspaper sale of 2,013,000 copies.

All Fleet Street waited for the reaction from Buckingham Palace. On the face of it, this was an astonishing intrusion into the family's grief. The pictures were private and could only have been stolen or bought by bribing a royal servant. Some thought that the *Mirror* would be arraigned for treason. Swaffer and Kenealy relished the prospect of going to the Tower. It would do a world of good for circulation – providing an ideal excuse for reprinting the pictures – new readers would need to see what all the fuss was about. Instead, Queen Alexandra emerged to say she had allowed the *Mirror* to print the royal deathbed pictures because it was her "favourite paper".

However, The Chief was coming to dislike the paper more and more. Northcliffe would frequently complain that the *Mirror* was "a ghastly mess" – especially on nights when Swaffer had simply jammed a hotch-potch of pictures on to the front page. But he could not afford to ignore the leaps in sales every time Swaffer came up with a really sensational set of pictures. The *Daily Mail* went to press earlier in the evening than the *Daily Mirror* and Northcliffe ordered Swaffer to offer his pictures first to the *Mail*. Swaffer hated this arrangement and he would conspire with his assistant Bartholomew to stop the *Mail* getting their best pictures. Once, Bartholomew smashed a photographic plate with his fist so that it could not be used by the *Mail* after he had finished using it to make plates for the *Mirror*. The act was so violent that he cut his hand and the blood flowed freely.

Like Swaffer, Kenealy could turn nasty when he was drunk and was famous for having hospitalised a cartoonist and causing $500 worth of damage during a fight in a New York bar. Physically, Kenealy was completely unlike the gaunt, tall, stick-thin Swaffer. He was a short and round neurotic man with a nervous cough and habit of tearing up pieces of paper as he talked at his desk, scattering them over his blotter and then carefully scooping them up and dropping them in a wastepaper basket. Kenealy told everyone that he thought Swaffer was insane. Sometimes they would be found arguing in Kenealy's cubicle, the shouting and swearing mounting steadily in volume and violence and ending up sometimes with chairs or punches being thrown, after which they would go to the pub and get drunk together, perhaps brawling again in the street before finally staggering back to the office – steaming drunk – to see how their respective deputies were getting on with the business of actually bringing the paper out.

Swaffer's rows with Northcliffe and fights with Kenealy were getting worse and more frequent. A new low was reached with a blistering row over the way the *Mirror* should handle the sinking of the *Titanic*. Swaffer read about the disaster on the news wires early on the morning of April 15, 1912, at the end of a long night spent drinking and playing cards in his office (Swaffer kept a bed in a sort of cupboard off the composing room and only rarely bothered to go home to his wife or to change his often filthy clothes). The problem was that the *Mirror* only had the official publicity pictures of the liner on file – and all the other papers would have them as well. Swaffer then remembered he had seen a set of 50 pictures of the *Titanic* in a photographer's shop in the Edgware Road. Realising the pictures would now be worth a fortune he rushed round and bought the lot before from the astonished shopkeeper before he heard the news.

Swaffer wanted to use every page in the paper – including the back – to display his *Titanic* pictures, but Northcliffe over-ruled him, claiming that such an important news story needed a well-written news report. Swaffer made the mistake of threatening to hit Northcliffe – a man who hitherto regarded even a raised eyebrow as insubordination, and failure to say good morning in the correct way as grounds for dismissal. But The Chief was prepared to take it from "The Poet" (as he sometimes called Swaffer in tribute to his bohemian ways) – so long as his will prevailed. There were no pictures of the *Titanic* on the back page of the *Mirror*. Even so, the next day the paper had far more pictures of the stricken liner than any rival and the sales again soared.

By now Swaffer felt that it was he – and not Kenealy – who ran the *Mirror* and who was responsible for its success and its profits. He began to complain about this constantly, demanding from The Chief the sacking of Kenealy and a big pay increase for himself. At the same time, his personal life was becoming more chaotic than ever and his drinking worse.

Swaffer was famous for cruising West End haunts like the Promenade

Bar at the Empire Theatre – once (but no longer) a famous haunt of gays and both male and female prostitutes in Leicester Square. "The extraordinary thing about it was that he very seldom reeled as he walked," an associate wrote. "He moved with tremendous dignity and with steady gait, standing upright and erect as a soldier until he either fell over backwards or flat on his face and passed out." Another said: "His grim, set, thin face was always a sickly pallor with eyes that glinted out of red sockets. He had a fierceness which hardly seemed of this world – a relentless implacable fierceness."

When after a particularly vicious drunken brawl Swaffer was barred from the Promenade Bar he ran a successful press campaign to have the Empire Theatre closed down. Swaffer wrote that his former watering hole was in fact "a den of vice, a sink of iniquity where ordinary, decent people cannot safely walk into the theatre without being accosted by all the riff-raff of the town. The good name of British theatre is at stake…"

The beginning of the end between Swaffer and Northcliffe came with a row over pictures of boxing and race riots. Swaffer produced what he believed to be "the perfect *Daily Mirror*" with no fewer than thirty exclusive photographs of the July 1910 heavyweight championship fight between Jack Johnson and Jim Jeffries in Reno, Arizona. Quite apart from the sporting aspect of the fight, there were sexual and racial overtones. Johnson, a black man, had scandalised America by keeping a series of white mistresses and his opponent, Jeffries, was a white man – "the great white hope" who, in the official promotional material for the bout, said his job was to "restore the athletic superiority of the white race". Johnson's victory triggered some of the worst racial violence in American history, with riots in dozens of cities, hundreds injured and several killed.

Swaffer signed off the paper's visual coverage of this "perfect" cocktail of violence, gambling, race and sex and then went drinking at a nightclub. He was tracked down and telephoned by Northcliffe who yelled: "I won't have one of those disgraceful fight pictures in my paper". It transpired that the advertisers had objected. Swaffer told him that if he wanted it changed he had better do it himself.

Soon after this, Swaffer annoyed Northcliffe even more by demanding that the paper's photographers should get more money. The photographers, paid only £3 a week, dared not confront Northcliffe themselves and left Swaffer to take up their cause. "You are a troublemaker," Northcliffe raged. Feeling that his time on the *Mirror* was running out, Swaffer then "sacked himself" and joined the rival *Daily Sketch*. There, he took a delight in scooping the *Mirror*, but in fact only lasted a year before landing a libel writ and leaving the paper to follow a diverse freelance career as a feature writer, theatre critic (unsurprisingly, so full of spite and vituperation that he was banned from many theatres) and columnist. Eventually, he gave up drink and embraced spiritualism, conducting a series of interviews with famous dead people "on the other side".

Swaffer's final revenge on Northcliffe came after The Chief's death in 1922. He published a book that purported to contain a long conversation with The (deceased) Chief transmitted through a medium, the gist of which was that Northcliffe had been entirely wrong and Swaffer had been utterly correct in every one of their many disagreements over the *Daily Mirror*. This amazing work, called *Northcliffe's Return*, remains a classic and a bestseller in psychic circles.

For a time in the 1930s Swaffer claimed to be the most famous and successful journalist in the world. He wrote and was paid for more than one million words a year and his work became increasingly left wing. He was an early and trenchant critic of fascism and he abandoned his earlier racism and became the strongest advocate in the British press of the American opera singer Paul Robeson, crusading for his right to kiss a white woman on stage during a performance of Verdi's *Othello*. Swaffer's freelance columns were printed in dozens of papers on four continents. He advertised himself as "the journalist with 20 million readers". Because of his spiritualist activities and later his general air of sanctimonious self-righteousness he picked up a new nickname – "The Pope of Fleet Street". After he died, the annual awards for excellence in British journalism were named after him until, in the 1970s, everyone forgot who he was.

Over the years there has been a lot of debate over the direct political influence wielded by newspapers and their owners. In the period after the Second World War, at least, it is hard to find examples of laws enacted solely and unambiguously in response to the demands of newspaper owners or journalists.

The exception is the 1946 Witchcraft Act which repealed – in those days before the abolition of hanging – the penalty of death by burning at the stake for psychics, dream interpreters, tarot-card readers and soothsayers.

The Act was repealed by a Labour government as a direct and explicit favour to Hannen Swaffer, the Pope of Fleet Street and the journalist who more than anyone else created the tradition of photojournalism which was to be – in an age before television and even movies – the very corner-stone of the *Daily Mirror* and tabloid journalism throughout the world.

3 GHOULS, CRIMINALS... ANIMALS BENEATH CONTEMPT

In 1905 Alfred Harmsworth had been elevated to the House of Lords as Baron Northcliffe after donating money and giving political support to the Liberal Party. On his fortieth birthday, already one of the richest men in the country, he had decided that politics and not newspapers was his ultimate destiny.

But the new Lord Northcliffe had no ambition to become Prime Minister. That carried the danger of being voted out of office. Instead, he saw himself as a potential kingmaker, using the opinion-forming power of his newspapers to pull strings behind the scenes.

Lord Salisbury's quip that Northcliffe was a man who created newspapers "written by office boys to be read by office boys" still rankled. Ownership of the *Mail* and, especially, the *Mirror* was becoming more and more of an embarrassment. After outrages like Swaffer's boxing pictures, Northcliffe's mother Geraldine would complain to him directly. She once sent a cable to him in New York saying: "I cannot make up my mind which of your two principal papers is the more vulgar this morning."

In 1905, the year of his ennoblement, Northcliffe had bought the "serious" but loss-making *Sunday Observer* as part of his quest for political influence and establishment acceptance. Three years later he bought *The Times* – the only paper in the country that was reputedly read by the King, the Prime Minister and the Archbishop of Canterbury. Ideally, he would have disposed of the *Mail* but he could not afford to, because he needed the profits to pay for the thundering losses made by *The Times*. Instead, he resolved to make the *Mail* a more "serious" paper and sell off the *Mirror*.

The *Mirror* was beyond redemption. The very idea of a "picture paper" was beyond the pale in polite society – seen as a violent, hopelessly vulgar and an essentially low American colonial intrusion into British life. In the years before the First World War all journalists (except the "gentlemen from *The Times*") were seen as horrible and uncouth people. But the photographers who made up the bulk of the workforce on a "picture paper" like the *Mirror* were even worse. They could be set upon in the street as "peeping Toms" and "ghouls" if they turned up at the scene of train crash or similar disaster. Swaffer later recalled how "reporters from *The Times* would not speak to a press photographer and especially not to us. They worked for penny papers. We were a halfpenny, and a picture paper. It was a dreadful crime. In those days the photographer was regarded as an animal beneath contempt".

For Northcliffe, the lightweight *Mirror* did not have anything like the same political clout as *The Times*. It still had a high proportion of women readers – and they did not even have the vote. Its less-educated working-class readers of either sex – attracted by the pictures, sensationalism and simple writing – did not yet have a political party to represent them. The *Mirror* was "a good paper for cab drivers," Northcliffe would say. "The *Mirror* does not count as a real newspaper," he would then complain, partly to explain why it had caught up with and then overtaken the sales of his beloved, but increasingly staid and respectable *Daily Mail*.[9]

Northcliffe began to cut his links with the *Mirror* in 1910, soon after Swaffer had printed the deathbed pictures of Edward VII. The Chief floated the *Mirror* on the stock market, raising capital for investment in the *Mail* and *The Times*. Four years later, on the eve of the First World War in 1914, Northcliffe sold his remaining, controlling block of shares to his younger brother, Harold Harmsworth, who was raised to the peerage as Lord Rothermere in the same year. The sale price was £100,000 – the exact sum he had lost on the original launch of the paper. Northcliffe said he was glad to be rid of the *Mirror* – his "bastard offspring".

Rothermere had none of the bombastic charm or flair of his older brother. He was profoundly ugly, with droopy eyes and heavy jowls – features that in later life made him look like a dyspeptic bulldog. His role in the Harmsworth family had been that of book-keeper and economiser, keeping accounts for his older brother's publishing ventures right from the start with *Answers*. He had little interest in journalists or newspapers – except as a source of cash that could be used to speculate on the London and New York stock exchanges.

Rothermere was a stingy man – obsessed with the cost of glue and string. It was later said that the whole Harmsworth press empire was built on Rothermere "shrewdly investing what he had saved on paperclips" used by his older brother and his editors. But it was not all frugality: in private Rothermere enjoyed the high life and kept a series of mistresses.

He was always ready to spend heavily in order to avoid complications in his private life. When he had trouble with one of his mistresses, he tried to pay his cousin £10,000 to take her off his hands by marrying her, complaining that "old mistresses are more expensive than old masters". He used the *Mirror* to nakedly hype or denigrate shares he planned to sell or buy and to boost or destroy the theatrical careers of his mistresses.

Under Rothermere, the *Mirror* suffered sudden budget cuts, self-defeating economy drives and constant editorial interference. The outbreak of the First World War meant Rothermere was more preoccupied with stock market speculation and with his job as the first Minister for Aircraft than with the detailed editing of his newspaper. The Air Ministry job was the latest gift from Lloyd George, the Liberal politician who the Harmsworth brothers had helped into power and who had given Rothermere his peerage.[10]

After Swaffer left the paper his assistant and – in effect – apprentice Harry Guy Bartholomew had taken over as picture editor and continued his mentor's brilliant run of success. The First World War was a gift to Bartholomew and a picture paper like the *Mirror*. The paper's circulation of 1.2 million just before the war jumped to 1.7 million in the first year of fighting. Ed Flynn, the editor who had taken over when Kenealy died in 1915, set out to make the *Mirror* "the forces paper" and arranged for distribution in the trenches. The soldiers, Flynn later said, liked the way the paper continued to carry lots of "slice of life" picture stories of ordinary life back home in England. Some said it was the only thing that kept them sane. The home audience were meanwhile enthralled by War Picture Specials including the sinking of the German battleships *Blucher* and *Emden* during the naval battle over the Falkland Islands; the shooting down in flames of a German Zeppelin airship off the coast of Norway; the collapse of the Russian army (the *Mirror* was the only London newspaper to have a reporter and photographer on the Eastern Front) and pictures of the first German daylight air-raid over London.

The *Daily Mirror* came out of the First World War in a very strong position. It had the highest sale of any daily paper – now well over a million regular daily sales – a reputation for reliable reporting and an unbeatable position as the pioneer of "picture journalism". In the next two decades the total number of national newspaper sales doubled from five million to ten million as people switched from reading local to national papers. Despite the economic depression of the 1930s, ad income also trebled from £20 million in 1907 to £59 million in 1938.

But, despite these excellent prospects, Rothermere neglected the *Mirror*, closing its northern offices in Manchester and failing to invest in new presses or in hiring journalists. One reason was that in 1922 he had inherited the *Mail* from Northcliffe.

Once again the *Mirror* became the poor relation inside a large newspaper empire.

4 HERALD OF DOOM – THE FREE GIFT WAR

By April 1922 Northcliffe had begun to go completely insane. Swaffer visited his old tormentor and wrote: "his vitality had gone, his face was puffy. His chin was sunken, and his mouth had lost its firmness. He lost his temper during a speech, because someone dropped a plate or something. He was a different man. The fires that burned within him had burned too fiercely all those years. People who heard him knew it was the end."

Others realised something was wrong when, without warning, Northcliffe began to object to the number of "coarse, abominable and offensive" adverts in the *Daily Mail* and appointed the paper's front-desk commissionaire to the new position of "chief censor of advertising" with orders not to let such adverts into the building. This followed a widely reported public speech in which Northcliffe claimed that the German economy would be bound to collapse unless something was done to increase the price of eels.

By June 1922 Northcliffe had fallen into a deep state of psychotic para-noia, babbling constantly about supposed attempts by German or Bolshevik Russian agents to poison or shoot him. He was convinced that his private secretary was a foreign agent who had fired a shot at him while they had both been standing on the platform of Boulogne railway station. Northcliffe took to carrying a loaded Colt revolver, keeping all six chambers loaded and sleeping with his finger on the trigger. He once fired it at his dressing gown in the middle of the night, after mistaking the shadow it cast for an intruder. Finally, he moved into a guarded and fortified hut built on the roof of a neighbour's house in Carlton Gardens.

Lord Northcliffe died on August 14, 1922, age 57. The official cause of death was given as heart disease brought on by a rare bacteriological infection that could also cause brain damage. But it is much more likely that he had died of tertiary syphilis, a condition for which he had been treated in secret since a visit to Germany in 1909, the year after he had taken over at *The Times*.

In 1922, just as Northcliffe died and Rothermere inherited his papers, there was another change in the shape of newspaper ownership in Britain, which was to have a deep impact on the *Mirror* and the shape of the national press as a whole. The socialist *Daily Herald* was taken over by the TUC and, later, with the backing of self-made millionaire Julius Elias's Odhams Press, was re-financed and began "buying readers" on a scale not seen since the days of the *Tit-Bits* and *Answers* "free insurance" schemes. The insurance offer was a popular as ever, and the *Herald* followed up by reviving that other staple of Northcliffe's early years – cash-prize competitions. It was reckoned that, because of the insurance and competitions, each new *Herald* reader cost the paper £1.

The *Herald* spent £3 million a year on "promotions" at the peak of its campaign. A big part of the cost was the army of door-to-door canvassers who tramped the streets collecting coupons and subscriptions and providing cash insurance and competition-prize pay-outs and, eventually, dishing out other free goods as diverse as ladies' silk stockings and complete canteens of stainless-steel cutlery. Many canvassers were unemployed ex-servicemen. Between 1924 and 1935 the number of people employed by the newspaper industry increased by almost three-quarters and two in every five people working in the business were door-to-door canvassers.

The *Herald* had fired the first shots in the free-gift war but the other papers were prepared to fight fire with fire. Lord Beaverbrook, owner and creator of the *Daily Express*, led the counter-attack. "I shall fight them to the bitter end," he said. The *Express* matched or bettered each *Daily Herald* free offer and put even more canvassers into the field. The *Express* specialised in simply giving away money by turning copies into numbered lottery tickets. In 1928 the courts outlawed newspaper lotteries so the papers switched to offering yet more free gifts – the canvassers were despatched to offer cameras, tea-sets, laundry mangles, encyclopedias, tea kettles, overcoats, children's shoes and boots to all comers. The story was told of how one canny coal-miner in South Wales had clothed his entire family for free and furnished much of his house by entering newspaper competitions, clipping newspaper coupons and taking out multiple newspaper subscriptions. In March 1933 the *Herald* offered a sixteen-volume edition of the collected works of Charles Dickens "decorated with real 22-carat gold" for 11 shillings plus *Herald* coupons. The *Mail, Express* and *News Chronicle* retaliated with Dickens at 10 shillings, 9 shillings and falling… Eleven million sets were sold, used to prop up beds and decorate the suburban mantelpieces of the house-proud and could still be found clogging up second-hand bookshops generations later.

By then Rothermere had been sucked in and was spending heavily on promotions to protect the *Mail*'s readership from being "poached" by the

Herald or the *Express*. This form of Mutually Assured Destruction was costing the national papers at least £3 million a year, wiping out the operating profits of the entire industry. The *Mirror* also joined in, but Rothermere was less prepared to spend on the picture paper. Circulation fell away and the paper was soon locked into a downward spiral that looked terminal.

Rothermere would not invest in the *Mirror*. Instead, he used its reserves to buy other businesses. In the single year of 1929 the *Daily Mirror* company made investments outside its core business of £8 million – including buying shares in the *Daily Mail* Trust, paper mills and even a mining company in Newfoundland. In 1925, Rothermere had used *Mirror* money to set up the Anglo-Canadian Pulp and Paper Mill Company in Quebec, buying rights to cut timber in much of south-eastern Canada. Rothermere's plan was to supply the booming newspaper market of New York. It seemed like a sound venture, but it ran into the great Wall Street Crash of 1929 after which Hearst could not pay his bills. Several New York newspapers closed after advertising revenues collapsed and Rothermere's Canadian paper mill was soon in trouble as well.

In the meantime every available scrap of cash and much talent was diverted away from the doomed *Mirror* and re-directed towards the *Mail*. Rothermere was convinced that maintaining the health of the *Daily Mail* was the best hope of saving his empire from financial ruin – that, and the need for a strong man to take over in politics. A man who would stop the rot, end the economic crisis and put the country back on its feet.

5 A HELPING HAND

"Dear Lord Rothermere,

"I should like to express the appreciation of countless Germans, who regard me as their spokesman, for the wise and beneficial public support which you have given to a policy that we all hope will contribute to the enduring pacification of Europe.

"Adolf Hitler
December 7, 1933"

★★★

"My dear Fuhrer,

"Everyone in England is profoundly moved by the bloodless solution to the Czechoslovakian problem. People are not so much concerned with territorial readjustment as with dread of another war with its accompanying bloodbath. Frederick the Great was a great popular figure. I salute your excellency's star which rises higher and higher.

"Yours Sincerely,
Rothermere.
October 1, 1938"

The owner of the *Daily Mirror* had first been converted to the cause of fascism in 1931 after his attempt to set up his own right-wing political party – the United Empire Party – failed. In disappointment and frustration Rothermere turned to Oswald Mosley, the leader of a right-wing Labour Party splinter group called the New Party and offered him the full editorial backing of the *Daily Mail* and the *Daily Mirror*. The alliance brought into being the British Union of Fascists – the official UK wing of the international movement that saw Hitler, Mussolini and Franco in power in Germany, Italy and Spain.[11]

Rothermere's move towards the extreme political right began at the end of the First World War. He was uneasy with the populist line taken by the *Mirror* during the war, its support for the Liberal peace settlement and Lloyd George's high-spending social policies that followed. In 1919 Rothermere replaced the campaigning Ed Flynn as editor with the more compliant Yorkshire grammar-school boy Alexander Campbell. The years that followed were to be the worst period in the *Mirror's* history, marked by the Free Gift circulation war and falling sales, lack of investment, the naked "puffing" of Rothermere's business interests and the deadening effect of his long screeds of right-wing political propaganda.

Rothermere's first political campaign after the First World War was against the Treaty of Trianon, which had carved up the old Austro-Hungarian Empire. Finally, he was offered the Crown of Hungary by the new republic's authoritarian military junta, after a *Mirror* campaign in favour of a "Greater Hungary". He commandeered a page in the *Mirror* to tell all of England that he had been "assured that, in view of the prevailing enthusiastic mood of the Hungarian people, a plebiscite in my favour would be practically unanimous." Nevertheless, he told the junta they would be better off appointing somebody of their "own race". Rothermere's authoritarian admirers contented themselves by naming a fountain in the centre of Budapest after him.

Rothermere's next political campaign involved the establishment of the Anti-Waste League, a committee of right-wing worthies dedicated to cutting back government spending and reducing taxes. The League was launched with an article in the *Mirror* on October 4, 1920, which read: "The House of Commons must listen to the irresistible cry of the people – no more waste!" Rothermere was convinced that Lloyd George's "Homes Fit for Heroes" social policies would in time bankrupt the country and pave the way for a Bolshevik revolution.

In 1929, just a few weeks after that year's general election, Rothermere – exasperated by the Conservative Party's failure to embrace the idea of strengthening the British Empire by means of Empire free trade and terri-fied by the election of a Labour government – joined with Lord Beaverbrook to launch the United Empire Party. The aim was to gain enough votes and parliamentary seats to force the Conservatives to get rid of their moderate and mild-mannered leader Stanley Baldwin and move to the right.[12]

In October 1930 an Empire Free Trade candidate backed by Rothermere and Beaverbrook beat the official Conservative candidate at a by-election in South Paddington. The result was a sensation and for a while it looked as though Baldwin would have to step down. Everything depended on the result of the next by-election, Westminster St George's in March 1931, where the Conservatives were again facing a strong chal-lenge from a United Empire Party candidate. Rothermere's latest obsession was the rise of nationalism and the independence movement in India, led by Mahatma Ghandi. He used the *Mirror* and the *Mail* in an attempt to turn the by-election into yet another referendum, this time on whether or not the government was doing enough to suppress Ghandi. Under the headline GANDHI IS WATCHING ST GEORGE'S the paper said: "this fanatic leader of a fanatic Indian horde knows that St George's is a test of opinion of the people of Britain on the vital problem of whether India is to be surrendered or governed. Put Petter [the UEP candidate] in and you put Ghandi out!"

Baldwin decided to make the power of the press lords an issue in the election. The Conservative leader told a public meeting that Rothermere and Beaverbrook's papers were not newspapers at all, but "engines of propaganda" used for pushing their own business and political agendas. "What they aim at," Baldwin said, "is power, and power without respon-sibility, the prerogative of the harlot through the ages."[13]

Losing the St George's by-election took the wind out of the sails of Rothermere's United Empire Party. Baldwin stayed as Prime Minister and Rothermere began to court Oswald Mosley as his best hope for political change. Rothermere was present at the first meeting of the "January club" – a dining club for industrialists willing to back Mosley. At about this time Rothermere began travelling to Italy and Germany frequently, attending fascist and Nazi party rallies. In 1933 he marked the coup that brought Hitler to power by describing in his papers how Germany had been:

> rapidly falling under the control of its alien elements. In the last days of the pre-Hitler regime there were twenty times as many Jewish govern-ment officials in Germany as had existed before the war. Israelites of international attachments were insinuating themselves into key posi-tions in the German administrative machine. It is from such abuses that Hitler has freed Germany.

There were important lessons, Rothermere wrote, that the British could learn from the Nazis: "Under Herr Hitler's control, the youth of Germany is effectively organised against the corruption of Communism," adding: "It was with some similar purpose that I founded the United Empire Party in England, for it is clear that no strong anti-Socialist policy can be expected from a Conservative party whose leaders are themselves tainted with semi-socialist doctrines". The pro-Nazi article was headed 'Youth Triumphant'.

Rothermere went public with his support for Mosley by writing an article headlined HURRAH FOR THE BLACKSHIRTS, published in the *Daily Mail* on January 8, 1934. The article said that Mosley's aim was to "bring Britain up to date" following the examples of fascist Italy and

Nazi Germany – "beyond all doubt the best governed nations in Europe today." Rothermere added: "Britain's survival as a great power will depend on the existence of a well-organised party of the right, ready to take over responsibility for national affairs with the same directness of purpose and energy of method as Mussolini and Hitler have displayed."

The *Mirror* joined the campaign a few days later. Under the slogan GIVE THE BLACKSHIRTS A HELPING HAND Rothermere praised the movement, saying Mosley's opponents did not know the facts: "If they had visited Italy and Germany, as I have done, travelling around and observing the national life in all its respects, they would find the mood of the vast majority of the inhabitants was not cowed submission, but confident enthusiasm." The article ended by listing the addresses of Blackshirt recruiting offices around the country, urging all readers to join.

Whenever Mosley gave a big speech the *Mail* and the *Mirror* made it either the lead or second lead article on the main news pages, and there were often unsigned editorials echoing what Mosley had said. In a front-page story marking a big Mosley rally in London the *Mail* said: "Mosley proved himself last night the paramount political personality in Britain... if he can win so completely the support of such an audience as faced him last night, he can win the country."

The *Sunday Pictorial,* which Rothermere had launched as the *Mirror's* photographic sister paper in 1915, ran a gushing picture special showing British fascists happily at work and play inside "The Black House" – the headquarters-cum-barracks of Mosley's para-military Blackshirts. Another Rothermere paper, the *Evening News,* ran a "Why I Like the Blackshirts" competition with cash prizes and free tickets for a Blackshirt rally given for the most enthusiastic entries... and the *Mirror* ran a photographic beauty contest to find Britain's best-looking female fascist.

Mosley and Rothermere's shared interest in aviation led to the formation of a Fascist Flying Club based in Gloucestershire. More bizarrely, Rothermere had tried to make money for and from the fascist movement by launching a joint cigarette manufacturing and distribution business with Mosley.

According to this plan he and Mosley would manufacture cigarettes and the Blackshirts would supply to the shops, "protecting" them from rival gangsters who, at the time, were fighting for control of the cigarette trade. The plan had its origins in Rothermere's need to use the huge capacity of his recession-hit Canadian paper mill. The whole business would be used to finance the recruitment of Blackshirt street fighters and at the same time make a healthy profit for Rothermere. But the venture collapsed when at the last minute Rothermere got cold feet over the cost of setting up the necessary factory, causing him to fall out with Mosley.

The peak for the fascist movement came in the summer of 1934 with a large rally at Olympia in London – massively advertised and promoted by both the *Mail* and the *Mirror*. Mosley took centre stage and the proceedings were based around great displays of Union Jacks and fascist insignia, patriotic music blasting from loudspeakers and hecklers being beaten up in the aisles by a Blackshirt "honour guard" as Mosley raved on in the manner of Hitler at a Nuremberg rally.

But after six months of boosting the Blackshirts in 1934, the *Mail* and the *Mirror* both suddenly fell silent on the matter. Rothermere said in public that he could no longer support a movement which was coming more and more to believe in dictatorship and the corporate state. But this was an excuse. Rothermere and Mosley had quarrelled over money in the wake of the cigarette fiasco. Rothermere was also starting to worry about loss of advertising revenue from Jewish-owned enterprises like Lyon's corner tea shops (the MacDonald's of their day) who refused to advertise in pro-fascist newspapers. Mosley told Rothermere that he should run headlines in the *Mirror* and *Mail* about the JEWISH THREAT TO BRITISH FREEDOM OF THE PRESS. It would increase sales, Mosley said. But Rothermere thought better of it.

Rothermere's break with Mosley dealt a severe blow to the fascist movement in Britain. Membership of the BUF reached 40,000 in 1934 after the *Mail* and *Mirror* campaigns, but collapsed to 5,000 after Rothermere for purely commercial reasons withdrew his support in the summer of 1934. But the change of direction did not mean that Rothermere had turned his back on either anti-semitism or fascism. He wrote privately of how "the Jews are everywhere, controlling everything". If anything, his editorial and propaganda support for Hitler grew stronger after his break with Mosley in Britain. Soon after the 1934 "Night of the Long Knives", when Hitler massacred the leaders of a rival faction of the Nazi party, Rothermere flew out to Germany to meet Hitler personally. He wrote about the meeting in the *Mail* saying that Hitler was a "simple and unaffected man" who was "obviously sincere" in his desire for peace in Europe. Rothermere had in fact found Hitler to be "a perfect gentleman" – a gentle, ethical vegetarian who neither drank nor smoked. "There is no man living whose promise given in regard to something of real moment I would sooner take." Rothermere made several more trips to Germany to visit Hitler and other leading members of the Nazi regime. According to the historian SJ Taylor Rothermere gave Hitler numerous gifts including a jade bowl with an accompanying note "to Hitler the artist", acknowledging the Fuhrer's indifference to worldly possessions.

When war broke out Rothermere might well have been interned along with Mosley as a threat to national security. Instead, he was found a meaningless and official mission to Canada on aircraft ministry business, to keep him out of the way. After that, he faced more or less forced exile to the Bahamas where he died of cirrhosis of the liver on November 26, 1940.

A month before Rothermere's death the first bombings of the London Blitz had begun, orchestrated by his personal friend Herman Goering, head of the Luftwaffe. Rothermere kept a commemorative photo of them both smiling and shaking hands during a stay at Goering's headquarters.

To the last, Rothermere regretted the fact that Britain was fighting against, instead of joining, Hitler in his crusade against Bolshevism, Jewishness and for the creation of a New Order in a united Europe.

His last words were: "there is nothing more I can do to help my country now".

6 BART... EL VINO'S VERITAS

The bulky figure of the *Mirror's* Editorial Director Harry Guy "Bart" Bartholomew wearing a crumpled three-piece suit, grinning demonically, his chubby features flushed red with whisky, creeps out from a side door and advances stealthily across the newsroom floor. In one hand he is carrying a massive, very solid-looking plank. The other hand is raised towards his mouth, index finger touching his lips, mouthing an exaggerated, silent "shhhh" to anyone who might be watching. Bart sneaks towards toward the crouched figure of *Mirror* editor Cecil Thomas, who is studying a pile of page proofs and wrapped in earnest discussion with the *Mirror's* chief sub-editor and technical team. Bart continues to advance and then rushes the last few steps, lifting the plank with both hands, swings it like a baseball bat and brings it crashing down on the back of Thomas's head with murderous force.

People who had not seen Bart perform this trick before were apt to go into shock. One who saw it for the first time found the act so violent that he almost fainted. But no real harm was done – except to Thomas's pride. The "plank" was a fake – made out of balsa wood.

Bart would explode into loud and strangely joyless laughter – more like a bark or a shout – as Thomas brushed the balsa fragments from his head and shoulders. Thomas would shrug sheepishly. "I don't really mind... It seems to amuse Bart and it does no harm."

It was a tribute to Rothermere's lack of interest in the *Daily Mirror* that "Bart" had risen to become the first "inky" – journalists' jargon for a printer or a newspaper production man – in modern times to become editorial director of a national daily newspaper. Rothermere had shared his older brother's disdain for "picture papers" after he had inherited Northcliffe's remaining stake in the *Mirror* in 1922. He considered selling the paper, but worried that a rival such as Beaverbrook or the *Daily Telegraph's* Berry family might turn it into a competitor and rival for the *Daily Mail*.

Through the 1920s the paper's circulation declined as Rothermere starved it of the money needed to compete in the Free Gift circulation war. At the same time, in order to keep advertising revenues up, Alexander Campbell, appointed in 1920, was told to aim the paper at the "well-to-do middle classes who annually holiday for a month in Scotland or the South of France, enjoy the long weekend, have tea at the tennis club and motor in the country". In the rest of Fleet Street the *Mirror* had once again become something of a laughing stock, derided as "The Daily Sedative" – a silly, insignificant little Tory newspaper that ran quaint front-page pictures of "girls in pearls", county cricket matches and brass bands playing music to caterpillars.

In 1931 Campbell retired and, at Rothermere's bidding, the board installed Leigh Brownlee as editor. Brownlee was a former schoolteacher and ex-county cricketer with little experience of journalism and still less of editing. After this masterstroke Rothermere hyped the paper for a final time and sold his residual stake in the paper at an inflated price, confident that it was no threat to the *Mail* and would soon close. Under Brownlee's leadership the standard of the *Mirror's* journalism dropped to not much more than a snooty parish magazine for the county set – full of picture specials of minor aristocratic weddings and social events – enlivened only by the occasional picture-based feature showing the Blackshirts at work and play in their London "Black House" headquarters. This uninspiring fare alternated with great tracts by Rothermere – no longer the owner but still pulling the strings via his appointees on the board – extolling Hitler, predicting national disaster and complaining how England was going to the dogs.

Through all of this "Bart" had bided his time, carefully studying Rothermere's management methods and divide-and-rule approach to handling the board of directors. He had been a member of the board since 1913, a reward for his work in rescuing the original *Mirror* as Swaffer's assistant. But, whereas Swaffer had marched up to Northcliffe, demanding the editorship, Bart had kept his head down, as the organiser of photographers and an ever-helpful technical specialist who was no threat to anyone.

By 1934, with Rothermere's influence starting to wane, the Rothermere-appointed board started to panic about falling sales and impending closure. Bart grabbed the latest circulation crisis to make his move. His picture operation was running smoothly and seemed to represent the only thing that was worthwhile about the paper, or that offered a chance of success in future. He carefully courted each of the directors, taking special care to gain the confidence of John Cowley, the lacklustre and ageing newspaper executive who "came with the flotsam" when Rothermere had bought the *London Evening News* and whom he disposed of by making chairman of the *Daily Mirror* board. In his memoirs, fellow director Cecil King said of Cowley that he was a man "without ability" who had "no initiative of his own and who simply sat there to see that Rothermere's wishes were carried out".[14]

Bart persuaded Cowley and the others to make him editorial director in charge of both the *Daily Mirror* and *Sunday Pictorial*, with the right to make circulation-boosting changes and to appoint the editors. Bart assured Cowley the changes would not be too dramatic – he would do nothing that would upset the now more distant but still feared figure of Rothermere. It was a lie: he was planning to change the paper out of all recognition and in so doing to create the modern *Daily Mirror* and the model for popular journalism throughout much of the world for the rest of the century.

★★★

Harry Guy Bartholomew – known to all as "Bart" – was born in 1878 and joined the *Daily Mirror* in 1904 as a photographic technician. He was almost entirely uneducated and all his life he found it difficult to express himself clearly in writing. It was sometimes claimed that Bart had never read a book in his life and found conversation with anyone with more than an elementary education uncomfortable, if not impossible.

According one man who knew him at the time, Bart was "vulgar, semi-literate, cantankerous, suspicious and jealous of any who withstood his authority, a man with a passion for crude practical jokes, and a ruthless determination to trample on anyone who got in his way". He was also a heavy drinker, never seen without a glass of whisky near to hand and granted his own "standing place" at the Fleet Street wine bar El Vino's – which others approached at their peril.

But Bart was also a practical man, a technical "genius" according to some, who liked working with his hands. He was fascinated by machinery and was drawn to the newspaper business because – one hundred years ago – it was a hotbed of the very latest technical innovation. Photography was in its infancy and advances in printing and page creation were being made all the time. In some ways the technical side of the newspaper business was similar in those days to the electronics, computer and telecom businesses at the start of the twenty-first century – technical frontier territory.

Hannen Swaffer was Bart's first boss at the *Mirror* and remained his great inspiration. In the years before the First World War the men worked together to pioneer American-style photojournalism and turn the *Mirror* into the world's biggest-selling picture paper. Bartholomew came to Swaffer's attention because of his boundless energy, physical bravery and –

importantly – a capacity for alcoholic drink that almost matched that of Swaffer himself. Looking back at the early days of the *Daily Mirror* Swaffer remembered that he and Bart had been a double act. "We would work day and night, if necessary, to get our pictures ready for the next day's paper," Swaffer wrote, adding: "I had the ideas and Bart was the master technician."

Bart's greatest technical achievement was undoubtedly the "Bart-McFarlane" (better known as Bartlane) system – jointly developed with the New York *Daily News*'s production expert Captain McFarlane. It was used for transmitting photos by radio, meaning that the *Mirror* could obtain American pictures in a matter of minutes or hours, rather than days or weeks. Bart used the system to receive the first telegraphic photos sent across the Atlantic – blurry pictures of yachts competing in the America's Cup. Soon the system was perfected and the *Daily Mirror* and the New York *Daily News* began trading pictures almost daily.

Despite Bart's growing fame in Fleet Street and influence in the world of photography, his early life remained a mystery. When pushed, he would claim his grandfather had been a cab driver from Horsham in Surrey and that his mother had been a singing teacher. But he never mentioned a father, and could be touchy about the subject. Throughout his life there was a rumour that he was one of Northcliffe's many illegitimate sons. Some even saw a physical resemblance.[15]

Bart also liked to spread the story that he was half-Jewish – and then deny it. Nobody discovered if there was any truth in the claim and some put it down to a type of anti-Semitism. He was a scheming man, determined to rise to the top in journalism. He may have imagined that to get to the top he would, in some vague way, have to make himself acceptable to the Jews. Rothermere had warned that Jews were "everywhere, controlling everything".

Bart's family life was another mystery. He had married a Scottish widow, an austere Presbyterian called Bertha Broome who was 13 years his senior, which led people to say that Bart had a double life – filthy mouth, roaring temper and hard drinking at the office; but mild-mannered and sober at home.

When Bart took control of the paper in 1934 circulation had dropped from a peak of over two million after the First World War to less than 800,000. The paper at that point was losing about 100,000 of its ageing readers every year. They were simply dying out, and the rate of decline was increasing. Even the complacent board could work out that the paper was set to have exactly zero readers by the year 1940.

Leading the demands for change on the board was the influential and aristocratic figure of Cecil Harmsworth King, the paper's 33-year-old advertising director and nephew of Northcliffe and Rothermere. King told the *Mirror* board that it was becoming practically impossible to sell any advertising because the paper was no longer attracting any sort of audience the ad agencies wanted to reach. King and Bart formed an alliance aimed at transforming the *Daily Mirror* into a New York tabloid, a direct copy of the *Daily News*, America's most popular newspaper.[16]

In September 1934, with King's support, Bart was duly appointed editorial director with a general brief to change the paper's direction and increase sales. Editor Brownlee was shown the door at once and Cecil Thomas was appointed as Bart's very own "yes man". But the new and real power relationship at the *Mirror* was to be between the implausible combination of Bartholomew and King, soon to become the new lords of Fleet Street. Within a few short years they were to create "the biggest-selling newspaper in the universe" and lay the foundations of Tabloid Britain.

PART TWO:
Death, New York-style

7 DEATH, NEW YORK-STYLE

Ruth Snyder was the first woman in the twentieth century to be executed by means of the electric chair at Sing Sing prison in New York. The date of her death was January 22, 1928. She was 33 years old. Ten minutes later, her lover Judd Gray was executed in the same chair.

Snyder, described at the time as a "stunning ice-cool blonde", had been convicted of conspiring with Gray to murder her rich but ancient husband (and former boss) – the millionaire publisher of a motorboat magazine. The murder had been carried out in cold blood. The motive was sexual frustration and greed for money. Snyder and Gray faked a break-in, chloroformed Old Man Snyder, tied him up, smashed his skull with an exercise dumbbell and – for good measure – garotted him with picture wire. The lovers then ransacked the apartment. Judd roughed Ruth up a little and then tied her to a bed where she was later found faking hysteria and gabbling about being overpowered by an intruder "with an Italian-type moustache". The mystery Italian had made off with a quantity of diamond jewellery given to her by the Old Man.

Snyder and Gray planned to clean up with an insurance claim, keep the jewels and double their money by selling them later. Things started to go wrong for them when the case attracted the interest of Joseph Medill Patterson, editor of the New York *Daily News*. Patterson specialised in re-opening unsolved murder cases and, caring not a jot for libel, he named Snyder as the murderer – "The Iron Widow" and "The Bloody Blonde" – and egged on the police to find the evidence that would send her to the electric chair.

In due course and in circumstances that have remained murky, the police found the missing jewellery hidden under Snyder's bed and made an arrest. The police may have obtained the jewels from Gray who, after being tracked down by *Daily News* reporters, had attempted to save his own life (without success as it was to turn out) by fingering Snyder and providing the evidence needed to confirm Patterson's unerringly accurate hunch. The *Daily News* had the inside track on the trial and played the story big. In the end the jury took hardly any time to reach their verdict. The penalty was to be death by means of the electric chair.

The Bloody Blonde spent her last night on death row screaming and banging her head against the bars of her condemned cell. In the morning she was dragged along the corridor to the room containing the electric chair. The windowless execution chamber was like a chapel – a small, plain white-walled room with rows of polished pews facing, in the place of the altar, the starkly simple form of the electric chair. The pews were occupied by sober-suited witnesses whose job was to see that justice had been done while preserving, as far as possible, the dignity and privacy of the prisoner's final moments. To one side was the electrocution apparatus, tended by the official executioner. Above the single heavy oak door the room's only decoration – a hand-drawn sign commanding "SILENCE".

Snyder was soon silenced by a leather mask and gag placed in her mouth. She was then pushed down into the chair and fastened in place with belts across the arms, chest, thighs and legs. The first electrode was strapped around her forehead, above the mask. Then a second electrode was attached just above her right ankle and the two shots of 2,000 volts applied.

The most vivid memory of the witnesses, arrayed in those church pews in front of this dreadful spectacle, was the noise and the smell. Once Snyder's jolting form had fallen silent there was "a sustained sound like bacon frying". A sweet, sickly revolting smell of burning hair and flesh filled the room, mixed with the smell of Snyder's violent and inevitable release of faeces.

The next day the *Daily News* gloated over the execution with a single word headline:

DEAD!

Beneath the headline there was a single full-page poster image of Ruth Snyder, back arched, a cloud of fumes around her ankles, strapped into the electric chair at the point of death. The picture had been obtained by a *Daily News* reporter posing as a witness. He had strapped a camera to his leg and at the crucial moment lifted his trouser leg and pressed a bulb in his pocket to set off a flash and get the picture.

The DEAD! edition of the New York *Daily News* broke all records, adding over 300,000 extra sales, temporarily giving the paper by far the highest circulation per head of population achieved anywhere in the world at the time. DEAD! proved beyond doubt the commercial value of the newspaper formula of huge, shocking pictures appealing to the rawest of human emotions next to massive, violent, shouting headlines set in big black type.

Harry Guy Bartholomew had long been an admirer of the *Daily News* and its New York rival, the *Daily Graphic*. The moment "Bart" gained control of the *Daily Mirror* in 1934 he began planning the transformation of the genteel Tory paper with its dwindling band of 800,000 readers bequeathed by Rothermere into a roaring New York-style tabloid capable of selling perhaps ten times as many copies.[17]

By 1934 the *Daily News* had perfected all the elements of the modern tabloid. While the *Mirror* remained stuck in a time-warp, suffering under the dead hand of Rothermere, impoverished by insurance and cash give-aways, the *Daily News* was also being sharpened on the anvil of red-hot competition. Hearst launched the New York *Daily Mirror* as a picture paper and the fray was joined by the *Daily Graphic* – known in the trade as the Daily "Porno-Graphic" because of its pioneering work in printing gratuitous pictures of nude and semi-nude girls.[18]

The daily war between the New York papers to grab readers meant that New Yorkers were bombarded with pictures and stories about nude dancing girls who liked to bathe in pools filled with champagne or randy bigamist businessmen who recruited whole harems of 15-year-old hill-billy child brides. During the sex-drenched 1927 separation trial of gangster "Daddy" Browning and his moll "Peaches" Heenan Browning, the *Daily Graphic* printed every line of testimony and doctored a photo to make "Peaches" appear nude.

No such thing had ever been seen in a newspaper, and it put on a quarter million readers overnight. The *Daily News* meanwhile concentrated on sex and scandal stories among the film stars of Hollywood. In contrast Rothermere demanded that the London *Daily Mirror* "avoid sensationalism" and serve up instead his increasingly cranky and boring right-wing political campaigns (Squandermania! Imperial Tariff Protection! Justice for Hungary!).

Standing in the way of Bart's American revolution was the *Mirror's* board of directors, still dominated by the unimpressive John Cowley and the mediocre and conservative men put in place in the 1920s by Rothermere. Bart's only ally on the board was Cecil Harmsworth King, Rothermere's nephew, who had risen to the position of advertising director through sheer nepotism. Fortunately for Bart, King was to be an enthusiastic supporter of the revolution. King, writing in his memoirs, said that at the time the *Mirror* was facing closure through falling sales because his fellow members of the board "no longer had the stomach for popular journalism".

As Bart's editorial plans unfolded, it was King's job to handle the board. Rothermere's nephew was much more of a diplomat than Bart could ever be. He also had the advantage of his family connections and the

Harmsworth name. Instead of confronting the board directly King brought in the London branch of the American advertising agency and market research company J Walter Thompson to advise on the way forward. The agency recommended a complete re-launch, with a new editorial agenda based on "human interest" and an expansion of the features section, which needed a total re-design to appeal both to women and the younger generation.

The board nervously sanctioned change and approved the recruitment of the new staff needed to bring it about. Bart was allowed to introduce bigger, blacker headlines and, most important of all, more cartoon strips – an important ingredient of the New York tabloid formula.

There was tension when Bart marked the change of direction by running a horrific *Daily News*-style picture of an American lynching on the front page. Bart had waited until late at night before putting the pages together, reckoning that the board would be in bed and therefore unable to object until it was too late. The old guard might wring their hands over this move towards "sensationalism" like this but if circulation went up they were unlikely to object unless direct offence was caused to Cecil King's uncle, the increasingly distant and formally powerless Lord Rothermere.

The crucial post of features editor in the new regime went to the intriguing figure of Basil D Nicholson, hired directly from J Walter Thompson where he had been an advertising copywriter. He was famous in the ad industry for his clever but cynical "Night Starvation" campaign for the hot drink Ovaltine. He basically invented the "night starvation" phrase, flamed it up into a supposed medical syndrome which could affect the healthy growth of children and sold tons of the stuff as a result. He was to adopt the same approach to feature-writing at the *Mirror* – it was a two-stage process: (a) think of a headline – the newspaper equivalent of an ad slogan; (b) write some "tosh" (to use one of Nicholson's favourite words) to "stand it up".

Nicholson was an Oxbridge intellectual, influenced by literary and artistic movements like surrealism. In some ways he treated the process of newspaper feature and headline writing as a type of surrealist poetry – which indeed it sometimes was. At the time, the American film trade newspaper *Variety* was famous for having run the headline HIX NIX STIX PIX – meaning something like "hicks (or yokels) don't like (nix) films about the countryside (stix pix)".

Nicholson looked the part of a 1930s avant-garde poet – always decked out in a bright green tweed suit, wearing octagonal glasses and never without an immense Groucho Marx-style cigar rolling around his mouth. He talked constantly in a stream of quick-fire wisecracks and insults and had a prickly, abrasive manner. It was said that he did not so much converse with people as cross-examine them. Nicholson got his job when Cecil King met him to try to sell him *Mirror* advertising space for Ovaltine. Nicholson turned the tables and started grilling King on why the *Mirror* didn't follow the example of the New York papers and run a lot more cartoon strips. Nicholson had studied the latest cartoon and graphic journalism techniques in New York and had seen at first hand the pull of cartoon strips in advertising created by J Walter Thompson on both sides of the Atlantic. King hired him on the spot.

Nicholson brought with him the advertising industry's obsession with market research. His first job was to fill a full page of the *Mirror* with American-style cartoon "strips" – each one aimed at a different segment of the target audience, and each gem such as Belinda Blue-eyes, Garth, Jane, Buck Ryan and Popeye tested in advance by market research. The cartoons were such a success that by 1936 the *Mirror* had one and half pages of strips in a standard forty-page edition. Cowley and the board sweated when rivals sneered that the *Daily Mirror* had turned itself into "a comic". But they could not argue with circulation figures that, for the first time in many years, were starting to show strong month-on-month increases.

Nicholson's other contribution was more intangible. He was what was known in the ad world as "an ideas man". His way of working involved long and often drunken lunches with cronies, trying out slogans and sketching poster layouts to go with them. He now treated the *Mirror*'s features pages in the same way and brought a dash of shock therapy to the prim and proper readers of Rothermere and Cowley's "Daily Sedative", with headlines like REVELLER VANISHES FOR DAYS – COMES BACK AS POP-EYED DRAGON SHOUTING "WHOOPEE! WHAT A NIGHT!" or MATCH-MAKING MAMMIES SHOO SPIN-STER LOVELIES TO GIBRALTAR TO GRAB A JACK TAR HUBBY. It didn't matter much to Nicholson that the stories run beneath these headlines sometimes did not make much sense.

Such an extrovert and openly bohemian figure in an important posi-tion was bound to excite the interest of Bart who took an instant and deep dislike to his new features editor. Bart, it was said, took exception to Nicholson's "lack of awe" in his presence. Others watched with jaws on the floor when in an editorial meeting Nicholson dismissed Bart's tech-nical inventions such as the mighty Bartlane picture transmission system as second rate and far worse than similar systems used in advertising. Bart was rendered almost speechless, but sought to silence Nicholson by fuming and spluttering that a new version of his famous photo-transmis-sion system would be able to "do anything". Nicholson asked, in a voice dripping with sarcasm, "Ohh, *anything*? Are you sure? Will it, for instance, make love to a guinea pig?" This was a brave thing for somebody to say to their boss, especially a boss with a sense of humour which stretched only as far as smashing people over the head with a balsawood plank. Everybody in the room sniggered and Nicholson was a dead duck.

Bart was a bully and, as a production process man, did not much like, trust or even talk to journalists. He was a hard man to please. Once he issued an edict that, as part of the *Mirror's* perennial search for younger readers, journalists on the paper should not write about anybody over the age of thirty. Later, Bart found out that the news editor had rejected a great story about a poverty-stricken old woman who had committed suicide because she had lost her Sunday best hat and had nothing to wear in church. He went berserk. When it was explained that the story did not fit with his previous order banning mention of the over-thirties he stormed: "Never do what I say ever again!" He wasn't about to take any cheek from some poet "toff" like Basil D Nicholson.

The next day Nicholson read a job advertisement Bart had placed in the *Daily Telegraph*. It asked for applications for the new post of *Daily Mirror* Deputy Features Editor. The ad asked for a man who was "ready to take charge" shortly from the current *Daily Mirror* features editor. Blood chilled as people worked out that Bart was not only advertising for a replacement for Nicholson before telling him he was sacked, but announcing in public that he planned to bring in Nicholson's replacement as his deputy, then sack him and then promote his new deputy over his head.

The man who benefited from Bart's sadism was a chipper 22-year-old Welsh feature writer called Hugh Cudlipp who, at the time, was Features Editor of the *Sunday Chronicle*, having lately been a district reporter in the northern fleshpot of Blackpool. When Cudlipp phoned to ask about the job Nicholson told him: "Can you start today? Otherwise I might be fired before you get here."

So Cudlipp, the callow youth who one day would be hailed as the *Mirror's* greatest-ever "genius" editorial figure, slid into the side door of the *Daily Mirror* under these least promising of circumstances, almost unnoticed. The paper was still seen by most of Fleet Street as the absolute pits, a cast-off and embarrassment thrown away first by Northcliffe and then by Rothermere, filled up in desperation with horror pictures and Yank cartoon strips, organised by Bart, the semi-literate printer, and his editor sidekick Cecil Thomas, run by Cowley and the worst board of directors in British newspapers and destined for the knackers' yard one way or another, sooner rather than later.

But for Cudlipp, only 22, it was a tremendous opportunity. He arrived at the *Mirror* in August 1935. Bart waited until Christmas before getting rid of Nicholson – ritual sackings of rivals or perceived under-performers timed for Christmas Eve were to become an established part of Bart's management methods. Just before he left, Nicholson – by then deeply paranoid – took Cudlipp up on to the roof, so as to avoid being overheard by Bart or one of his many spies or toadies. Nicholson told Cudlipp he was being sacked, and he added: "Bart wants to see you now. I think they want to give you my job. Take it or everything we've done will be wasted".

So it was Hugh Cudlipp who got the chance, as he later put it, to "hijack the hearse at the gates of cemetery", and to "be on the barricades when the tabloid revolution began" at the *Daily Mirror*. Cudlipp made a small fortune and was able to live the high life in the process. Nicholson, the creative spark who did more than any other to light the fire, hit the bottle, disappeared for two decades, then re-emerged in a terrible state and resorted to sending begging letters to the newspaper.

He died friendless, alone and in poverty.

8 LOW-RENT BABYLON

Before the 1920s Blackpool had been much the same as any other seaside resort. It was a place to enjoy the traditional, genteel delights of the Edwardian English seaside – bathing machines, pleasure gardens, donkey rides, Punch-and-Judy shows on the beach, tea shops, light classical concerts, zoological gardens, military bandstands and music-hall "turns" at the end of the pier.

In the 1930s, while other such resorts suffered enormous economic damage, Blackpool boomed, entering a golden age, becoming the very symbol of the British working-class at play and in their element. Blackpool sold itself as the place where everything was the biggest, the fastest, the tallest, the weirdest and tastiest – Coney Island by the Irish Sea. The famous Blackpool illuminations – at first nothing more than a demonstration of the technological wonder of the electric light bulb – began in 1912. The town's most famous attraction – the Pleasure Beach – had been built in the 1920s by local businessman W G Bean as "an American-style Amusement Park".

In 1931, when Hugh Cudlipp, the future *Daily Mirror* editorial director, arrived there as a reporter for a Manchester-based regional paper, another entrepreneur opened the first foreign branch of "Ripley's Believe it or Not" – the chain of freak-show "museums" featuring what purported to be two-headed babies in jars, a copy of Ruth Snyder's Sing Sing electric chair and lovingly created waxwork tableaux of hideous car-smash and medical-accident victims. The attraction was a massive hit – a visit to the regularly updated vista of ersatz carnage becoming a high point of the annual holiday for millions.

In 1930 Blackpool had thrills – the literal "sensationalism" of the new Grand National switchback ride on the Pleasure Beach, a copy of New York's Coney Island Cyclone, carried a genuine health warning about the danger of heart attacks from excitement. It had the voyeuristic horror of the popular freak shows; the sentimentality of the music hall – the

Blackpool Grand theatre was the biggest Music Hall outside London, home in the 1920s and 1930s of Gracie Fields and big American musicals like *Rose Marie*, the *Desert Song* and *No No Nanette*; it had booze – in the form of massive bars the size football pitches and, above all, it had sex – in the form of dance-halls, the tunnel of love and dozens of picture houses. It was a low-rent Babylon with thousands of dingy, cheap bedrooms in "boarding houses" that could be hired by the night.

This was the culture in which the young Hugh Cudlipp came of age – living away in digs, running the Blackpool district office of the Manchester *Evening Chronicle*, working with a midget cameraman called Moishe Saidman, and dressing like a Hollywood *film noir* version of a newspaper man, complete with trilby, silk waistcoat, white trousers and spats, while filing endless reports about prostitutes soliciting on the Golden Mile, drinking draught champagne – available all year round in Yates's Wine Lodge on the Promenade. He stayed only two years in Blackpool and later described the experience as his "university". When he came to shape the *Daily Mirror* after the Second World War Cudlipp would create a cocktail from the sex, fun and sensation, saucy-postcard Blackpool agenda with dollops of comical class-war politics, freak shows, cute animal pictures and sports results to create an unbeatable combination.[19]

Cudlipp had been born at 118 Lisvane Street, Cardiff, in 1913, the son of Willie Cudlipp, a travelling salesman who supplied groceries to corner shops in the South Wales valleys. The family was far from well off. Hugh, his younger sister Phyllis and his two older brothers, Percy and Reg, used to take it in turns to be bathed in front of the fire in the tin bath in the back room of the cramped Lisvane Street terrace. Hugh was five when his brother Percy went into journalism as a local newspaper reporter, twelve years old when Percy made it to Fleet Street. His other brother, Reg, eight years his senior, was to become editor of the *News of the World*.

Percy's success encouraged the two younger brothers, and also showed them the way. Percy steered Reg into a reporting and sub-editing job on the *Penarth News*, a tiny local newspaper in Cardiff, long since closed. In 1927 Hugh Cudlipp left school to take his brother's place on the paper. A year later he moved to the larger circulation *Cardiff Evening News*. The letter of recommendation from his old editor said Cudlipp was a "hard worker" who was "strictly temperate". The first assessment, at least, was to be true for most of his life. The job lasted only one year – the *Evening News* closed down in the aftershock of the Wall Street crash and the onset of the depression. The sudden closure of a person's place of work followed by the threat of unemployment is an awful experience for anyone. But for Cudlipp the memory was searing. On the day he was due to leave the paper, the 16-year-old lad went into the editor's cubicle to collect his expenses and found his boss suspended from the ceiling with the window cord around his neck, face purple, eyes popping. Cudlipp's last job for the paper was to cut the cord with a penknife and call an ambulance. The editor was revived in hospital, but the experience gave Cudlipp a haunting and vivid fear of the effects of unemployment and newspaper closure.

The teenage Cudlipp moved to Manchester after being fixed up with job as a district reporter on the *Evening Chronicle*. Before taking his Blackpool posting, Cudlipp briefly toured the surrounding Lancashire cotton towns, reporting on the crime, ill health and social problems which, he thought, resulted from grinding poverty. He also had a short spell as a reporter in Salford, covering the local courts, which were full of the results of unemployment and poverty – pathetic thefts, domestic violence, suicide and the victims of back-street abortionists.

By the time he got to Blackpool, Cudlipp was developing a reputation as a "good operator" who could construct a good yarn – he boasted of "my See Salford and Die masterpieces" – and was prepared to go to any lengths to get a story. His most famous stunt in Blackpool was to "kidnap" a football star, holding him incommunicado on a fishing boat in Blackpool bay and running the story of the MYSTERY OF THE MISSING FULLBACK. A week later, the player was returned to dry land, giving Cudlipp an even better headline: THE CHRONICLE FINDS MISSING FULLBACK: EXCLUSIVE INTERVIEW. The footballer had simply wanted to get away from it all for a few days and had been happy to play along.

In 1933 Cudlipp packed his stick of rock, Kiss Me Quick hat and dirty postcards and took the train to Fleet Street. He had seen national newspaper reporters at work from time to time in Blackpool – sent up by head office, for example, to try and get a sniff of his very own MISSING FULLBACK scam. He did not think much of them – but he was impressed by the amount of effort they put into fabricating huge, fraudulent expenses claims and the success they boasted in getting editors to cough up.

Cudlipp wanted to move on to national newspapers and, at the same time, made the crucial decision to specialise as a newspaper production expert and feature-writer, rather than an ambulance-chasing news reporter which, more and more, began to look like a mug's game to him. He got plenty of advice from his older brother Percy who had risen to become Assistant Editor of the *Evening Standard* in London. In March 1933, Percy helped steer Cudlipp into the London features department of the *Sunday Chronicle* where he was trained in newspaper production by the *Chronicle's* layout and design expert James Drawbell. He showed a natural flair for the visual side of journalism and, almost at once, was recognised as an exceptional headline writer.

Having honed these skills, in August 1935, Cudlipp applied for and got the job of *Daily Mirror* Deputy Features Editor "ready to take charge", when Bart advertised it. As planned, Basil Nicholson was sacked as features editor as soon as Cudlipp had shown that he was ready to take over the job. At Christmas 1935 Hugh Cudlipp became the features editor of the *Daily Mirror* at the age of 22.

At the time Bart was already running his shock-horror New York *Daily News*-style poster front pages featuring lynching, murder and disasters. Cudlipp had been shown copies of the *Daily News* on the day of his appointment, and had been told that was the formula they were going to follow. The J Walter Thompson contingent had installed the American-type cartoon strips and Cudlipp began to re-style the features pages along the lines of the sex-and-sensation, saucy-postcard agenda of the Golden Mile and Ripley's Believe it or Not. Cecil King had already got rid of the screeds of right-wing political propaganda insisted upon by Rothermere, making the *Mirror* in the early 1930s an essentially non-political paper. "Our best hope," King later wrote, "was to appeal to young, working-class men and women... If this was the aim, the politics had to be made to match. In the depression of the thirties, there was no future in preaching right-wing politics to young people in the lowest income bracket."

Looking back in the 1950s, the newspaper historian Roger Manvell said the *Mirror* under Bart and Cudlipp "left no holds barred in exploiting the readers' interests in sex, violence and sensationalism. The great black headlines screamed blue murder and stories of lurid human interest pushed all but the most sensational current news out of pages that used cheesecake pictures of girls and banks of strip cartoons to jack up the circulation". Francis Williams, editor of the rival *Daily Herald* at the time, was later to write that the *Mirror* in the 1930s had displayed "a frenzied gusto in dredging the news for sensational stories of sex and crime and a complete lack of reticence in dealing with them". The features pages were dominated by picture-led stories with headlines like: 6' 4" WIFE BOUNCED 3' 11" MIDGET ON HER KNEE ONCE TOO OFTEN and STARS WEEP AS $60 A DAY CHIMPANZEE IS BURIED IN SATIN COFFIN and the all-time classic: MAN FIRED FROM CANNON HITS OWN WIFE.

The news agenda changed from Rothermere's United Empire and Blackshirt campaigns to the price of a cup of tea in the nation's cafés. When tea went up by a ha'penny from tuppence to tuppence ha'penny the story was run in massive headlines on page one and a national campaign was launched. By 1937 Bart had transformed the genteel, right-wing *Mirror* of the 1920s and early 1930s into a "daily affront to bishops, magistrates, schoolmasters, the retired élite and the combined forces of officialdom and respectable society". The new *Mirror* was packed with human interest stories – issue after issue had no political news at all. There was virtually no foreign news – it had a column called THE ONE MINUTE WORLD NEWS TOUR which consisted almost entirely of "funny old foreigners"-type single-paragraph snippets from papers around the world. In 1938 the paper refused to print the Queen's Birthday Honours List, describing it as "a dull catalogue of names. True, they are worthy names, but many people who have put all they know into bettering this great country of ours are not there. They are shunned…"

As features editor, Cudlipp placed enormous emphasis on readers' letters, which were used as both a cheap source of material and as a type of market research. In 1938 he introduced the *Mirror*'s "Live Letters" section – edited by the Old Codgers who would invite readers to send in written questions on any topic they liked – a straight lift from Northcliffe's original *Answers to Correspondents On Every Subject Under the Sun,* which had been such a hit in the 1880s. Bart made it one of the *Mirror*'s strictest rules that every one of the thousands of letters that poured into the paper had to receive a personal reply. Questions were followed up to such an extent that eventually the paper hired a woman to sit on a hen's egg for a week to answer a letter-writer who wanted to know if it was possible for a woman to incubate one. A suitably broody female volunteer was hired to do just this, the paper keeping up a running photographic commentary until it was concluded that, no, no matter how still she sits, a woman cannot hatch a hen's egg.

The letters revealed that thousands of women had been attracted by the *Mirror*'s new sunny and sexy approach – and this was a surprise to some. But the new female readers were not the Edwardian gentleladies of the original *Mirror.* They were from the new army of secretarial "working girls" who had come into the workforce in the 1930s. The paper cleverly targeted this new market by running editorial campaigns in favour of better conditions for secretaries: "Big business walks in silk stockings, but they are threadbare and have holes in the feet," the paper complained, adding that secretaries "did all the work, but didn't get the pay," in most offices. Cudlipp arranged for the Old Codgers to be joined by the American writer Elizabeth Meriwether Gilmer, who was hired to provide *Mirror* readers with the first female-friendly modern newspaper "agony aunt" feature under the pen-name Dorothy Dix.

The Dix column quickly moved in the direction of sex: "We are going to get to the bottom of this love business," Dix announced, soon after the column was launched. Readers were asked to fill in a questionnaire on how they behaved when they were courting. Dix claimed that 50,000 replies enabled her to tell readers that girls had their first kiss at the age, on average, of fifteen and a quarter and that it usually took place between 6 p.m. and midnight.

Another of Cudlipp's innovations with added female appeal was PERSONALITY PARADE by Godfrey Winn, a freelance women's magazine writer. The feature balanced the editorial mayhem and murder of Bart's news pages by talking entertainingly about Winn's profoundly humdrum life with his mother and his pet dog Mr Sponge, pottering about in his garden in the suburbs and preaching the gospel of "This Happy Life". Winn was homosexual and therefore viewed with great suspicion by Bart who gave him the nickname "Winifred God". Eventually, Winn became a big star and was head-hunted by the *Mirror's* more up-market rival, the *Daily Express*, for a huge sum.

With Dix and Winifred looking after the female readers, Bart and Cudlipp began to add more and more cheesecake pictures of girls, usually with some essentially fabricated news angle. Any excuse would do – dancers showing off their legs in some new or "record-breaking" variety show, or winners of endless local and national beauty contests – all edging carefully towards the "Health and Efficiency" style of the New York "Porno" *Graphic*. The sex theme was pushed further when Bart and Cudlipp printed what were later believed to be the first-ever naked female breasts to appear in a national daily newspaper. The photos illustrated a supposedly anthropological pictorial study of "native life" in Africa, featuring two nude African girls washing in a stream.

After the African boob outrage the *Mirror* was denounced by a rival newspaper, the *Daily Sketch*, and accused of being "sensational, ribald and pornographic". The *Sketch* lined up vicars in support of its campaign, as a form of publicity. The Bishop of London got behind the *Sketch*, saying he how much he welcomed a "newspaper free from vulgarity, suggestiveness and sensationalism". If anything, the campaign backfired on the *Sketch*, a would-be popular picture-led rival to the *Mirror* – it was like free advertising. Vulgarity, suggestiveness and sensationalism had not previously been on offer beyond the confines of Blackpool's Golden Mile. Now the *Mirror* was offering plenty of it to anyone, any time.

The *Mirror's* "sensational" coverage of one child abuse case led to a man being almost lynched by the paper's readers. A sadistic father had forced his young son to hold live coals. When the paper published pictures of the injuries to the child's hands, two thousand people found and besieged the house, screaming vengeance. There was shock at the scale of the reaction, but satisfaction too in the *Mirror* newsroom that the paper was starting to have an impact. Sales began to climb sharply and the paper began to move strongly into profit for the first time in a decade.

In 1938, in tribute to Bart's success, Cowley and the *Mirror* board offered him a pay rise and editorial and managerial control of the *Mirror*'s ailing Sunday sister paper, the *Pictorial,* as well as the *Mirror* itself. Bart turned them down, convinced that "the *Pic*" had been so ground down by the old regime that it was beyond redemption. Instead, the post was offered to Cecil King, who became editorial director of the *Pictorial* with the idea of finding a day-to-day editor.

Bart was delighted. He had needed King's support to become editorial director of the *Mirror* and found his aristocratic manner and Harmsworth blood useful in smoothing relations with the board of directors when that had been important. But, now that Rothermere had gone and the share-holders were happy with the dividends and profits the *Mirror* was once again providing, he had less need of his old ally and began to plot against him. Bart made his low opinion of King known to the *Daily Herald* editor Francis Williams, calling King "an adding machine that thinks it's Northcliffe". Cowley was approaching retirement age and Bart was deter-mined to become chairman of the company. He wanted King, his only real rival, out of the way and reasoned that saving the *Pic* would be a chal-lenge too far for King.

The immediate question was: who would edit the *Pic* under King's direction? Bart, with exaggerated and utterly insincere generosity, told King he could take "anyone you like" from the staff of the *Mirror* to help turn the *Pic* around. In fact, Bart intended to see all the likely candidates and tell them that if they took the *Pic* job he would see to it that their careers were destroyed. Several senior *Mirror* journalists turned King down until, finally, he asked Bart if he could have Cudlipp as his editor. Bart graciously agreed. But the minute King left the room Bart went to see Cudlipp's door and said to him: "Here's a laugh. Cecil King is going to send for you shortly and ask you to become the editor of the *Pictorial.* As if you'd leave the *Mirror*! Go and see him. But come and see me afterwards."

Cudlipp did indeed go and see King. He accepted the job, later wondering how Bart could have thought any 24-year-old journalist offered the chance to edit a national paper could be deterred by "threats from a 54-year-old megalomaniac". He then went to see Bart, plucking up the courage needed to tell the old tyrant of his defiance.

"Seen King, Cudlipp?" Bart asked with relish, awaiting the story of his aristocratic rival's latest humiliation. "Did he offer you the job?" Cudlipp nodded, yes. Bart, delighted, brought down his fist on his desk and cackled: "What did you say, Cudlipp?"

When Cudlipp said he had accepted the job. Bart became "almost breathless with rage" and issued a threat: "I'll tell you this, you'll not get any help from me, no help at all…" After that, Bart tried to keep King and Cudlipp out of the *Mirror* as much as possible and confound them whenever he could. But to his intense annoyance the *Pictorial* under Cudlipp began to put on circulation at a faster rate than even the revived *Mirror*.

The reason was that at the *Pictorial* Cudlipp pushed the sex and sensation even further, in competition with the salacious *News of the World*, soon to be edited by his older brother Reg. Typical headlines included: MANIAC KILLER SLAIN IN HIS FLOATING SOUTH SEAS HAREM. Cudlipp later said his efforts to give the paper more sex content had been more important than any other change he made at the paper. He managed to get a picture of a topless woman in the *Pic* – becoming the first editor to do so, thirty-five years before "Page Three" entered the language and notwithstanding Bart's anthropological African maidens. Cudlipp simply printed "a study of springtime", featuring a topless girl in a garden surrounded by apple blossom. Cudlipp claimed he got permission from the Cowley, the chairman, by showing him the picture and getting him to talk about the apple blossom. Cowley owned an orchard in Kent and, as Cudlipp told the story, was so distracted and interested in the horticultural aspect of the picture that he approved publication without further thought.

But now, given complete editorial control, Cudlipp also gave "the *Pic*" a harder political edge to go along with all the sex. His first scoop came only a few weeks after taking over the paper, when he became the first to announce the resignation of Anthony Eden from the Chamberlain Government. Cudlipp got the story by ringing up Eden at home at midnight and put it to him that he was about to resign. Cudlipp's reading of the surprised "Oh!" (as in Oh! how did you know about that? – as opposed to Oh! what the hell are you on about?) was enough for the paper to run the story. Cudlipp inserted trenchant opinion articles into the *Pic*, which had the advantage of being a very cheap way of filling the paper's columns. Normally, Cudlipp would wrap himself in the Union Jack, attack the Conservative government's failure to stand up to the military threat from Nazi Germany and castigate the other papers for supporting a policy of peace or "appeasement" of Hitler.

Cudlipp's own articles in the paper at the time included: THE WORLD IS SAYING WE ARE YELLOW – a bombastic, nationalistic rant, decrying the policy of disarmament, and IS THIS THE BRITAIN YOU ARE PROUD OF? – another war-mongering effort, listing the times since the First World War when the British government had caved in to military pressure when it should have stood and fought. Another Cudlipp article in the *Sunday Pictorial* praised Hitler for "putting six million Germans back to work and making a great nation fit" but said that readers ought to "deeply resent" German foreign policy. His persecution of the Jews was "disgusting". Cudlipp concluded: "I look upon Hitler in many ways as the Devil in human form. All the same, you must give the devil his due, because his success is the source of his dangerous power."

In July 1938 Cecil King and Cudlipp visited Winston Churchill at his home in Kent and planned out a political campaign against appeasement, demanding the urgent creation of a large army, air force and navy ready to fight Germany if the need arose. Churchill was signed up as a columnist for the *Mirror* and the *Sunday Pictorial*.

But when war itself broke out Cudlipp was to play no direct role at either the *Pictorial* or the *Mirror* because he was conscripted into the army.

For the time being the spotlight shifted back to Bartholomew and his titular editor Cecil Thomas, both of whom very nearly got the *Mirror* closed down amid charges of undermining national morale and the war effort and – such was the memory of Rothermere's influence at the paper – helping the Germans win the war.

9 POOR BLOODY INFANTRY

Harry Guy Bartholomew and Cecil Thomas sink into deep leather armchairs in an imposing oak-panelled office buried within the sand-bagged bowels of wartime Whitehall. It is March 1942, barrage balloons are overhead. The war is far from over, but there are signs that the allies are starting to get the upper hand in the war against Nazi Germany.

Through the gloom Bart and Thomas eye up the irascible figure of Herbert Morrison, the self-educated London Labour Party politician, East End MP and Home Secretary in the War Cabinet headed by Winston Churchill. They sit silently as Morrison thumbs through a dossier on his desk, pulling out a cartoon and squinting at it with evident disgust through his one good eye and says sarcastically: "in my opinion, very artistically drawn… worthy of Goebbels at his best".

The cartoon had been printed in the *Daily Mirror* a few days before-hand. It showed a muscular but exhausted merchant sailor clinging on to a driftwood raft facing a certain and horrifying death on the open ocean after, it seemed, his ship had been torpedoed by the Germans. The caption read: "The price of petrol has been increased by one penny – official". Some members of the War Cabinet accused the *Mirror* of delib-erately trying to undermine public morale. Others wondered if the paper was part of some secret underground German propaganda effort.

The *Mirror* had already officially put its case in writing. The cartoon was meant to help – not hinder – the war effort. The intended effect was to shame people into saving petrol. Nevertheless, the paper had been threatened with closure. Bart's plan was to listen to what Morrison had to say in complete and defiant silence… and then ignore him.

Morrison continues, saying the cartoon is "thoroughly wicked", adding that "only a fool or somebody with a diseased mind" could have produced such a cartoon. He turns to Thomas and in threatening tones says, "only a very unpatriotic editor could have passed that for publication". Thomas was almost provoked at this point. Morrison had refused to fight in the

First World War, citing political objections. It needled Thomas to be called unpatriotic by a cowardly Hun-loving "conchie".

Morrison explains that the Attorney-General has assured him there are legal grounds for closing down the *Mirror* because "the effect of the cartoon is to spread defeatism". The Communist newspaper *The Daily Worker* had been closed down for the same reason. Churchill had already ordered MI5 to investigate Philip Zec, the man who had drawn the cartoon, and to find out whether a group of fascists put in place by Rothermere, the recently deceased Nazi sympathiser, was still somehow secretly controlling the paper. They discovered that the *Mirror* stock was widely dispersed, with no one block of shareholders exercising control. They found that Zec was Jewish, and a man of pronounced left-wing and anti-fascist views. Bartholomew and Thomas remain stony-faced. Morrison warns them that, unless they edit the paper in a more responsible and reasonable way in future, he will close them down "at a speed that will surprise you". The *Mirror* executives are dismissed and make their way silently out of the building. Criticism of the way the government was running the war effort was toned down for a while and the paper continued to be published without interruption.

Under Rothermere the *Mirror* had — like most papers — been a firm supporter of the policy of "appeasing" Hitler adopted by the Conservative party and its leader Neville Chamberlain. The policy led to the signing of the Munich agreement with Adolf Hitler which, Chamberlain said, guaranteed "peace in our time" at the expense of acquiescing to Hitler's territorial demands in Europe. Once Rothermere was gone, the *Mirror* was essentially non-political. But by the late 1930s it could no longer afford to ignore the international situation and began to take an increasingly anti-Nazi stand. The *Mirror's* best staff writers Cudlipp, William Connor (working under the pen-name "Cassandra") and Richard Jennings began churning out effective and entertaining patriotic anti-Nazi and pro-war propaganda.

Jennings wrote punchy leading articles or "editorials" attacking Chamberlain, appeasement and the *Mirror's* rivals — "the Heil-Hitlerite organs of the British press". In September 1938, when most of Fleet Street was calling for an accommodation with Hitler, Jennings wrote in the *Mirror:* "The Dictators mean war. Be strong. Re-arm. Seek allies. Appeasement will not save us; it is leading to disaster." The criticism of Nazi Germany began to be as consistent in the *Mirror* as the praise lavished by Rothermere's *Daily Mail*. Eventually, Hitler complained personally to the British Foreign Minister Lord Halifax about the paper, saying it was complicating Anglo-German relations. Much later, it was discovered that Cecil King, Bartholomew, Cecil Thomas, Hugh Cudlipp, "Cassandra" and many other senior *Mirror* journalists had been put on a Gestapo "death list" for immediate execution in the event of a Nazi conquest of London.

On September 4, 1939, the day after the outbreak of war, the *Mirror* appeared with a roaring lion on its front page. Inside, the "Cassandra" page was set out poster-style: "WANTED! For Murder... For Kidnapping... For Theft and Arson – Adolf Hitler alias Adolf Schicklegruber..." The paper billed Richard Jennings as "The Most Important Journalist in Britain" and "The Man Who Made England Sit Up" because of his anti-appeasement warnings. Chamberlain, the architect of appeasement, was still in office as Prime Minister. The *Mirror* led the noisy campaign to drive him out and replace him with Winston Churchill. The paper declared: "In 1939 we cannot endure fools in high places as we did after 1914. The self-revealed blunderers must go."

But even after Chamberlain resigned (for "health reasons") and gave way to Churchill, the *Mirror* continued its campaign against the "bone heads" at the top of the British army and the "out-of-touch toffs" of the Conservative party and government who knew nothing of the reality of modern warfare and who had "got us into this mess in the first place".

"Cassandra" railed against "the encrusted barnacles in obsolete brass hats" who harmed the war effort through inefficiency and by imposing petty discipline on the rank and file of the services. Jennings on the leader page reacted to the early disasters in the war, such as Dunkirk, by denouncing "the men at the top – the discredited and inefficient survivors of the appeasement period" who were derided as "dope Ministers", "old blunderers", the "Men of Munich" and "the old loitering gang". In one leader Jennings wrote the telling words: "In these critical times dead wood isn't even of use for the coffins of those martyred through muddle."

Bartholomew had been determined to claim for the *Mirror* the role it had enjoyed during the First World War of being "the soldiers' paper". He understood the instinctive, practical, tribal working-class patriotism of the troops, the feeling that they were being led by upper-class idiot officers (the phrase from the First World War was "lions led by donkeys"), the yearning the troops had shown for news from home and the huge demand from families left at home for pictorial news of what was happening on the front line.

Bart had appointed Bill Greig to write a regular column dealing with soldiers' grievances, building on the proven success of the Old Codgers and Dorothy Dix letters features which were already part of the paper. Thousands wrote to Greig, and the letters came from wives and girlfriends as well as troops and sailors – down-to-earth complaints about delays, red tape, official insensitivity, inefficiency, arrogance. Inevitably, sex – or the lack of it – was one theme. The *Mirror* ran a campaign about VD – reporting that it was rife in the forces and calling on the Ministry to do something about it. And "Jane" – one of the cartoon strips Bart had introduced into the paper – was made far more sexy. Originally, the cartoon had been billed as "the adventures of a Bright Young Thing". During the war Jane frequently appeared semi-naked in a variety of coy but risqué situations. The newspaper commentator Bernard Levin later wrote that when he first saw "Jane" as a schoolboy it had been "the last word in naughtiness, the 1940s equivalent of what by the 1970s would have been unexpurgated editions of the Marquis de Sade".[20]

The *Mirror*, as a matter of policy, always took the side of the soldiers against the imbecilities of the "old men" and "ostrich-ism" of the officer class and the politicians. To the fury of the military high command, units where officers overdid "bull" and "blanco" were named, and officers' pictures printed. Alongside Greig, the *Mirror* hired Tom Winteringham as its expert on military tactics. He was given a column called THE WAR TO WIN THE WAR. Winteringham was a veteran of the Spanish Civil War who had fought on the republican side and experienced the new terror tactic of aerial bombing at first hand. After that, Winteringham warned that a more general war in Europe was inevitable. Based on his experience of the reality of 1930s warfare – as opposed to the memory of the First World War that guided the high command – Winteringham campaigned for the building of a network of air-raid shelters, a force of civilian air-raid protection wardens and the mass mobilisation of the population to form a Home Guard. In one of his first WAR TO WIN THE WAR columns he wrote: "How do we get a modern air force? Obviously the first thing to do is to get rid of the men at the top who know so little about modern warfare that they have prevented us from having modern dive-bombers".

Hugh Cudlipp later boasted that during the war the *Mirror* became "the bible of the services' rank and file, the factory worker and the housewife." He added: "No daily journal was in a better position to register the nation's pulse. All the clues were in the *Mirror*'s postbag from its readers." Reporters and executives – including Cudlipp – who had been called up were required to write secretly to the paper as often as possible, reporting on the mood and atmosphere in their units so that they could be echoed in the columns of the paper. As the paper gained momentum, Bart hired the future Labour cabinet minister Barbara Castle to tour British military bases organising "Question Time in the Mess" meetings that aired grievances which were then reported in the paper. By 1945 the paper claimed 11 million readers and 2.4 million sales – limited only by wartime paper rationing which capped the number of copies printed. Demand was naturally boosted by the war – not just because of hunger for news, but because of the sheer boredom and communal nature of life in wartime. The paper responded by giving people something to talk about and debate with the relative strangers in the barracks hut, on the wartime factory floor and in the communal air-raid shelter. The *Mirror* was quite unlike the *Daily Mail* or the *Express,* which were aimed at the solitary commuter strap-hanging on the train into the big city, or the solitary housewife at home. It was still less like *The Times* or *Telegraph,* designed with the silence of the private study, senior common room or the reading room of a gentlemen's club in mind.

Cudlipp meanwhile spent most the war in uniform, editing *Union Jack,* the British Army's answer to the American forces' morale and propaganda sheet *The Stars and Stripes.* Cudlipp's paper was designed as a passable miniature version of the *Mirror* complete with the "Jane" strip, football results and a letters page airing grievances and giving advice. He got carpeted only once – for running a court story about the divorce of an officer, revealing every detail of his sex life. *Union Jack* also had a cheerful anti-"Yank" tone – complaining that the British troops in Italy needed a special allowance so they could afford to compete with the Yanks in buying the favours of local women.

At the end of the war Cudlipp was given the OBE and the honorary rank of Lieutenant Colonel and was one of those adjudged to have had "a good war". Cudlipp's private papers at the time show that he may also have joined the intelligence services, or at least was approached to do so.[21]

Towards the end of the war, Cudlipp's thoughts naturally turned to his future. As far as he was aware his old job as editor of the *Sunday Pictorial* was still on offer – in fact his position was protected by the law, which guaranteed that no returning soldier could be sacked or taken back on worse conditions than those he had enjoyed before being called up. But King wrote hinting that greater things were in store. "I believe more people are more seriously-minded than they were before the war," King wrote, "but there are formidable numbers, at home anyway, who are at least as feather-brained as ever. I am not arguing that instruction should not be given, but our main function is – and is likely to remain – entertainment". A few months later, King wrote again to Cudlipp delightedly giving him the news that John Cowley, Rothermere's "trusty" chairman of the *Mirror* board, had died of Bright's disease. A brief power struggle had resulted and Bart had become chairman, with King in the key role of head of advertising and finance director.

"There are various projects under discussion and Cowley's departure will mean a great impetus for all plans for the future," King wrote. A few weeks later King wrote again saying, "we have been discussing various post-war publications and under the new regime you feature very much more prominently."

"One thing is very certain about the new step up," King wrote, "and that is that we are all going places!"

10 FORWARD WITH THE PEOPLE

Some thought it significant that the *Mirror*'s Geraldine House head-quarters on Fetter Lane, just off Fleet Street, and named by Northcliffe after his mother, had been the only newspaper offices to have been bombed by the Luftwaffe during the Second World War. The premises of the "Heil Hitler Press" – as the *Mirror* called most of its rivals – had been miraculously spared. If the German air force's plan had been to wipe out the *Mirror*'s journalists then their aim was good, but their intelligence hopeless. It was rare for the top brass of the *Mirror* to be found in the office. The paper was to a large extent planned and edited in the nearby pubs. If the Germans had wanted to knock the *Mirror* out of the war they should have dropped a bomb on El Vino's wine-bar – the place where Bart carried on much of his business and where, more often than not, he could be found drinking steadily for hours at a time.

By the end of the Second World War, El Vino's had become a British journalistic institution. It was owned and run by a florid-faced eccentric called Frank Bower, customarily decked out in a bowler hat, black Edwardian frock coat, striped trousers and a silk waistcoat. Bower would fawn over important regulars like Bart or star writers like William Connor – "Cassandra" of the *Mirror*. Bower would protect favoured clients' privacy by glaring suspiciously from behind the bar with tremendous rudeness at everyone else who entered the place. Sometimes, he would suddenly yell at a stranger: "Out of my house this minute, sir, and do not let me see you in here again".

Bart was such a regular customer that he had claimed by squatter's rights ownership of a square of floor-space near the door. He would stand there every day, drinking whisky with the company's senior accounting clerk who was Bart's only apparent friend and confidant at the *Mirror*. No other regular would ever dare stand in "Bart's place", even when the *Mirror* chief was not there. New customers would get black looks from Bower or his staff if they strayed into the space. They certainly would not be served.[22]

Naturally it was in El Vino's that one of the modern *Mirror*'s most significant front pages was devised. One fine day just before the 1945 general election, *Mirror* news editor Garry Allighan was standing in the wine-bar with Michael Foot and Nye Bevan, leaders of the socialist left-wing of the Labour party, drinking and talking about the forthcoming election. Allighan was himself the Labour candidate for Gravesend. The wartime national coalition lead by the Conservative Churchill, but staffed by many Labour ministers, was about to be dissolved and it was widely thought that Churchill, the great war leader and national hero, would lead the Conservatives to victory at the polls.

Allighan was not so sure. He thought most people in the forces were likely to vote Labour because they blamed the pre-war Conservative policy of "appeasement" for causing the war in the first place. Philip Zec, the *Mirror* cartoonist who had drawn the "Price of Oil" cartoon which had caused so much grief for the paper during the war, caught the national mood, especially in the services, brilliantly with another cartoon. It showed a wounded British soldier emerging from the devastation of the battlefield, his bandaged arm in a sling, looking heroic but sorrowful and holding out a battered and dirty laurel crown bearing the words "Victory and Peace in Europe". The soldier said to the readers: "Here you are, don't lose it again". It became one of the most famous images of the war.

Then, ten days after the death of Hitler, the *Mirror* adopted the slogan "Forward with the People" and ran a leader, picking up the victory theme and saying: "There are shining victories to be won in the cause of peace and social justice. We shall reach new freedom not by submitting to economic slavery but by doing our duty faithfully while we lead a full, enjoyable life. The bill has to be paid, but we shall work and we shall play..."

The market research that had been playing such a big role in editorial decisions at the *Mirror* ever since the days of Basil Nicholson showed 86 per cent of the population to be in favour of the Beveridge report, which proposed a National Health Service. The overwhelming feeling was of "no return to the 1930s" – the "hungry decade" of unemployment, grinding poverty, fascism and war. The *Mirror*'s daily sacks of letters told the same story in more detail.

So Allighan, Foot and Bevan were standing in El Vino's, under the beady eye of Frank Bower, puzzling over the best way for the *Mirror* to help Labour win the election, without actually telling anyone how to vote. Allighan told Bevan that the entire campaign had to be based on an appeal to women voters: "Sod the servicemen," he said. "Most of them will vote for us, anyway." But their wives and girlfriends didn't "know their arses from their elbows" when it came to politics, he said. The danger was that, without discussing it with their husbands, the women would vote for Churchill simply because he was the only name in politics they had heard of. "If we could get the wives on our side we'd be home and dry," Allighan said and suggested a headline directed exclusively at women voters, telling them to cast their ballot for Labour – because it was what their husbands would have wanted. Bevan said it was a brilliant idea: "Go and tell that to Bart… explain it to him". The result was the front-page headline VOTE FOR HIM, published on polling day in July 1945. It told readers to cast their vote for "the men who won the victory for you".

The paper warned:

You failed to do this in 1918. The result is known to all. The "land fit for heroes" did not come into existence. The dole did. Short-lived prosperity gave way to long, tragic years of poverty and unemployment. Make sure history does not repeat itself. Let no one turn your gaze from the past. The call of the men who have gone comes to you. Pay heed to it. Vote for them.

The overwhelming majority of servicemen were found to have voted Labour, but what turned the election into a completely unexpected landslide and total rout for Churchill was the number of proxy votes cast in Britain by wives on behalf of men still away in the services, just as Allighan thought.[23]

The political impact of newspapers is endlessly debated, but it seemed clearer in 1945 than at any time before or since that a single newspaper – the *Mirror* – had a decisive impact on the outcome of a general election. The myth – at least – was born of the *Daily Mirror's* immense political power and its importance to the Labour party.[24]

The paper's skill in judging the mood of times seemed to sweep it along on the crest of a tidal wave of generational and political change. The *Mirror* shared in the glory of Labour's 1945 unexpected landslide, which brought the welfare state, greatly expanded education, social security and the first efforts to clear the slums and get rid of the rigid class system of the 1930s. Wartime restrictions and paper rationing meant that the *Mirror's* circulation was being held at an artificially low level. But everyone seemed to sense that there was massive potential demand for the paper.

None of these developments, or his own success in at last capturing the chairman's position he had coveted for thirty years since first joining the board, made Bart any less misanthropic, or feel more secure in his job. If anything, he was more paranoid than ever – increasingly suspicious of his old ally Cecil King. When Rothermere and Cowley were still in charge of the paper, Bart knew that a tactical alliance with King was essential in his dealings with the board. But, when Cowley died in 1944, Bart, at the age of 66, made himself chairman as well as editorial director and started replacing the Rothermere-era directors with his own placemen. Philip Zec the cartoonist and Cecil Thomas, his titular editor, joined the board. King moved up the ladder as well, adding the role of finance director to that of advertising sales. Bart's private loathing of King – the aristocratic "toff" who owed his job at the *Mirror* and his place on the board to family connections – began to come to the fore.

Bart was not wrong in feeling paranoid. The moment Cecil King joined the *Mirror* in 1926 he had determined that he would make a success of the "bastard offspring" of his uncle Northcliffe's empire, proving to the rest of his family that he was worthy of the Harmsworth name. It was true that King owed his position on the paper to nepotism, pure and simple. He had also grown up in the expectation that Northcliffe would leave him a lot of money. But when his famous uncle died in 1922 all Cecil got was £500 as his share of the £5-million bequest.

King was therefore forced to keep up aristocratic appearances on the relative pittance of a salary provided by the advertising job at the *Mirror*, arranged by the family. At his shooting lodge in Aberdeenshire he kept on the wall a huge portrait of Northcliffe as a young man. The physical likeness was such that visitors often mistook the man in the painting for King himself. People who knew King well also knew that he longed to step into his uncle's shoes one day.

In the meantime he explained away his lack of fortune and the humiliation of his long apprenticeship in the advertising department at the *Mirror* (and other, even more humble, clerical positions in the family firm) by saying that people ought to remember that Northcliffe himself once had to "push a wheelbarrow full of second-hand books for sale down Farringdon Road" to make a living.

As the opportunities of the 1950s and the post-war boom began to open up before him, King began to eye an even greater prize – that on the success of the *Mirror* he could build a second Harmsworth newspaper empire that might outshine even the first.

Standing in the way was the ageing and increasingly uncertain figure of Harry Guy Bartholomew.

11 JUDAS ISCARIOT

Bartholomew pulls himself upright, tugs his collar against the cold and looks at the three other men standing against the grim exterior of Brixton prison, in south-west London.

"I bet that's the first and last formal meeting of newspaper directors ever held in a jail," he says, a characteristic thin, cruel smile playing on his lips. With a nod towards the others he pulls open the rear door of his chauffeur-driven car, tosses a pile of documents on the back seat, struggles in after them and orders the driver to set off.

It is December 1949 and three members of the *Mirror* board – Cecil King, Hugh Cudlipp and Philip Zec – are left waiting for their own cars. They have just been inside on a visit to see Silvester Bolam, editor of the *Mirror,* who is currently serving a six-month sentence for the crime of contempt of court. Inside the prison the directors waited in the visiting area until Bolam was brought before them by a prison warder. Bart needed Bolam's signature on a pile of documents and the guard looked at each document before Bolam was allowed to sign.

Bart seemed to take pleasure in the fact it was Bolam and not himself who was behind bars, which might have been more just. Bolam was in prison and yet he had nothing to do with the article in the *Mirror* – a front-page story about a major and grisly murder, which was likely to seriously affect or "prejudice" the jury against the accused. He had not even been in the building when the article was discussed, written and approved (by Bartholomew). But, according to the law of the land, it was the named editor of a newspaper who had to take responsibility for what was in the paper. And that was Bolam the editor, not Bart the "editorial director".

When the hapless Cecil Thomas had suffered his last plank bashing and retired as editor of the *Mirror* in 1948, Cudlipp – with his good war and tremendous success at the *Pic* – seemed to be the obvious choice to take the editor's chair. But Bart had already decided to get rid of him. The young Welshman had defied him by taking the *Pictorial* job in the first place and then embarrassed him by making a success of it, saving Cecil

King's bacon into the bargain. Bart had been required by law to offer Cudlipp his pre-war job as *Pictorial* editor. But there was no chance of him ever supporting Cudlipp's promotion to the top job at the *Mirror*.

Bart had forced the appointment of Bolam through the board instead. Having got his way, he published a gloating front-page "manifesto" under Bolam's name to mark the fact that the *Mirror* had overtaken the *Express* to become the biggest-selling daily newspaper in the country. Nobody except those in the know would have worked out that the manifesto was aimed not so much at the *Express* as at King. It was Bart's way of smashing a metaphorical plank over King's head in front of six million readers.[25]

King had made the mistake of gainsaying Bart by suggesting that the paper needed to change. They had got the formula right for the 1930s and the war, but the post-war readership would be different – better educated, more prosperous and more female. The paper would need a change of approach. It was a matter of slow, evolutionary change. But change there must be. The *Mirror* would have to become less sensationalist and more up-market and "aspirational" like the *Express*.

Bart took all this as a personal affront, and commandeered the front page at the moment of the paper's triumph over the *Express* to deliver a stinging reply. The "manifesto" lambasted (unnamed) "critics" (meaning King and Cudlipp) who, from their ivory towers or positions of privilege, accused the *Mirror* of being a "sensational" newspaper. The paper was sensationalist and proud of it: "We believe in the sensational preparation of news and views," the manifesto continued, "especially important news and views, as a necessary and valuable service in these days of mass readership and democratic responsibility. It means big headlines, vigorous writing, simplification into everyday language and the wide use of illustration by cartoons and photographs. Sensational treatment is the answer, whatever the 'sober' and 'superior' readers of some other journals may prefer. No doubt we shall make mistakes but at least we are alive…"

Bolam, however, was an intellectual – certainly by the standards of Bart – who loved explaining complicated issues like the economics of the National Health Service, foreign affairs or developments in science in clear, sharply edited language. Bolam could produce the "sensationalist" *Mirror*, of course, but that vision of the paper was Bart's and not his own.

Bolam had been picked out from relative obscurity at the paper to be Bart's mouthpiece. He was clever enough to do the job, without beoming any sort of threat to Bart. His main job was to transmit Bart's wishes to the staff. Bolam was a small, dapper man with a gnarled face and a goatee beard, a working-class Geordie with an economics degree who had started in journalism on the *Newcastle Journal* in 1926 and joined the *Mirror* as a sub-editor in the wake of the 1935 Bart "revolution". He was popular enough in the newsroom, mainly because he did what he could to shield the reporters and subs from the increasingly erratic and sadistic Bart. He was a decent if unspectacular man, everybody thought – a moralising Christian socialist who nevertheless had a liking for high living. There was a rumour that he was a lay Methodist preacher, though nobody at the paper could remember ever having seen him in a pulpit. He was, however, a supporter of Christian Action, a left-wing pressure group, and had acquired the nickname "Bish".[26]

The story that had led to his incarceration was the first really major murder trial of his editorial reign. It concerned John Haigh who became known as "Vampire Murderer" because of the way he drank the blood of his female murder victims. Haigh was arrested in March 1948 and charged with the murder of a woman in Notting Hill, London. Scotland Yard had tipped off the *Mirror* that Haigh was what would now be called a "serial killer". The story was perfect for the *Mirror* and, without consulting Bolam, Bart splashed the story on the front page under the headline VAMPIRE HORROR IN NOTTING HILL.

The legal problem came from the fact that the paper printed a clearly recognisable picture of Haigh in the process of being arrested and wearing handcuffs. The *Mirror* report called him a "monster" and a "maniac" who "cut the throats of people he had killed and sucked their blood through a lemonade straw" before dissolving their bodies in an acid bath. The rules governing what newspapers can say about suspects in criminal cases before a trial starts are very strict. Above all, nothing must be done to imply that a defendant is guilty before a jury has been assembled and evidence starts to be given under oath. The idea is to make sure that the accused gets a fair trial and that the "presumption of innocence" – that a man is innocent until proved guilty – is maintained. If a newspaper does anything to "prejudice" a jury, then it has committed the crime of "contempt of court" – a very serious offence that carries a maximum jail sentence of thirty years.

The judge in the Haigh case decided that the *Mirror* had committed "contempt" because the picture of Haigh in handcuffs, the headline and some of the details of his arrest would make any reasonable person – and all the members of the jury if they saw the paper – think that Haigh was guilty, even before a single word of evidence had been heard in court. Lord Goddard, the Lord Chief Justice, said that he had never seen a case of contempt of court that was "of such a scandalous and wicked character". During the contempt trial the judge peered carefully at the reasonable and unassuming Bish and, at one point, said that he did not believe he was the editor of the *Daily Mirror*. The judge wondered if Bish was really responsible for the words that had appeared in the paper. But Bolam loyally took the rap.[27]

Bolam was reinstated as editor when he came out of prison – which Bart presented to the world as a rare act of kindness and generosity. But by then Bolam was a completely broken man. He talked gamely of the way prison had given him "time to reflect". But the three months he had served of his sentence took their toll on his health and state of mind. His family suffered badly and his children were bullied when their school-mates found out their father was in prison. Bolam did not even have the potential mental prop of martyrdom to lean upon. The article he was being punished for was at best a stupid, reckless error and at worst carried a serious risk of undermining the precious and precarious right to a fair trial for no good reason other than newspaper sales and profits. He knew from the moment he put on his prison overalls that his career as a jour-nalist was over. He remained in place at the *Mirror* purely because of Bart and was all the more dependent upon him as a result.

With any sort of threat from the senior editorial ranks of the *Mirror* dealt with, Bart started plotting the removal of Cudlipp from the *Sunday Pictorial* and, if possible, King from the *Mirror* board. Bart expertly planned Cudlipp's sacking to happen at the *Mirror* senior staff's 1948 Christmas Eve party, held at Emile's, a Fleet Street restaurant. As usual, all present were drinking heavily. Cudlipp had two or three bottles of claret, but for once Bart drank hardly anything. Congratulatory speeches rolled out as the afternoon wore on, everyone was in an excellent mood because circu-lation had been climbing and the *Express* had been trounced. Cudlipp's *Pictorial* had been doing especially well, boosted by a series of articles he had commissioned from the public opinion research organisation Mass Observation on public attitudes towards sex. The results had been run as a series of lengthy illustrated features for six consecutive weeks headed "The Private Life of John Bull... Are Our Morals on the Decline?". The answer was basically, er, yes. Week after week headlines like: "Marriage-Love Outside Marriage-Divorce", "Sex Education", "Family Planning" and "Prostitution" decorated the front page. Sales went through the roof.

Now, in the restaurant, the celebration rolled on. Bart seemed to be joining in the mood of back-slapping and self-congratulation. He seemed particularly keen to make sure that everyone, and especially Cudlipp, was well oiled – going around the table filling glasses himself and insisting on toast after toast. Then his mood suddenly changed. He started asking Cudlipp why it was that he had "spiked" (meaning refused to print) an article written by Cecil King about a riot in Nigeria which had led to several deaths in the Enugo coalfield. King was in Nigeria supervising a chain of *Mirror*-owned newspapers he had established and ran in his capacity as finance director. Cudlipp blearily explained that Enugo was not much of a story for the readers of the *Pictorial*. Cecil had picked it up on his business travels. But Bart continued to goad and provoke Cudlipp – asking sarcastically if this was not just the sort of uplifting, serious, non-sensational material that people wanted these days. Cudlipp held his own and the exchanges started to turn into an ugly argument. As the relatively sober Bart wound up the legless Cudlipp the room fell silent, the temperature dropped by several degrees and the mood changed from bonhomie to nervousness. Eventually Cudlipp "erupted in a torrent of fiery rudeness" in the words of one of those present. Bart, a slight flicker of satisfaction apparent to some, stood quietly, pointed to the door and hissed calmly: "Get out of here, Cudlipp. You are dismissed." Back at the office the thin white envelope was already waiting for him.

Cudlipp later wrote that Bartholomew had fired him that day "with all the subtlety accorded to a tenth-rate sub-editor who turns up late on the first morning of a month's trial." In another letter to a friend, Cudlipp wrote: "The final Bartholomew-Cudlipp clash has come. The Field Marshal has hanged his General."

King returned from Nigeria a few days later, powerless to do anything. Cudlipp wrote in a letter to King: "Now there is only one cockerel in the barnyard I suppose Bart's hens on the *Mirror* will all know even more clearly when, and how often, and to whom to lift up their skirts."

Fortunately for Cudlipp, the *Mirror's* great rival, the *Daily Express,* was prepared to take him on at once. The *Express* editor Arthur Christiansen had in fact been making job offers in writing while Cudlipp was still in the army. The *Express* owner Lord Beaverbrook was said to be taking an interest in Cudlipp's career and finally wrote to him saying he had wanted his services for "many years" and now looked forward to working with him on "the sunny side of the street". Cudlipp went to work for the *Sunday Express* on a salary of £4,500 with an additional tax-free expense account of £1,500 but he kept himself up to date with office politics at Geraldine House through his former secretary Mary Ellison. She would write letters to him about the latest horrors, gossiping about Bart and King, signing off, "I couldn't be more depressed. Yours dejectedly, Mary".

By now Bartholomew was in his early seventies and was a hopeless alcoholic, scarcely coherent after 9.30 in the morning and nearly impossible to work with. The problem came to the attention of the board because he would turn up morose and drunk at official functions and boardroom lunches with distinguished guests. In his memoirs King recalled one boardroom lunch attended by Sir Lionel Hook, the head of the Australian Radio Control Board, at which Bart mumbled "all Australians are crooks" throughout the proceedings "mercifully so incoherently as to be nearly unintelligible".

King decided in December 1951 that Bart had to go and, as finance director, he was the only man who could or would act to get rid of the old monster. There would need to be a unanimous vote of the directors. King talked most of the board round, but right to the end Bart believed that Philip Zec and Bolam – men he had personally appointed to the board to shore up his position – would never move against him.

The end for Bart came when he arrived at his desk to find a letter from Cecil King, acting on behalf of the board of directors which Bart chaired, telling him to clear his desk and leave the building immediately – the style Bart himself had so often used when sacking people.

Bart flew into a fury and phoned Zec, demanding to know what was going on. Zec said he knew nothing, but told Bart he would go and see King, who told him that all the directors wanted Bart out. He was too old, his drinking was a serious problem and he was preventing the paper changing and developing. Zec protested, but King told him that Bart had to go sooner or later.

Zec – a fellow "sensationalist" and graphic artist – was the man Bart most respected on the board and so now he could do his old mentor what amounted to a favour. He was more likely to resign quickly if Zec – and not King – explained it all to him. Zec, filled with trepidation, agreed and advanced on Bart in his office where he was steadily putting away the whisky. He told him of the board's decision and Bart answered in two words: "Fuck off."

"Please be reasonable," Zec pleaded, emphasising that he would be well looked after if he retired without too much fuss. Bart had not amassed much money from working at the *Mirror*, and had no shares in the company or a proper pension scheme. Zec told him that King was prepared to pay £20,000 – a considerable sum at the time – if he went quietly. Anyway, Zec said, there was nothing he could do about it. The board's decision was unanimous.

"Bollocks," Bart sneered, sinking yet another glass of whisky. "You will never get Bolam to agree."

"Bolam has already agreed," said Zec.

At first Bart refused to believe what he was being told. But slowly the reality started to sink in. Bolam was such a weak man that he had been swayed by King and – doubtless – other conspirators. The defection of Bolam hurt Bart more than anything else. It was an act of pure and apparently unprovoked treachery, since Bart had picked him out and promoted him, giving him the job of editor in the first place and then "rescuing" his career after his spell in prison: "Bolam – Judas Iscariot – Bolam – Judas," he began to mutter, repeating the phrase over and over, as though in a daze. It was interesting, Cudlipp later reflected, that in the only classical or literary allusion Bart made during his life, he compared himself to Jesus Christ.

Eventually, Bart realised that his position was hopeless and he broke down in tears. Zec talked him round and Bart got ready to leave the building for the last time. He left the task of gathering his belongings to his secretary but there was one removal job he wanted to carry out himself. On his wall he had accumulated a treasured collection of framed caricatures of *Mirror* editors and other senior people painted in gouache by Ralph Sallon, the famous cartoonist.

Bart was getting ready to take the pictures to his car when King called to find out why he had not yet left the building. Bart explained that he was just taking down the Sallon paintings. But King – for the first time in his life – was able to contradict him. The drawings, the new chairman-elect said, were valuable, they had been drawn in company time and belonged to the *Mirror*. They were to stay. And Harry Guy Bartholomew was to leave the *Mirror* empty-handed.

After Bart had gone, the normally reserved and tight-lipped Cecil King allowed himself the slightest tremor of exultation. In an interview he said: "I had only one real battle here and that was when I wanted to get rid of the previous chairman. One year later he was in the street and I was chairman."

At a press conference to explain the changes in the *Mirror*'s senior management, a journalist asked if it was true that Bart was an "illiterate and a drunkard". Cudlipp had objected: "That's not fair. He was *semi*-literate, and he wasn't drunk *all* the time."

★★★

In his book *English History 1914–1945* AJP Taylor, the greatest English historian of the twentieth century, commented that the importance of the *Daily Mirror* was that it had enabled "for the first time" the mass of the English public to find their own voice. "The *Mirror* had no proprietor," Taylor wrote. "It was created by the ordinary people on its staff and especially by Harry Guy Bartholomew, the man who worked his way up from office boy to Editorial Director."

Shortly after Bart's departure, Cecil King commissioned a semi-official history of the *Daily Mirror,* written by the *Mirror* reporter and Labour MP Maurice Edleman. It was, until very recently, the standard work on the subject.

Edleman's book naturally quoted AJP Taylor's accolade, emphasising the *Mirror*'s historic importance. But the quotation was printed in the following, slightly truncated form:

> The *Mirror* had no proprietor. It was created by the ordinary people on its staff… The *Daily Mirror* gave an indication as never before what ordi-

nary people in the most ordinary sense were thinking. The English people at last found their voice.

At the *Daily Mirror*, Harry Guy Bartholomew, the paper's creator in its modern form, had been officially written out of history, to be replaced by three dots on a sheet of paper.

Bart was never heard from or seen again at the paper. He retired to a modest cottage in Norfolk where he drank himself to death within a few months.

PART THREE:
In the Land of the Legless

12 SPREADING THE WINGS

Cecil King's first act as the chairman of the *Daily Mirror* at the start of 1952 was to bring Cudlipp back from Beaverbrook's *Express* newspapers, giving him back his job of editing the *Sunday Pictorial* with, soon afterwards, promotion to the board, taking Bart's old job as editorial director, making him editor-in-chief of both the *Mirror* and *Pictorial.* "Let's get together and make a dent in the history of out times," King wrote in the letter of reappointment.

Cudlipp had found his three years working for Lord Beaverbrook frustrating – in his position of managing editor of the *Sunday Express* he had not really been allowed near the front page, or to do much journalism at all. He had been a victim of Beaverbrook's policy of "stockpiling" talented or experienced national newspaper journalists in order to deny rivals of their services. The *Express* had huge numbers of journalists on the staff, all on good wages, and there was rarely enough work to go around.

But his stay on "The sunny side of the Street" as Beaverbrook liked to call the *Express*, had been instructive. He came back to the *Mirror* with a deep understanding of the *Express* titles, their strengths and weaknesses, the personalities involved… and whom he and King might headhunt.

The *Express* was admired by journalists throughout Fleet Street as a self-confident, positive and exciting newspaper. Tony Miles, later the editor of the *Mirror*, remembered that, when he started his career in the 1950s, his mates on the *Mirror* regarded themselves as the scruffy urchins looking through the window at the gold-plated wonders of the *Express.* In contrast to the run–down Geraldine House rabbit-warren offices of the *Mirror*, Beaverbrook had provided the *Express* with landmark sleek black glass-and-chrome offices in both Fleet Street and Manchester. Beaverbrook also had the man regarded as the greatest editor of his generation – the legendary Arthur Christiansen, a master of layout and newspaper design, crisp writing and clever headline-writing. Cudlipp copied all these techniques and, at one point in the 1970s, planned to make Christiansen's son editor of the 1970s *Daily Mirror* as a sort of genetic manifestation of his desire to re-cast the *Mirror* as a younger version of the *Express* of the 1940s and 1950s.

In January 1949 the *Mirror* had reached daily sales of 4,187,403 and had moved almost a quarter of a million ahead of the *Daily Express*. It was an achievement, but the *Express* was not too worried. Beaverbrook's flagship was adding more sales as well, but at a slightly lower rate. Where the *Express* was still ahead of the *Mirror* was in the value of its advertising. The *Express* had always appealed to a more middle-class audience, originally in competition with Northcliffe's *Daily Mail* (sales of which had dwindled under the first Lord Rothermere and his son Rothermere II). Cudlipp said the *Express* sold to the man with a car and a garage. The *Mirror* sold to the man who made the car and the garage.

King and Cudlipp were obsessed with the *Daily Express* and the success of its owner, Lord Beaverbrook – by the 1950s acknowledged as the last and greatest of the old-style press barons. King knew the premium the *Express* was able to charge advertisers desperate to reach a mass middle-class audience. At the same time both he and Cudlipp were beginning to think about the changing shape of the working class. The younger generation – the "baby boomers" born after the war – would grow up with all the benefits of the welfare state and the 1944 Education Act, which was set to extend the length and quality of free education for ordinary people. Bart's *Mirror* – with its diet of bawdy pictures, Yank cartoons, crime stories and vituperation at the expense of the nobs and toffs – had been a great act for the 1930s. But it was unlikely to work in the coming New Britain of the 1950s and 1960s with its welfare state and the Labour government famously elected in 1945 with the *Mirror's* help.

The political battle between the *Mirror* and the *Express* had been set out in that election and until the end of the century the two papers continued to support the Labour and Tory parties respectively. In the 1945 election the *Express* had backed Churchill and run a smear campaign against Labour saying that if they got into government they would set up a "Socialist Gestapo". It cut little ice. The *Express* was at the time still remembered for its pro-appeasement stance before the war and, in particular, a front page printed just before the outbreak which declared THERE WILL BE NO WAR THIS YEAR. When the legislation finally bringing the National Health Service into being was passed the *Mirror* marked the event by commanding national celebrations under the banner headline THE DAY IS HERE! The *Express,* in contrast, had run the knocking headline MIDNIGHT – AND THE FREE-FOR-ALL BEGINS.

However, the *Express* entered a golden age in the 1950s, despite losing first place in the circulation stakes to the *Mirror*. Beaverbrook had invested heavily in new presses in both London and Manchester. There was a huge editorial staff, including a large number of foreign correspondents, as part of a Great Value, "more of everything", editorial strategy. Under Arthur Christiansen – regarded by tabloid folk as greatest "technical" journalist ever - the paper recovered and sales rose towards four million. Christiansen's formula was simple. The *Express* was "aspirational" – it exuded optimism and faith in the future, and brought its readers into vicarious contact with the alleged glamour of the rich and powerful "beautiful people" it specialised in writing about and photographing.

With Bart out of the way King and Cudlipp began to remodel the *Mirror* as a more modern version of the *Express*. But, at the same time, King was preoccupied with the early stages of building his Harmsworth Second Empire, running a chain of newspapers in West Africa and in Australia and with playing a role in national politics. So Cudlipp played a larger and larger role in shaping the paper - as he later put it himself, "allowing the paper to spread its wings". The *Mirror*, Cudlipp said, was "already acknowledged as audacious and irreverent, now it elbowed its way into national and international affairs at an exciting time with a panache that avoided pomposity and punditry".[28]

Changes were noticed in the newsroom at once. Rare species such as university graduates – and even women – were seen on the editorial floor for the first time in fifty years. A clutch of female Oxbridge "bluestock-ings" joined the *Mirror*. They were not hands-on journalists used to knocking on doors, but experts in politics and diplomacy who were supposed to give the paper's coverage greater depth. One of the first was Shirley Williams, the future Labour cabinet minister. Another was Diana Houston-Boswall, a diplomat's daughter, and Anne Lloyd-Williams, a chief constable's daughter who later became the *Mirror*'s Royal Correspondent. Then there was the remarkable Betty Tay who wrote about animals and set up the immensely popular *Mirror* Pets Club. Tay clinched her appointment as a reporter by turning up for interview in full riding rig and riding a horse up Fetter Lane, tying the reins to the orna-mental wrought-iron gates that led to the paper's headquarters.

Alongside the bluestockings, Cudlipp brought in cronies picked up at various stages of his career – from local papers in Cardiff, Manchester and Blackpool to his army pals and colleagues at the *Express* and *Pictorial*. One was the upper-class sports writer Peter Wilson, who came over from the *Sunday Pictorial* to become sports editor. Wilson had joined the *Mirror* on the same day as Cudlipp and "Cassandra" in 1935. He was famous for his boxing reports which, it was said, concentrated so much on the crushing and clashing of bone and the gushing of blood from noses that his reports was "like reading about a road accident". Wilson shared another charac-teristic of Cudlipp's in-group – he was a prodigious drinker, even by the standards of the time. Waddling around, baying in his upper-class accent, wearing a cape, sporting a bright red, bulbous drinker's nose and carrying a silver-topped swordstick, Wilson struck an odd figure, like a creature from another age.

Some members of the Bart regime, of course, had to go. There was a Bart-era column in the paper Cudlipp didn't like called "The Man With A Thousand Secrets". After reading this column one night in his office Cudlipp called the columnist up and said: "Hey – want to know a real secret? You are fired". And he put down the phone. But, if he liked the paper, it would be champagne, macadamia nuts and Havana cigars for the newsroom heroes of the week, all served on a trolley pushed by Mr Lucas, the office butler.[29]

Even before Cudlipp had returned to the paper he had decided that "Bish" Bolam should be replaced as editor. He had wanted to lure Edward Pickering from the *Express* where he had been one of Christiansen's deputies. But Pickering said he wouldn't come and Cudlipp decided that the editorship should go to Jack Nener, a rough-tongued Welsh sub-editor. Nener had started in journalism at the age of 14, starting as a reporter on the *South Wales Daily Post* in Swansea. He was a fully paid-up member of Cudlipp's South Wales "Taffia".

Cudlipp wrote to King putting forward Nener's name, saying that he was not a perfect choice for editor, but would do until such time as the *Mirror* could develop some home-grown talent. King replied, saying he agreed: "It is becoming clearer every day that the *Mirror* is drifting badly under Bolam. Nener is a good old warhorse with the qualities of courage and energy (and God knows the paper needs them) but he could not hold down the editorship without a great deal of help from you".

So Nener was rocketed into the editor's chair, under the overall charge of Cudlipp. "Bish" Bolam was once again dealt with harshly. An announcement was drawn up saying that he had "resigned due to a disagreement with the management". The night he was sacked Bolam went, for once, to the pub brandishing his brush-off cheque, proclaiming himself rich and ordering champagne. "Cassandra" walked in and Bolam shouted out for him to join the party. "Come and join the wake," Bolam said. "I've just been paid off and we're celebrating." "Cassandra" looked at him with contempt and said coldly: "Sorry. I don't drink with jail-birds." Bolam, who had never really recovered from the shame, professional ignominy and physical strain of his prison sentence, died suddenly and prematurely three months later.

Jack Nener struck some as being like a Hollywood central casting director's idea of tabloid editor – crinkly silver hair, dapper bow-tie, gravelly voice, volcanic temper. All he lacked, really, was the green eyeshade.

He was a technical perfectionist with a total Bart-like ink-under-the-fingernails understanding of the newspaper production and printing process. This was especially important at the time because newsprint was still rationed and the paper was restricted to eight pages. There was no room for padding and the editing had to be very tight to get everything in. Nener concentrated his own efforts on the evening – between six p.m. when the first edition had to be printed to reach Cornwall, rural backwaters and the north in time for the morning, and the more important final editions, produced later in the evening and distributed mainly in London and the south.

During the morning and afternoon he would pretty much leave things to his deputy – the equally ferocious Joe Grizzard, known as the "Israeli commando" because he was Jewish and, it was widely known, a keen amateur pistol shot. Grizzard was a strict disciplinarian who roared around the office criticising everything and everybody. One of his sayings was the demand that somebody who had not shaped up (i.e., a "useless bastard") should be "flogged to death with syphilitic spiders".

When the first edition came off the press everyone would brace themselves for the customary whirlwind arrival of Nener. He would storm in from the pub f-ing and blinding, rushing around the newsroom tearing the paper up, screwing up pages, angrily kicking them around the floor and shouting: "I can't fucking understand a fucking word of this!" If he got completely out of control, Grizzard would snarl, "OK, Jack – we've got all that – now, it's your turn to get the fucking tea." Nener would growl but obediently take his turn in obtaining a huge steel jug of tea from the canteen and bringing it back to the newsroom while others made changes to the paper.

Individual bollockings were horrible while they lasted, but never really nasty. Nener once carpeted the paper's science reporter, Ronnie Bedford, for mentioning in a story smoke coming out of the chimney of a steam train. He dragged Bedford into his office, brandished the offending piece of paper. He went spare: "What the fuck is this? Smoke comes out of a fucking funnel, not a fucking chimney. Chimneys are what you have on houses..." In fact, Bedford was right and later left on the editor's desk a page from an encyclopedia showing that only ships had funnels. Nener went bananas again – "Who the fuck left this here?" But it blew over. Unlike Bart he did not hold grudges or plot revenge or the downfall of those he worked with.

Nener swore all the time. When in full flow he could not and did not finish a sentence without the f-word. Once he was called at home on Sunday morning by one of his deputies and the phone was answered by the family's foreign *au pair* who Nener was teaching to speak English. "No possible for Meester Neener to come," the girl said, adding innocently: "He fix now zee fucking vacuum-cleaner". Another time Nener paid a surprise visit to the home of Noel Whitcomb, the *Mirror* society columnist who lived in genteel splendour in Hampstead. As it happened Whitcomb's wife – who quite possibly had never heard a swear-word in her life – was enjoying afternoon tea with the wife of a Mayfair art dealer and an extremely cultivated and reserved American widow. "Do you live in Hampstead, Mr Nener?" asked one of the ladies with immense politeness over the bone china. "Fuck, no!" said Nener, cheerfully. "I live in an ordinary fucking house in Wimbledon."

In the newsroom Nener kept up constant banter with his deputies, Grizzard and, especially, Dick Dinsdale. The double act was often unintentionally hilarious. Dinsdale was overheard one day telling Nener: "What we need at this paper, Jack, are a few Young Turks." Nener's face crumpled in pained consideration. "I can see we need new people," he said finally, "but why in fuck's name do they have to be Turkish?" Nener's lack of reading was shown up in other ways. The subs at the *Mirror* had at one point taken to using the silly phrase "Flashman, you are a bully and a liar, and there is no place for you here!" from *Tom Brown's Schooldays* to cheer up the tedium of putting the pages together. Nener overheard the subs saying this one day and rushed off to ask Dinsdale, "Who's this fucker Flashman then?" Dinsdale said he didn't know and asked: "Is he a reporter or a sub?" Nener replied: "I don't give a fuck what he is, but get rid of him quick. Apparently he's a fucking bully and a liar."

Nener had his own ideas about the *Mirror* and Cudlipp let him get on with it most of the time. According to one senior journalist, Nener's approach involved an attempt to keep the old wartime spirit going. His version of the paper "loved charladies, patted doggies, cooed at babies, drank beer with coal miners, stuck two fingers up at the toffs and stood for no nonsense from uppity foreigners". It also saw, after a few years, the introduction of the Andy Capp cartoon strip featuring a work-shy, beer-swilling, cloth-capped, Geordie wife-beater permanently on the run from the rent collector – parodied when it was still running in the 1980s as "Sid the Sexist" in *Viz* magazine.[30]

Following Cudlipp's example, Nener made sure the paper had its daily quota of sexual interest. The feature writer Donald Zec once saw Nener hovering around the picture desk, skipping from foot to foot (Nener had gout and this made it difficult for him to stand still) waiting for the picture editor to come off the phone. Eventually the picture man covered up the phone and asked: "You want something, Jack?" Nener growled: "Yes… I need some tits to go with the rail strike story".[31]

Nener's *Mirror* was also obsessed with film stars and gave a lot of space to film reviews. The *Mirror* critic Reg Whitley became famous for his pithy style and his dismissive review of a filmed version of *Hamlet* starring Laurence Olivier is still regarded by some as a masterpiece: "Top actor in a classic yarn about a foreign prince who goes potty. All right for some." The word "classic" figured in his reviews more or less as a health warning. Much more to his liking was the standard Norman Wisdom comedy, boosted by Whitley as "a rip-roaring, laugh-a-second funathon, a whizzo romp for our Norm and just the job to tickle the fancy of all the family". Another essential part of the mix was horseracing, betting and tipping. For a while, Nener employed the services of a man called John Godley who claimed he could "dream winners" and – for the first couple of weeks of his tenure at the paper – this seemed to be true, such was his luck in picking horses.

Cudlipp had bigger ambitions for the *Mirror* and would over-rule Nener from time to time, in order to put more politics into the paper. This came mainly in the form of special "SHOCK ISSUES" devised by Cudlipp himself as what amounted to a cross between advertising posters and political pamphlets. The SHOCK front pages made a lot of impact, not least amongst journalists, and much of the *Mirror*'s later reputation as a serious paper which dealt with social issues in a big yet entertaining way rested on them. The first *Mirror* "shock issue" was produced in 1960. It was a detailed account of the suffering of horses shipped from Britain to the butchers of France and Belgium and most of the day's edition was devoted to the subject. The *Mirror* followed up with SHOCK ISSUES dealing with slum housing, race and child abuse.

Cudlipp claimed the SHOCK ISSUE as his very own invention, designed as "an exercise in brutal mass education". In 1964 a SHOCK ISSUE on poverty was hailed as having have a significant impact on the outcome of that year's general election. The front page featured a down-trodden-looking woman hanging out washing in a filthy walled back yard, six feet by nine. The whole edition was turned over to emotive examples of people right across the country enduring real poverty and blighted lives. This was after 13 years of Conservative "never had it so good" rule. The SHOCK ISSUE given over to an *exposé* of child abuse and neglect was entitled "THE HIDDEN HORROR – The fight to end cruelty in BRITISH homes" also had huge impact, doing much to put the problem on the political agenda for the first time. Other SHOCK ISSUES dealt with the "suicide cult" of "ton-up" teenage motorcycle clubs, the neglect of the elderly and the problem of poorly equipped youth clubs. The effect on sales of the SHOCK ISSUE front pages is hard to judge. They certainly did not add as many sales as conventional big news stories such as events in the life of the Royal Family. In 1953 the *Mirror* had sold over 7,000,000 copies of an edition marking the

Coronation of Elizabeth II. But the SHOCK ISSUES certainly made the paper conspicuous on the news stands.

During general election campaigns and at times of international crisis, Cudlipp would emerge on the editorial floor himself – sleeves rolled up – taking over the editing of the paper (or at least the front page) himself. General elections were handled by setting up a special editorial unit consisting of star writers like "Cassandra" and link-men to the leading figures in the political parties, especially Labour politicians. Cudlipp would become the day-to-day editor of the paper during the campaign, with the editor in charge of the rest of the paper. A lot of energy would go into brain-storming, sketching out with big thick pencils dozens of versions of the front page on big pieces of paper. According to one journalist at one of these sessions Cudlipp ran through ideas "at the speed of light". He would "deliver an inspired headline while applying a match to his eight-inch Bolivar cigar. Ash would hardly have formed before he had designed an entire centre-spread."

Cudlipp's most subtle election campaign was his first one as editorial director – marking the 1955 general election. Labour had no chance of winning and so he came up with the clever headline KEEP THE TORIES TAME – asking people to vote Labour to ensure that Conservative majority was small enough to prevent its less populist and more hard right-wing faction taking over in government.[32]

In 1956 Cudlipp again took charge during the Suez Crisis, making the *Mirror* the only paper to oppose the Conservative Prime Minister Anthony Eden's military action against the Egyptian leader Nasser, who had nationalised the Suez Canal. The anti-war campaign cost the *Mirror* an estimated 70,000 daily sales which, Cudlipp thought, was a price that had to be paid "to keep the paper on the side of the Labour party and progressive opinion generally."

In 1960 Cudlipp created one of his most famous poster front pages, commenting on the decision of the Russian leader Nikita Khrushchev to rudely walk of out a session of peace talks in Paris. In huge type the *Mirror* said:

Mr K!
(if you will pardon an Olde English phrase)
DON'T BE SO BLOODY RUDE!
PS: Who do you think you are?
Stalin?

The Cold War was a constant theme for Cudlipp, who always took a hard line. When Khrushchev's head of secret police Serov was due to visit

London, in 1960, the editorial director pushed Nener to one side and "Cassandra" was given the whole front page to castigate Serov as "an odious thug", "the Himmler of the Soviet Union", a "grisly creature" and a "revolting butcher".

Circulation continued to mount through the 1950s, for one thing because there was very little effective competition. Down-market stood the under-funded and struggling *Daily Sketch* – a quixotic attempt to produce a popular but "clean" and moralistic, pro-Imperial and right-wing paper for a mass working-class audience. Apart from its right-wing agenda and the fact that it sold for a higher price, the *Sketch* was a straightforward copy of the *Mirror*, almost indistinguishable in terms of design and writing style: "It is the only example of a carbon copy costing more than the original," Cudlipp used to say of the *Sketch*. By the late 1950s it was so ineptly edited and constrained by its 1930s Imperialist politics that it hardly mattered – its sales trapped around one million and falling.

Another potential rival, the socialist *Daily Herald*, was also in rapid decline. The dead hand of editorial control by the trade unions (who partly owned it) and the Labour party meant that it was a boring read. Many of its readers had been "bought" in the promotional giveaway circulation wars of the 1930s. Now that the free gifts were no longer on offer, the *Herald's* readers began to desert in droves – many rushing into the waiting arms of the newly pro-Labour *Daily Mirror*.

The *Herald* did not represent serious competition for the *Mirror*. The *Daily Express* was still increasing in circulation, though at a slower rate than the *Mirror*. The *Express* therefore saw no desperate need to compete head to head. Cudlipp had achieved his slight nudge up-market and advertising revenue was also flooding in.

It seemed that everything the paper touched turned to gold. And it was time to start celebrating.

13 BREAD OF HEAVEN

Mike Randall, later the editor of the *Daily Mail*, used to tell the tale of his interview for the job of features editor of the *Daily Mirror* in 1953, the year Jack Nener took charge. In fact, he could not remember everything that happened in complete detail – the reason being that the experience was soaked in a fog of alcohol.

Randall remembered for sure that he had been given champagne and caviar while he waited for the interview with Nener and his deputies to take place. He was thus feeling fairly relaxed when he went into the office chosen for the interview itself. Nener straight away offered him more champagne, to put him at his ease. Since the bottle was open for reasons of hospitality there was no harm in Nener having a glass or two as well.

The interview went well and Randall was told that he had got the job just before lunchtime – and just in time, therefore, for extended celebratory "welcome on board" drinks in the office with his new colleagues, senior executives and journalists at the *Mirror* – "all copious consumers of beer or wine or both". Then it was time for lunch – with appropriate wine accompanying each course. The midday meal, as was often the case at the *Mirror,* was "leisurely" and continued until just before pub opening time. Over pints and chasers it was time to think about the future of the *Mirror* features department and the challenges ahead. By this time Randall was of course completely pissed and he later claimed that he did not really sober up until he left the paper three years later.

The tradition of heavy drinking at the *Mirror* had been established by Bart who, in turn, had learned the art of functioning in a newspaper office while completely hammered from Hannen Swaffer – the archetypal drunken hack. Cudlipp had been a heavy drinker since his days in Yates's Wine Lodge in Blackpool. Cecil King was also a steady boozer who, like his uncles, suffered medical and health problems as a result. In Cecil's case he at one point lost all sensation in his enormous feet. In hierarchical organisations like newspapers everyone tends to take their lead from the man above them. So the booze cascaded from the top downwards. Ability to drink was seen as an essential part of the job. For reporters it was supposed to work as a type of truth serum. The idea was to get whoever you wanted to talk to into the pub, pump them full of booze, get out the notepad and wait for the quotes to roll out.

After going out drinking "on the job" it was then essential for reasons of career progression to drink with colleagues after work, or arrange to take possible employers (or be taken out by them) for "a drink". Every paper had its own pub, generally a no-go area for staff from other papers. The *Daily Mail* had the White Swan (known as the Mucky Duck); the *Telegraph* had the King and Keys. By the 1960s, the *Mirror* needed two pubs – the Printer's Devil and the White Hart (always called "the Stab" as in the "stab in the back"). Inside each pub there were invisible boundaries separating areas to be occupied according to pecking order. Any reporter straying towards a group of tables rightly occupied by executives would be given the cold shoulder. If he did it again he could get the sack.

Drunkenness could cause industrial accidents, even in the apparently safe environment of a newsroom full of typewriters. The theatre reviewer Fergus Cashin was famous for having taken a slug from a whisky bottle before yelling "I am surrounded by the inky fingers of mediocrity" and smashing his fingers down on his typewriter in the manner of a concert pianist, only to have them slip between the keys so they ended up mangled in the machinery in a bloody mess.

The whole of Fleet Street reeked with the distinctive "grey, serious smell of newsprint" wafting out of air vents and mixing with the fumes of "warm beery breath" from doorways of pubs, the former *Observer* journalist Michael Frayn remembered.

Cudlipp started his regime at the *Mirror* with a crack-down on hard liquor. Bart had been destroyed by whisky and Cudlipp resolved he would not go the same way. After, in addition, being threatened with demotion or even the sack by King, Cudlipp substituted champagne and dry white wine, which he seemed to think of as (at least compared with neat whisky) a non-alcoholic thirst-quencher to be gulped down at any time of the day. Brandy was still allowed, following the topsy-turvy logic that, since it is made from grapes, it is closer to wine than to other types of hard liquor.

One reason Cudlipp had chosen Nener to become editor, it was believed, was that he was a fellow boozer and great company in the pub. The journalist Alan Watkins, who was briefly at the Mirror Group in the 1960s, said that by then the paper had evolved a semi-official job of "editorial drinking partner" – a whole host of people who were employed just so that senior journalists like section editors, heads of department and senior correspondents would have somebody to drink with or go to the pub with at any time of the day.

Nener was thought of by others at the paper as a man with "hollow legs" – meaning that he could consume the required vast quantities of alcohol but show few signs of drunkenness – until, that is, he started singing. Mercifully the choruses of "Bread of Heaven", "Land of My Fathers" and "Keep a Welcome in the Hillside" were mostly restricted to private drinking parties at Cudlipp's fabulous Georgian mansion in Cheyne Walk which he had desecrated by turning the basement into a pub called The Chelsea Pensioner. It was decorated like a sort of Wild West saloon bar complete with 20-ft polished bar, brass rail, spittoon and a pet parrot called Bertie in a cage trained to squawk, "Buy the *Daily Mirror.*" The "pub" took its name from a life-sized waxwork Chelsea Pensioner in full uniform sitting in a rocking chair. Cudlipp's wife Eileen was prevailed upon to play the part of an Edwardian barmaid as Cudlipp, Nener and drinking-buddy-of-the-day would lead the communal singing around an open-topped upright honkytonk until one evening somebody was sick into it, gumming up the works and ruining the instrument's less than delicate tone for good.

Many of the paper's star writers were also extremely heavy drinkers. William Connor – "Cassandra" – according to Randall often missed his deadline because he needed to "sink a pint or two to try to relieve the blockage". Everyone above the very lowest level in the pecking order had a booze cabinet and some got fridges when they became available. One of the paper's most talented page designers, a man called Harry Keeble, had a fridge full of Pouilly-Fuisse – and kept an oxygen cylinder and mask next to his desk in case he needed to sober up quickly. The sports editor Peter Wilson was a legendary drinker. Michael Grade, the 1980s TV mogul who briefly had a job as a sports reporter at the *Mirror* in the 1960, remembered going to Wilson's house for dinner. Grade had resolved not to drink too much – but was defeated by the series of dishes put in front of him – soup laced with sherry, followed by steak swimming in brandy sauce, a rum sorbet rounded off with Stilton cheese floating in port. "They put me to bed utterly pie-eyed, even though not a drink had passed my lips all evening".

Much of the drinking was paid for by the lavish expense accounts given to most journalists. The system worked like a free hole-in-the-wall cash dispenser system, long before ATM machines became common on the high street. Noel Whitcomb said that he came to look upon the *Mirror* more as a highly congenial private bank than an employer. He found that he could basically bank his salary and live high on the hog off "exes". Expenses had to be accounted for at the end of the week, but this was largely a formality. At the end of his first week working for the *Mirror* in 1953, features editor Mike Randall took a deep breath and put in an expenses claim for the massive sum of £12 – more than the average industrial working wage at the time and twice what he had been allowed to claim by his previous employer, the *Sunday Graphic*. To his horror Randall was pulled to one side by managing editor Harold Barkworth who was clutching the claim and looking angry. "Mike, this really won't do," Barkworth said. "Sorry, Harold – what should I cut it down to?" Randall asked. "Don't be a bloody fool," Barkworth snapped. "Double it – or else you will be letting the side down." Randall obediently doubled the fictitious expenses claim and later said he wrote some "fine fiction" while he worked at the paper. The standard method was to buy or steal sheaves of empty bills from Fleet Street restaurants, which were filled in as a record of entertaining some non-existent VIP whenever some cash was needed to go down the pub or finance a dirty weekend in Brighton.

The expenses fiddles got steadily worse as time went by, especially when various forms of statutory wage freeze came into fashion. It reached the point, according to Christina Appleyard, who was a *Mirror* executive for a while, where some reporters would even put the services prostitutes and call-girls down on "exes". The abuse was seen as a way of paying people "cash in hand", avoiding tax and keeping down "official" salary rates. Cudlipp condoned it all. According to legend he welcomed on board one new writer with the words: "as far as entertainment is concerned, put down anything you like except the Archbishop of Canterbury. He's mine".

The greatest ever single expenses fiddle was reckoned to have been attempted by David English, a *Mirror* reporter in the 1950s who later went on to become Sir David English, the respected editor of the booming *Daily Mail* in the 1980s. English claimed a huge sum for "hire of lifeboat" needed to cover a shipwreck off the coast of Cornwall. He was only found out when the lifeboat crew wrote to complain about his article – which had criticised the rescue operation in a mild way – saying it was a bit rich to be attacked in the paper after all the help they had given English – including free use of a motor launch so he could write his story.

The *Mirror's* expenses largesse was made possible by the paper's growing sales and profitability. By the mid-1950s Cudlipp was in a position to poach any writer in Fleet Street and then pay the increasingly huge wages they demanded to stay. Frequent raids on the *Express* brought over some of those who, like Cudlipp himself at one point, had been "stockpiled" by Beaverbrook. Soon the *Mirror* was as lavishly staffed as the *Express* and this was seen by Cudlipp not as an economic weakness but as a source of journalistic strength and competitive pride.

The paper's growing circulation meant that by-lined writers and columnists became – in the pre-television age – some of the biggest celebrities and stars in the country in their own right. One of the first was Marjorie Proops who picked up the pre-war mantle of Dorothy Dix with a Nener-and-Cudlipp-inspired mission to keep up the paper's sex content. Cudlipp's own "What does John Bull really do in the Bedroom?" series had slaughtered a good many taboos a few years earlier, providing a healthy sales spurt for the *Pictorial*. The general idea was that Marje Proops would provide similar stimulation for the *Daily Mirror* every day. Proops had originally been hired as a fashion artist in 1939, then had developed into a columnist in women's magazines and in the *Daily Herald* before moving over to the *Mirror*. Her first ever column was about divorce and looks tame in retrospect: "Funny the way, when a marriage breaks up, it's so often the little things that bring it to an end," she wrote, "not the sordid infidelities or the harsh cruelties or the squalid, searing scenes". The "squalid, searing scenes" were to come later. Proops's own 20-year adulterous affair with the *Mirror*'s legal manager was well known to *Mirror* staff long before she decided to go public about it in 1993.

The *Mirror*'s greatest superstar of the 1950s was "Cassandra" – William Connor, the former JWT advertising writer who had worked with Cudlipp on *Union Jack* during the war. "Cassandra" had a tough job filling a column five days a week and his style varied from the whimsical to the utterly scathing. The first line of his first column after the war began with the words: "As I was saying before I was so rudely interrupted…"

The "Cassandra" column was headed by a tightly cropped close-up of his eyes, seen through the thick-rimmed NHS-type specs he wore in real life. He developed a tight writing style based on a technique known as the "delayed drop". His articles would often start with some innocuous observations that would go on for a couple of sentences, lulling the reader into a false sense of security before delivering the literary equivalent of a smack in the gob. One typical example of his technique was an article demanding the abolition of hanging (a defining political stance in the 1950s, and one seen as electoral suicide). It was printed on June 30, 1955 and marked the forthcoming execution of Ruth Ellis:

It's a fine day for hay-making. A fine day for fishing. A fine day for lolling around in the sunshine.

And if you feel that way – and I mourn to say that millions of you do – *a fine day for a hanging.*

The article finished with the word, "The hands that place the white hood over her head will not be our hands. But the guilt – and guilt there is in this abominable business – will belong to us as much as to the wretched executioner paid and trained to do the job in accordance with the savage public will."

Although generally liberal-minded, "Cassandra" was a man of his times, he would now be thought of as a "sexist" and certainly a homophobe – a trait he shared with both Cudlipp and King, whose loathing for "poufs" and "queers" was so intense that the wearing of suede shoes would render a man suspect. In the paper, homosexuals were routinely described as "sex perverts". When Godfrey Winn, the gay columnist, had worked for the paper "Cassandra" had done his best to persecute him, leading Winn to defend himself by saying, "I may be *queer*, but I'm *sincere.*"

In 1956, "Cassandra", in line with the *Mirror's* house-style loathing of homosexuality, wrote an amazingly vituperative and entirely unprovoked attack on the pop piano player Liberace, the Elton John of his times, an obviously (but not admittedly) homosexual stage performer known for his flamboyant, diamond-encrusted costumes and tremendously effeminate stage presence. For no apparently good reason "Cassandra" launched into an extremely violent verbal attack on Liberace:

He is the summit of sex – the pinnacle of masculine, feminine, and neuter. Everything that he, she and it can ever want… [he is a]… deadly, winking, sniggering, snuggling, chromium-plated, scent-impregnated, luminous, quivering, giggling, fruit-flavoured, mincing, ice-covered heap of mother love… He reeks with emetic language that can only make grown men long for a quiet corner, an aspidistra, a handkerchief, and the old heave-ho. Without doubt, he is the biggest sentimental vomit of all time. Slobbering over his mother, winking at his brother, and counting the cash at every second, this superb piece of calculating candy-floss has an answer for every situation… a sugary mountain of jingling claptrap wrapped up in such a preposterous clown.

"Cassandra", Cudlipp and the *Mirror* had assumed that the article was legally safe because it was merely the columnist's honest opinion – however rudely expressed. In a free country readers were free to agree or disagree. But Liberace's lawyers claimed the article deliberately gave the impression that Liberace was homosexual, which was a matter of fact (either he was, or he wasn't), which the *Mirror* had to prove (which it couldn't). As a result a libel jury ordered the *Mirror* to pay Liberace the tax-free sum of $22,400. Asked if he had found the case upsetting the pianist coined the now famous phrase: "I cried all the way to the bank."

The Liberace case was a temporary set back which came at a time when the *Mirror* was facing a far more serious problem – a severe potential dip in advertising revenue threatened by the end of paper rationing and the launch of commercial television. During the war all British newspapers had their circulation frozen at pre-war levels so as to reduce the total amount of newsprint being brought into the country. Most of it came across the Atlantic from mills in Canada and, as such, it was a drain on foreign exchange and also competed for space on the Atlantic convoys with more important cargoes such as wheat. Papers had a choice – they could print fewer copies, or reduce the number of pages (some papers, notably *The Times*, decided to keep the pages and print fewer copies). After the war the fix on pre-war circulation was lifted and rationing eased, but limits on the number of pages stayed in place. This arrangement actually suited many in the newspaper business. The effect of rationing was to choke off space available for sale to advertisers, putting up the price. At the same time, newspapers were so thin that the tabloids, in particular, could be read from cover to cover in a matter of minutes and it was common for people to buy two or more papers. In 1956 it was announced that newsprint rationing would end completely on January 1, 1959. This meant increased competition for advertising and for journalists and, crucially, for the extra skilled print workers who would be needed to produce bigger newspapers.

The launch of ITV in 1956 was another threat. It would inevitably compete for advertising revenue with all the papers – but especially with the *Mirror,* which was chasing the same mass audience that the new commercial TV service was after. There was no advertising on the BBC – it provided news, but its agenda was so up-market and its tone so upper-class that it was no sort of competition for the *Mirror.* ITV – and its news element – was in contrast deliberately designed to be the "*Daily Mirror* of the airwaves".

Advertising was Cecil King's speciality and he reacted to the spectre of extra competition by commissioning a massive market-research exercise. The upshot was that the *Mirror*'s wartime readership was ageing, that the other papers and ITV were bound to compete hardest for younger readers and the paper therefore had to target younger readers. At the same time King decided to make a strategic investment in ATV – the London ITV company – so as to hedge their bets and get board-level information about programme-makers and stars, and accurate financial information about ad sales.

To see off the ITV threat, the *Mirror* went through an official mini "re-launch" in 1959 under the heading "Youth Revolution". The idea was that, as in the 1940s the *Mirror* had been the "soldier's paper", in the 1960s it wanted to be the paper of "youth". From the mid-1950s onwards Nener had made various painfully hip attempts to appeal to the young, even though he suffered from the key handicap of hating pop music and being completely unable to differentiate Bill Haley and his Comets from Elvis Presley and his Jordanaires.

"Loud. Violent. Unpredictable. Sizzlingly ALIVE. And that's what grips the vibrant youngster of 1955," the paper wrote in some desperation. There was a series on how young people were developing a language of "their" own, the influence of American slang and such horrors such as the spread of the use of the expression "OK" instead of "yes". There were jazz clubs and coffee shops. Beat music had become the symbol of a growing hostility between the generations. The *Mirror* attacked a local magistrate who wouldn't allow a licence for teenage dances – it was a straight return to the lambasting of the fuddy-duddy boneheads and colonel blimps in the upper ranks during the war.

On October 12, 1959 the paper announced that it was a "New *Mirror* ... sparkling NEW ideas, NEW features, NEW contests, NEW writers...". The blurb read: "Sit back folks. Just look – and listen". The new *Mirror* said it was "Gay... Buoyant... and moves with the times". Mostly the paper moved ahead with the OLD features and the OLD writers, though particularly whiskery items like the "Jane" (eternal age 24) cartoon were pensioned off (to be replaced, in her case, by the less successful Patti). As part of the re-launch, Mike Randall's features department organised the first *Daily Mirror* Pop Festival. But Randall got it badly wrong. He thought that Cliff Richard was far too "way out" for *Mirror* readers. Top billing went instead to the unbelievably square crooner Jimmy Young, later a Radio 2 DJ. But the paper was trying. An association with Bill Haley and the Comets promised the readers "We are going to rock around the clock" and made a free offer of records and tickets to *Mirror*-organised concerts. The paper got 50,000 responses – its biggest "reader response" success since the mad days of the 1930s cash give-aways.

The *Mirror's* handling of youth was far from sure. Cudlipp was now reaching his fifties and had been editing newspapers for more than a quarter of a century. Like Cecil King, his outlook was shaped essentially by the 1930s – the poverty and the saucy seaside postcard – and the trauma of the war. It must have been hard to adjust to the new genera-tion of "baby boomers" born at the end of the Second World War and by 1960 starting to leave school as teenagers and joining the newspaper-reading public. But the paper was saved by the even more inept handling of what was to become known as the "generation" gap by its only signif-icant rival, the *Daily Express*.

By the end of the 1960s the *Express* was a fantastically old-fashioned newspaper. According to people who worked there at the time "it reeked of old age" and this probably enabled to *Mirror* to cruise on without much competition and without having to really change direction. Beaverbrook was 81 years old in 1960 but still trying to play an active role in the paper, foisting upon it an essentially 1930s Conservative agenda – including the idea of keeping the British Empire in existence – which the new gener-ation found hard to fathom let alone support. In 1964 Beaverbrook died, but his "dead hand" continued to exercise an influence beyond the grave. The paper became a by-word for "old-fashioned", its readers were dying out and circulation plummeted through the 1960s.

At the end of the decade of the 1950s, the declining sales of the *Express* – especially in terms of young readers – left the field open and allowed the *Mirror* to continue to grow. Cecil King was clever enough to appreciate intellectually the need for a blood transfusion of youth-appeal in a way that appeared to elude Beaverbrook and the *Express*. But the paper was more profitable than ever and King, as finance director, hardly knew what to do with all the cash. One *Mirror* executive later remembered meeting King in the late 1950s and overhearing a conversation about finance. Ad sales were so strong, a minion was reporting to King, that the paper could easily put up its rates. King replied by vetoing a price increase saying that the paper already "all the money it could ever need".

Cecil King was starting to think of ways of spending the huge profits the *Mirror* was making by the late 1950s. In 1961 he moved the *Mirror* from its ramshackle headquarters in Geraldine House to the modernist splendour of a new purpose-built status-symbol tower block overlooking Holborn Circus, near Fleet Street in central London. The move was puffed in the paper itself in the edition of March 8 as THE HOUSE THAT 14,000,000 READERS BUILT (readership being regarded as much larger than circulation). The building, known as Holborn Circus, was described as "the finest, most efficient newspaper headquarters ever known".

A small lake of champagne was consumed at the opening party. The "new London landmark" had been commissioned by King and built for £9 million, cash. The paper had so much money that it did not need to raise a single penny from the banks. It was built by Owen Williams, the architect who had also built Wembley stadium, was famed for his concrete bunkers during the Second World War, had designed parts of Heathrow Airport and also much of the UK motorway system including Spaghetti Junction. But, most importantly, Williams had designed the *Daily Express's* stunning modernist black glass and metal offices in Fleet Street – an exuberant monument to the paper's wealth and power in the 1930s when it had been built. The new *Mirror* building was probably five times as big and just as ostentatiously modern in its design.

King, ever erudite, quoted the inscription on the wall of Tamburlaine's mosque in Samarkand: "Oh unbeliever! look upon our buildings and weep!" Cudlipp wrote King's speech for the official opening ceremony, leaving out this particular quotation. But he did manage to get King to describe the new status symbol as "the Taj Mahal of journalism". Had Cudlipp been clever? Or had he made a mistake?

He must have known. The Taj Mahal is a tomb.

14 1964: THE GOLDEN AGE

1964 *Nelson Mandela is sentenced to life imprisonment, Muhammad Ali (still known as Cassius Clay) beats Sonny Liston to become World Heavyweight Champion, Khruschev falls, the Americans attack the Gulf of Tonkin, escalating the Vietnam War, the contraceptive pill is declared officially safe for use and the Beatles have 19 hit records in Britain and the USA within a twelve-month period...*

And on June 9, 1964 it is announced that the *Daily Mirror* is regularly selling more than five million copies a day. The *Mirror* had become the biggest-selling daily newspaper in the world.

The paper began to print the boastful slogan "World's Biggest Daily Sale" just under the front page logo where the phrase "Forward With the People" had once been emblazoned. Cudlipp had wanted it to say "Biggest Daily Sale in the Universe". But Cecil King had objected: "How do you know?"

The sales success was a personal triumph for King and Cudlipp. Out of around 52 million popular newspapers sold every week, the Mirror Group sold 41 million (this included Cudlipp's old paper the *Sunday Pictorial*, which was renamed the *Sunday Mirror* in 1964).

Cudlipp arranged for a celebration of the Five Million Milestone to take place at the Royal Albert Hall. Thousands of celebrities, politicians and other VIPs were invited – a sea of tuxedos and evening dresses on the floor of the Albert Hall with Cudlipp above them all in the Royal Box waving, jabbing the air with one of his truncheon-sized 1960s media-mogul cigars, swigging champagne, waving, smiling and giving the thumbs up like a Roman Emperor to assorted glitterati arrayed respect-fully before him. According to later legend the Beatles themselves had been shown into the Royal Box and Cudlipp, seized by hubris, is supposed to have said, "Get those long-haired fuckers out of here!" The story was later told to illustrate Cudlipp's growing egomania and a declining grip on the popular market: in 1964 John Lennon was on his way to claiming that the Beatles were "bigger than Jesus Christ"... and

Cudlipp was starting to act as though he was bigger than the Beatles.

The *Mirror's* sales' success had come to a large extent at the expense of the ageing *Daily Express* which, although it was still selling over three million copies a day, had been thrown into chaos in 1964 after the death of Lord Beaverbrook. The *Express* was carrying – and continued to carry – a huge amount of fat. In 1968 it had 415 journalists to produce the regular 18-page edition – and ten of those pages were advertising.

Cudlipp was leading the continuing assault on the *Express*, helped by Lee Howard, a new and more intellectual editor who replaced Jack Nener when the "old warhorse" retired in 1961. At Nener's farewell party, a typically boozy affair, he made a farewell speech saying: "I wasn't a bad editor. But my fuckin' tragedy was that I was no fuckin' good with expenses."

Lee Howard's original name was Leon Krislovsky. He had been born in Battersea in 1915, the son of Russian immigrants. He changed his name in 1939 to make easier to join the Royal Air Force, where he served with great distinction as an intelligence photographer and navigator, specialising in low-level raids, using a specially adapted Mosquito fighter-bomber which, he said, used to fly through enemy territory at less than 50ft. His most famous assignment was to take photos of the damage done during the Dambusters raid. He was regarded as a war hero and won the Distinguished Flying Cross. After the war he became a novelist and married the *Financial Times* journalist and literary agent Sheila Black.

Howard's appointment was popular with most people at the *Mirror*. He had worked his way up the production side of the paper, working on the all-important sub's desk – always the powerhouse of a popular paper – where he had a reputation for putting in extremely long hours and being completely unflappable. His trade mark was shirt-sleeves and bright red braces. Apart from that, anyone might have thought him the editor of a broadsheet paper like the *Guardian,* which probably fitted his politics better than any other. In contrast to Nener's frenetic approach and generally uncouth manner, Howard was a quiet, modest and thoughtful man who was seen only rarely on the newsroom floor – most of the day-to-day editing was done by the night editor Geoff Pinnington who came in at about 3 p.m. in the afternoon to see what the reporters and feature writers had come up with, shaping it all into an actual newspaper. When the paper hit the five-million mark he was in the chair but, as the champagne corks popped, he wondered in his anxious way why the *Mirror* wasn't selling eight million a day – the total size of the popular market. "What is it that makes three million people turn their back on us?" he would muse.

Howard was unfailingly courteous to all and never displayed anger, even when things went wrong. He was described in a rival paper as being an "easy-going, amiable, deceptively intelligent man who has restored an atmosphere of cheerful bonhomie in the *Mirror* offices." In contrast to Nener's erratic foul-mouth bollockings – often conducted in public – Howard would deal with people who were not cutting it by calling them into his office, pouring them a strong drink and then requiring them to sit in a particular chair – he called it his "penitent's stool". He would then deliver some well-thought-out criticism with a gentle but insistent demand that matters improve. The session would end with Howard pointing again to his drinks cupboard and the words: "There's the bar, ducky, get yourself a drink." Howard called everybody, including Cudlipp, "ducky", "doll" or "daahling".

As an editor, it was later thought, Howard had two major drawbacks. He was more or less the same age as Cudlipp and was of the same wartime generation. It was only in comparison with the *Express* that they looked young and it meant that the editorial direction was in the hands of men who were well into their fifties. But the arrangement suited Cudlipp. There was no way that Howard, at his age, could entertain ideas of succeeding him as editorial director. Another problem was that Howard was the third editor in a row (counting Bart as editorial director) who had, by anybody's standards, a drink problem. People remember seeing him plonk a bottle of Scotch in front of himself and down it in one sitting as others might drink a bottle of wine. Howard had a reputation as a "workaholic" – staying in his office at the *Mirror* until the small hours. But many knew that much of this time was spent drinking. It was reckoned by some that much of the hard work was delegated to his far more sober deputy, the ex-fashion editor Felicity Green (nicknamed Ferocity Green) – the first woman in Fleet Street to reach the rank of deputy editor and reach the boardroom.

Drink took a terrible physical toll on Howard. He steadily put on weight and eventually became grossly fat – at least 20 stone, people reck-oned. His appearance disgusted him, he could barely stand to look at himself and he developed a dread of mirrors. Howard's wife Sheila Black – who was herself bulky – once confided to a *Mirror* reporter that she and Lee had been forced to commission a specially reinforced steel bedstead to cope with the physical strain. By the time Howard ran away with his girlfriend to live in Rome he was drinking several bottles of whisky a day and was seriously ill.

As the paper became more successful, "office lunches" increased in frequency – called by Cudlipp to celebrate sales milestones, an anniver-sary of some sort or the coming of goings of important members of staff. Office lunches started to be held at the best hotels – the Ritz, Savoy, the Café Royal - with twenty or thirty present. Staff would arrive at about

12.30 and drink martinis or gin and tonic, waiting for Cudlipp and Howard to turn up some time after 1 p.m. The editorial director would then say: "Let's have a glass of Charlie." A team of waiters would crack open dozens of bottles of Bollinger and the drinking would continue until four or five in the afternoon, through the food and then the speeches about whatever it was. Often, Cudlipp used these occasions to sharpen his trade-mark technique of unrestrained invective. Sometimes he went too far and sacked people – Bart style – for no other reason than to vent his spleen. But they were always reinstated in the morning – the reconciliation baptised in more champagne, naturally.[33]

"Ordinary" lunches could be just as alcoholic and were indulged in by people at all levels on the editorial side. Booking somebody interesting for lunch was an important task for the secretariat that supported Cudlipp – he went out every day with anybody from cabinet ministers to pop and showbiz stars. The *Mirror* celebrity interviewer Donald Zec was a good source of lunch companions. He might interview Tony Curtis or Peter O'Toole for the paper and then bring them along for lunch with Cudlipp in the lavish *Mirror* board dining room or a fancy restaurant in Soho. Sometimes a favoured member of the editorial floor would be brought along as well. Mike Molloy, a graphics and newspaper design specialist who became editor of the paper in the 1970s, remembered one lunch involving Zec, Cudlipp and Shirley MacLaine at which the wacky American actress had become boring in her demands that soft drugs should be legalised because they did no harm. She claimed that psychiatrists said that they were safe. "Psychiatrists?" Cudlipp told the baffled MacLaine in a tipsy imitation of what he thought a zonked-out hippie drug user might say: "We use them as stair rods in this building!"

The laid-back approach to the actual job of getting the paper out was made possible by the very large numbers of journalists hired over the years. It was not that people were lazy. The theory was essentially the wartime one of having enough troops to deal with an emergency – when it would be all hands on deck with all available men working round the clock. There was some sense in this. It meant that the paper was always ready to rise to the occasion and could an amazingly good job, throwing dozens of reporters into the field to cover all the angles of a really big story such as a disaster or a general election. The end of paper rationing in the 1950s meant that all the papers had added extra pages and desperately needed extra journalists. The *Express* and *Mirror* in particular had gone head to head in hiring and "stockpiling" as many journalists as possible – to deny them to the enemy if nothing else. The journalists' union had been strengthened (the first national journalists' strike over pay had come in 1955) and its operation of a "closed shop" meant that it was virtually impossible to sack journalists once they had been employed – not that the Cudlipp wanted or needed to get rid of anybody. Cudlipp had a sentimental dislike of sacking people, having experienced this fate early on in life. The *Mirror* had plenty of money to pay the generational layers of journalists it had accumulated.

The approach to hiring new talent could nevertheless be lax in the extreme. The famous 1970s *Mirror* foreign correspondent John Pilger tells of how he got his job on the paper basically because it was facing a cricket match against the *Express* and needed a spin bowler. He approached Michael Christiansen, one of Lee Howard's deputies, to see if there was any work. Pilger had the good fortune to catch him after a "long Fleet Street lunch". The minute Christiansen noticed Pilger's Australian accent he boomed, "You're just what we want – an Australian!" After some head-scratching Pilger was found a "job" sub-editing articles about programmes on pets, fishing and gardening (only) on the television page. For this he was given a full-time position and salary (necessary to qualify for inclusion in the team) despite the fact it would have taken any conscientious person about five minutes a day. To top it all, Pilger, even though Australian, knew nothing at all about cricket and couldn't play. But by that time he was on board and stayed on board – later providing reports from Vietnam and Cambodia, which were to be among the paper's finest moments. Pilger played an important role on the paper as it adopted a more serious agenda from the mid-1960s onwards with plenty of foreign reporting mixed in with the fluff and "tosh".

The key development was the design and launch by Cudlipp of "Mirrorscope" – a pull-out "paper-within-a-paper" which was designed to match the *Express*'s coverage of current affairs, the arts and science. King was keen on the development, seeing it as an outlet for his more academic interests. After the war the *Mirror* had published a series of pamphlets under the general title of *Spotlight,* as in "Spotlight on Africa". Titles included the Common Market (at King's insistence, the *Mirror* was to campaign for Britain to join), the future of television, the future of the press and the future of education. Mirrorscope was in some ways a development of the pamphlets – an indulgence but, at the same time, a supposedly hard-headed commercial move.

Some *Mirror* readers were likely to be put off (or at least not attracted) by Mirrorscope. But the beauty of it, according to plan, was that these people could simply throw it away (which they did, the top decks of London buses being littered with copies). The main part of the paper still contained a Bart-and-Nener-like mixture of sex, crime, sensation, football results and strip cartoons. Over time, the balance between Mirrorscope and the rest of the paper might change, in line with market research that predicted the younger working-class generation would be better educated and more demanding. Cudlipp collected around Mirrorscope a group of younger journalists marked down to evolve into the home-grown *Mirror* talent he had thought so lacking in the 1950s. They included the future editor Mike Molloy, who introduced a more sophisticated magazine-like design to the paper, and Tony Miles, who wrote an up-market gossip column called The Inside Page, modelled on The Londoner's Diary, the *Evening Standard's* celebrity and society gossip column.

The logical conclusion of Mirrorscope was an entirely new newspaper – and that new newspaper was to be the *Sun*, which, in one form or another, was to become the symbol, flagship and very essence of Tabloid Britain.

But decidedly not in the way King and Cudlipp had hoped or expected.

15 BORN OF THE AGE WE LIVE IN

One of the stranger and more symbolic attempts of the 1960s *Mirror* to introduce its readers to The Good Life was the creation in 1962 of the *Mirror* dinghy. This was a relatively cheap, DIY self-assembly, single-mast sailing dinghy that readers could order in kit form through the paper. It was designed by Jack Holt and Barry Bucknall, a celebrity television DIY expert.

It was a great hit and a huge success – in a way. According to one yachting magazine it "caused sailing in Britain to expand at an enormous rate. Soon thousands of their little red sails criss-crossed lakes and rivers, sailed by their builders". The problem was that hardly any of those builders were *Mirror* readers. It was reckoned that most *Mirror* dinghy owners were readers of the *Daily Telegraph* (*Times* and *FT* readers could afford proper yachts). Because production was subsidised by the *Mirror* – no profit was ever factored in – it ended up costing the paper a fortune.

The question of why the *Mirror* – a paper whose sporting agenda had hitherto consisted of football, boxing, Walthamstow dogs, all-in wrestling – should make a strategic push into the world of yachting remained a mystery to some. The answer was that Hugh Cudlipp had himself taken up sailing and power-boating as a hobby. One evening, after the sun had fallen below the yard arm, he had been drinking with some bigwigs at the Royal Yacht Squadron. "What this country needs is a decent basic boat design," somebody had said. It was the Idea that launched 10,000 ships. A light-bulb went off above Cudlipp's head and the *Mirror* Class dinghy was born.

Cudlipp had taken to the high seas as part of the millionaire lifestyle he now enjoyed as creator of the Biggest Selling Daily Paper in the (known) Universe. In addition to his mansion in Cheyne Walk – overlooking the River Thames near Parliament (and a few doors down from Cecil King) – Cudlipp had another even more grand pile further up the Thames at Sonning – built on stilts over the river and complete with acres of grounds and mooring for his ocean-going motor launch and other river-craft.

Cudlipp was now living the life of a millionaire media mogul and was a fixture on the more egalitarian-meritocratic circuits of London society

– showbiz and finance rather than aristocrats and diplomats. In June 1961 he was given the accolade of being photographed by Henri Cartier-Bresson as part of an extensive eulogy printed in the society magazine *Queen*. The black and white pictures showed him in glamorous and archetypal 1960s groovy-tycoon poses and situations: on the phone with a huge cigar in a Dr No-type command centre with huge personal switchboard; in evening dress in the newsroom urgently correcting proofs in the manner of the young Citizen Kane, surrounded by furrowed-browed shirtsleeves-and-braces acolytes; emerging from his Cheyne Walk pad, ruffled and carrying suitcases – obviously *en route* for a secret assignation with Mr Big of the underworld and/or international espionage network; relaxing on his boat in rugged Ernest Hemingway style and feeding his pet parrot Bertie – the one that squawked: "Read the *Daily Mirror*."

Cudlipp also indulged himself with numerous sexual affairs. In April 1962 his 47-year-old second wife Eileen Ashcroft killed herself with an overdose of sleeping pills and was found dead in the living room of her house in Chiswick, London. (Cudlipp's first wife Bunny, a teenage sweetheart, had died in 1938 while giving birth to a stillborn child fathered by her adulterous lover). Cudlipp had been unfaithful to Ashcroft throughout the entire marriage, conducting an endless series of affairs with two, three or possibly more women at a time. One *Mirror* executive told Cudlipp's biographer that if "Hugh had a fancy for the wives of his subordinates he was not above exercising a bit of *droit de seigneur*".

For a while Eileen Ashcroft (wife No. 2) and Jodi Hyland (wife elect) lived in a sort of permanent *ménage à trois* with – according to Cudlipp's biographer Ruth Dudley Edwards – Eileen doing the chores at the Cudlipp household. Dudley Edwards says that Eileen did not mind this arrangement (although she was no longer around to confirm this) because they had a modern, open marriage and Eileen took lovers too. Eileen had not been especially upset by Cudlipp's affairs and certainly had not committed suicide as a result. Others remember the situation differently.

Although the death was recorded as death by misadventure, it was an open secret at the *Mirror* that Cudlipp had driven Eileen to suicide. When police heard about the death they tipped off the *Mirror*'s crime reporter Tom Tullet, an ex-Scotland Yard copper and friend of Cudlipp's over many years. Tullet rushed to Chiswick, found the body and – so the story went – stole the suicide note and destroyed it in order to repay a favour to Cudlipp. Ten years earlier Tullet had been sacked by the Yard after he had been found selling information to Cudlipp, giving him the inside track on crime and court stories. Cudlipp took pity on him and set him up as a crime reporter. A few months later Cudlipp married the entirely blameless Hyland.

Cecil King had also used the wealth and power provided by the *Mirror's* success to indulge one or two whims. He had been in overall charge of the design of the *Mirror's* new Holborn building, earmarking for himself a huge private office that, together with various anterooms, corridors and private lift-shafts, covered a large proportion of the ninth floor. The room itself was as big as a small football pitch and many were later to complain of the intimidating effect of the journey from the door towards King's desk. The walls were lined with shelves of rare books about Africa. A safe contained King's collection of Georgian silver plate, bought at the company's expense as an investment. King's desk was amazing – an octagonal arrangement eight feet wide and built around two William Kent mahogany desks, reckoned to be worth £30,000 (the cost of a street full of suburban houses at the time) and the place was decked out with enormous hand-woven Turkish and Persian silk carpets, an eighteenth-century clock, numerous Chippendale mahogany armchairs and countless antiques and rare *objets d'art* collected during his seemingly endless travels to Africa, America and Australia on *Mirror* and, increasingly, government business. At a party given in King's office for some of the lower orders, features chief Michael Christiansen, a chain-smoker, noticed there were no ashtrays. At first he put the ash in his pocket, but then found a rough old pot and started using that. King rushed over and pointed out it was a 2,000-year-old Etruscan pot.

The centrepiece of the room was an Adam fireplace leading to a specially installed chimney in which King kept a real coal fire long after the Clean Air Act made this illegal in central London. Bob Edwards, editor of the *Sunday Mirror,* said that the room would have "damaged the ego of an oil sheik". But the most remarkable thing of all was the view. Through plate glass King looked down upon the dome of St Paul's Cathedral just to the right and the Blind Justice statue of the Old Bailey just to his left.

King was rarely seen by journalists or other humble folk at the *Mirror.* John Pilger remembered seeing him only late at night when he might spot King "sailing serenely across the editorial floor followed by assorted establishment figures – the Prime Minister or at least a member of the cabinet, the chairman of a great corporation, a state director of the arts…" King's diaries, published in the 1970s, showed how little time he spent doing anything connected with the *Daily Mirror.* That suited Cudlipp just fine. He had never really liked or trusted "the Old Wykhamist" as he called King. He knew that King was a ruthless operator who could and would dispense him with the same speed and cold steel he had applied to Bartholomew. He therefore had to watch his back – even when the *Mirror* was on top of the world.

Cudlipp viewed King with a mixture of admiration and fear. He told

King's biographer how impressed he had been by King's ability to think out his strategy for gaining control of the *Mirror*. "To an extravert from the other side of Offa's Dyke it was chilling – like watching a blind man playing chess," Cudlipp said. King did not mind being thought of as ruthless. "He was never impetuously or emotionally ruthless," Cudlipp added. "It was planned meticulously. If he decided to part with a colleague he would exercise extraordinary patience over a period of a year or more, gathering evidence and then choosing the moment to act – then he acted with the force and precision of a controlled explosion."

King's weak point was in judging how people might react to him. He was incredibly shy and Cudlipp claimed that he had to encourage King to speak off the cuff at small gatherings in the office as a type of therapy. King's fear of other people, Cudlipp thought, was down to his relationship with his mother – whom he hated. King said that even ten years after her death he would still wake up in the middle of the night in a panic thinking that she was still alive. He also claimed that he had a fear of using his hands because he had such a vivid association in his mind with the act of strangling her with them.

The important thing for Cudlipp was to humour King, but keep him away from the paper as much as possible. A *Mirror* political reporter, Frederic Mullally, remembered how Cudlipp would give King "short shrift" if the aristocratic director turned up for one of his regal progressions around the newsroom. "Keep Cecil nattering as long as you can when he stops by your desk," Cudlipp had once asked Mullally, adding: "He likes to be in bed by nine, so the longer you can keep him yapping politics, the longer he'll be off my back."

The biggest showdown between Cudlipp and King over the detailed editing of the *Mirror* and the *Sunday Mirror* came in July 1964. While Cudlipp was away on holiday King decided to intervene directly over a *Sunday Mirror* story about a homosexual relationship between Oswald Mosley's old friend and advisor, the Conservative politician Lord Boothby, and the Kray twins, the leading East End gangsters of the 1960s. The paper had a tip-off that Scotland Yard was investigating the gay relationship and, in addition, had pictures of Boothby and Ronnie Kray sitting next to each other. King, in Cudlipp's absence, chaired the editorial conference.

"What have we got for tomorrow?" King asked. The editor, Reg Payne, explained the Boothby story. He was sure it was true, but his Scotland Yard source was not prepared to come on the record. All they could say was that "a leading member of the House of Lords" was thought by police to be involved in a homosexual relationship with one of the Krays.

King was worried, but agreed that the story should be run. "I hope it is all true," King said. Payne assured him that the story was "copper-bottomed" so long as Boothby was not at that stage named or the picture used. The story was printed under the headline WHO IS THE MYSTERY PEER? That very evening, King was at a dinner party and was asked who the article was about. In front of witnesses, King said, "Boothby, of course." His remark got back to Boothby and that was enough to give him grounds to sue for libel. However, Boothby didn't want to go to court because the story was true. Instead, he wrote a letter to The Times denying everything. Cudlipp came back and took over the case. He gave Boothby £40,000 – a huge sum in any sort of libel action at the time – in damages in return for an undertaking that Boothby would not sue. The astonished gay Lord took the money and ran. All those associated with the affair read the settlement as a message from Cudlipp to King: "Don't touch my newspapers again."

Cudlipp kept King out of the editorial side, leaving the chairman free to concentrate on "strategy" and building up the Mirror Group into a huge conglomerate. King's empire-building began even before he saw off Bart and became chairman. As finance director in 1947, he had organised the acquisition of the Lagos Daily Times in Nigeria, then still a British colony, for £46,000 (far less than the cost of decorating his office a few years later).

In November 1958 the tantalising opportunity had arisen for King to buy the Amalgamated Press – a chain of consumer magazines – which his uncle Rothermere had sold to the owners of the Daily Telegraph to raise money during the pre-war depression. Cudlipp – who was on a visit to Russia at the time – was perfunctorily consulted about the move in the form of a telegram: "Thinking of buying Uncle's old business in Farringdon Street stop Cable your views but deal may have to be completed swiftly warm regards Cecil King". It did not matter what Cudlipp or any other member of the board thought. King bought the magazines, even though they were in a terrible state, had not made a profit for years and faced deadly competition from a rival magazine group, Odhams Press, which owned highly successful titles such as Woman and Woman's Own.

King's solution was to buy Odhams as well. That chance came in January 1961: Cecil King was watching the television news and saw an item about the proposed merger between Odhams and the Thompson Organisation, then the owners of The Times. Roy Thompson said on TV: "This is truly a marriage of convenience, a truly fifty-fifty partnership, an equally divided board and no chairman's casting vote." Thompson added that there was no chance of a counter-bid because nobody in the publishing world had enough money to make one, or the editorial expertise to run so many magazines. King later wrote that he took this as a personal insult and a challenge. "This was a bit much," he recorded in his diary, "so I reached for the telephone, alerted my colleagues and in fact we made a successful counter-bid." The next morning, a banker's draft for £38 million made its way to Odhams and the magazines were added to King's growing empire. Thompson had been humiliated but, more importantly, a virtual monopoly in women's and consumer magazines had been created.

King called the new company created by the *Mirror* acquisition of Odhams the International Publishing Corporation, better known to all by its initials IPC. He had achieved his aim of creating an empire bigger than Northcliffe's and far bigger than Rothermere's. The *Mirror* and *Sunday Mirror* were now only subsidiary parts of the new IPC conglomerate. Through it, King controlled over two hundred consumer magazines in the UK, France and the USA, nineteen different printing plants on three continents, eight book publishing companies, a large stake in ITV commercial television, a record company and several paper mills.

The creation of this virtual monopoly across such a range of media activities had to be cleared with the competition authorities and the government. The Conservative government had no objections but the Labour opposition, under the leadership of Hugh Gaitskell, still had to be squared. However, Gaitskell's party had a direct, vested interest in the creation of IPC. Odhams held a 51 per cent controlling stake in the Labour-supporting *Daily Herald* (the rest was owned by the Trades Union Congress). The *Herald* still had a circulation of over 1.5 million, was influential and was the only completely reliable gun in Labour's arsenal. The *Mirror* had supported Labour since 1951, but sometimes the support was lukewarm. And – unlike the *Herald* – the *Mirror* could change its political complexion any time King thought it expedient.[34]

Gaitskell correctly suspected that King wanted to close down the unprofitable *Herald* and scoop its million-plus readers into the *Mirror* fold – they would have nowhere else to go. The Labour party therefore threatened to push for a referral of the Odhams purchase to the competition authorities unless the *Mirror* board undertook to continue publication of the *Herald* as a Labour-supporting paper. King agreed to these terms with the stipulation that the *Herald* had to become profitable before 1970. Gaitskell was mollified and political problems with the merger melted away.

But losses at the *Herald* continued to mount. The paper was bleeding away at least £1 million a year and losses were climbing by the month as circulation and ad revenue continued their inexorable fall. Whereas the *Mirror* had been highly profitable and cash-rich, the new IPC conglomerate was more of a mixed bag. Many of its magazines and operations like paper mills were loss-makers or required huge capital investment.

King no longer found that he had money to burn. The *Herald* was suffering from the old newspaper problem of its customers dying. It also had the lowest proportion of women readers. This fact alone made it unattractive to advertisers since women did the shopping and were also in charge of what in ad industry jargon were called "major purchase decisions" (i.e., what brand of car or washing machine to buy, when to decorate the house and where to go on holiday). One of the *Herald*'s slogans had been "Put Your Trust in the *Daily Herald*". By the mid-1960s the joke in the advertising industry was that the paper was the one to use if you were selling surgical support: "Put Your Truss in the *Daily Herald*". The *Daily Herald* became known as King's Cross – it was a punishment he had to carry with him.

When Harold Wilson replaced Hugh Gaitskell as leader of the Labour Party in the early 1960s, King took the opportunity to re-negotiate the *Daily Herald* deal, offering him the continued political support of the *Daily Mirror* to oil the wheels. Wilson agreed to the re-launching of the *Herald* as an entirely new paper called the *Sun* which would appeal to the rising generation of left-wing readers. The plan fitted into Cudlipp's overall Mirrorscope project of capturing a more affluent readership from the *Express* and perhaps the *Guardian*, while not ditching the older, less well-educated wartime and pre-war audience in the meantime. If the newly re-launched *Herald* went well it could replace Mirroscope as IPC's ticket to the prosperous future. If the *Sun* did not work out, the experiment could be folded after four or five years, the deadline for the non-closure of the *Herald* having been passed, and the Mirroscope approached revived in the *Mirror* as an alternative.

Much of the thinking underlying the *Herald* re-launch was based on a vast audience research survey commissioned by Cecil King and called THE NEWSPAPER READING PUBLIC OF TOMORROW. It was produced by Dr Mark Abrams of Sussex University. The work confirmed what King and Cudlipp thought already – that young people were being brought up on television and were better educated than ever, with more "leisure time" to spend on hobbies (such as yachting) in future. Dr Adams concluded that Britain was rapidly becoming "a nation of steak-eating weekenders" led by a group of cutting-edge consumers he called the "pace-setters". These new Britons, born after the war and enjoying all the advantage of the Welfare state, would read IPC's consumer magazines, and might read broadsheet newspapers but would get most of their quick news and down-market entertainment from television, especially from ITV.

With all this in mind Cudlipp and *Herald* editor Sydney Jacobson began planning the launch of the new paper. According to Mike Molloy, Cudlipp and Jacobson came up with the name for the *Sun* when they were walking down a street near the *Herald* office, brows furrowed. They passed a pub with its sign swinging above – The Sun. "That's it, Sydney," Cudlipp yelped.

The launch campaign for "IPC *Sun*" (as it later became known, to distinguish it from the wildly different "Rupert Murdoch *Sun*" which came later) was yet another Cudlipp triumph, much toasted in champagne at every stage of planning and implementation. A saturation advertising campaign on TV introduced the nation to the Whole New Concept of young steak-eating pace-setters and their glamorous-yet-ordinary lives and interests. The adverts left everyone breathlessly awaiting a very clever, fashionable paper with a lot of appeal to women and young groovy people. The first edition, like the adverts, dwelt on the pace-setter's idea in a long leading article set out under headings such as "The New Thinking: The British public believe it is time for a new newspaper, BORN OF THE AGE WE LIVE IN. That is why the SUN rises brightly today", the paper said on page one:

> We welcome the age of automation, electronics, computers. We will campaign for the rapid modernisation of Britain…
>
> Look how life has changed. Our children are better educated. The mental horizon of their parents has widened through travel, higher living standards and TV…
>
> Steaks, cars, houses, refrigerators, washing-machines are no longer the prerogative of the "upper crust", but the right of all. People believe, and the *Sun* believes with them, that the division of Britain into social classes is happily out of date.
>
> *The New Women:* The present role of British women is the most significant and fruitful change in our social life. Women are no longer trapped between four walls. They are released from household drudgery by labour-saving devices, gadgets and intelligent home-planning. In 1938 only one married woman in ten went to work: the figure is now ONE in THREE and will soon increase… Women are the pace-setters now.

There had been great trepidation at the *Daily Express*, the paper that had the most to lose if the *Sun* turned out to be a success. But the new *Sun* was greeted dismissively in the *Express's* offices. It was an ad man's fantasy of what readers wanted, not a real, living, breathing newspaper. The first edition of the paper carried a splash "exclusive" story about the latest James Bond film *Goldfinger* – later seen as a serious miscalculation. Inside, the paper was a mess, mixing stuff about pop stars and bouffant hairstyles with odd snippets of bureaucratic trade union news. The paper had evidently fallen for its own hype – it ran features on how to brief an architect and consumer reviews of holidays in the West Indies, even though among its readership it had inherited some of the poorest people in the country.

The new *Sun* sold over three million copies on day one, following the massive promotional campaign and TV advertising. It was down to about two million on day two. Sales collapsed after that and soon the new *Sun* was even more of a liability than the old *Herald*. By 1968 the losses on the *Sun* were running at £1,750,000 a year. IPC had honoured their pledge to keep the *Herald* going in one form or another until the end of the decade and announced that the *Sun* would either have to find a new owner or be closed down at the first available opportunity in January 1970.

The last edition of the "IPC *Sun*" was produced on November 15, 1969. It was a blow to the journalists, many of whom experienced it as being like a death in the family. There was an official wake focused on the *Sun* pub, the Cross Keys. Somebody had hired a piper to play a lament and the hacks trooped across the road in a ragged line, following the piper through the bitterly cold night into the *Sun*'s offices. The editor who had taken over from Sydney Jacobson – Nener's old assistant Dick Dinsdale – was nowhere to be seen. He was not "prepared to face the music" was the sad joke.

Many of the reporters on the *Sun* had been seconded from the *Mirror*. Most had refused to serve unless they were assured of a berth back at the *Mirror* if the *Sun* failed, as many were sure it would. Cudlipp held a party on the ninth floor for the bloody but unbowed souls who were returning from the *Sun* to the *Mirror*.

"Are you happy tonight?" Cudlipp snapped at one of the returnees. "Why shouldn't I be, after spending five years in your bloody Siberia?" he replied.

All that remained now was for Cudlipp to safely dispose of the wreck.

16 ENOUGH IS ENOUGH

It is a fine spring morning in 1968. Labour Prime Minister Harold Wilson is standing next to his special assistant Marcia Williams in the State Room of No. 10 Downing Street, looking out of the back window over the buildings of Whitehall. They are discussing where MI5 will place their machine-gun nests when the time comes for the counter-revolutionary military coup. Harold thinks the top of Admiralty building would provide most cover. Marcia thinks Horse Guards parade has got a better command of Whitehall as a whole.

According to Marcia Williams's memoirs, discussion of a right-wing military coup to remove the 1964 Labour government had been a running joke between herself and Harold Wilson throughout much of their time together in Downing Street. They used to chat about it to cheer themselves up when, as was frequently the case, economic crises loomed and prospects for the government looked grim.

But sometimes both Wilson and especially Williams gave journalists the impression that the idea of a "plot" was more than a joke, and that there might actually be something to it. The subject of "The Wilson Plot" remains grist to the mill of the conspiracy industry and it is unlikely that anyone will really get to the bottom of it. But this much is clear: in the spring of 1968 the economic problems facing the UK had become so severe that some people in the interlocking worlds of the military, the treasury, the media, intelligence services and the City felt that emergency action might be needed. Something unpleasant was indeed stirring the higher reaches of the British establishment. And, whatever it was, Cecil King was near the core of it.[35]

King's part in these shadowy goings-on was to publish on May 10, 1968 under his own name an extraordinary front-page *Daily Mirror* article headlined ENOUGH IS ENOUGH demanding that Wilson should leave office immediately. This was followed by similar articles in the Mirror Group's Sunday titles, and there were plans to provide free advertising and editorial support to a new business- and military-led committee of national salvation, whatever it might be called. The role of this unelected body would be to take the action Wilson had refused to countenance – draconian measures against the trade unions, huge cuts in public spending in order to cut interest rates and shore up the value of the pound, and rebuilding the strength of the armed forces.

Under his own name King wrote in the *Mirror* that Wilson and his government had "lost all credibility, all authority". He demanded that Wilson should resign as Prime Minister and Labour party leader. The article, coming from a loyal Labour-supporting paper like the *Mirror,* had enormous effect. It did not cause the Prime Minister to resign and for many years it was viewed as a one-off brainstorm, a momentary act of madness and misjudgement by a man succumbing to the Northcliffe-Rothermere-Harmsworth family characteristic of becoming barking mad in later life. (Others explained it away as a personal act of spite against Harold Wilson. It was known that Cecil King had expected a hereditary peerage from Wilson, in return for the paper's support for Labour. But Wilson offered him only a life peerage. King turned it down demanding "all or nothing". He got nothing.)

King had never really been a supporter of the Labour party. Before the war the *Mirror* had been an essentially non-political paper, vaguely "on the side of the underdog" in the phrase that King himself used. He had loathed the Labour post-war leaders Atlee ("a complete drip") and Gaitskell ("a vain man without substance or principle") but supported Wilson, briefly, because he seemed less objectionable than the Conservative party at the time.

In 1964 Wilson received political support from the *Mirror* on a scale never seen before – super-loyal, clever, funny and effective. Cudlipp had also been involved in writing Wilson's speeches, including a famous one to the Labour party conference which talked about "the white heat of technological revolution" as part of a speech about the need to modernise British industry and society. Wilson was elected with a majority of just five, but within two years went to the polls again and won a landslide.

Wilson had promised King that a Labour government would arrange for rapid and full British entry into the European community – an unpopular idea with the public at the time, and one previously opposed by Gaitskell. But when in office Wilson back-pedalled on Europe, King's admiration soon evaporated.

Talk of unconstitutional action against the Wilson government had been rife in Whitehall since at least 1967, as Wilson's government ran into a severe economic crisis and deep cuts in Britain's armed forces and reports from spies in Russia convinced some in the intelligence world that members of Wilson's cabinet – and perhaps Wilson and

Marcia Williams themselves – were working to destroy the country and had to be removed.

In March 1968 King held meetings in Paris with French politicians, bankers and newspaper publishers around the country. Alerted to the fact that King was up to something funny, Cudlipp got the paper's Paris correspondent Peter Stephens to keep tabs on King's activities in the form of a series of confidential memos. Stephens reported: "Cecil explains that eventually there will be a dictator in Britain 'perhaps not next year, but it is certainly coming because parliament is totally discredited'."

In another memo Stephens reported that King was bitterly attacking Wilson as "a liar, an untrustworthy man, and ruining the country" predicting that "the Labour Party will collapse" but regretting that the Conservatives were no alternative. At a restaurant on the Riviera with Raymond Comboul, deputy chairman of *Nice Matin* newspaper group, King burst into a bitter personal attack. Comboul asked if King would continue to use the *Mirror* in his campaign to oust Wilson. King answered: "Oh yes. I think everyone agrees with me on that."

One way forward might have been to somehow force Wilson out of government, resulting in a general election that would put the Conservatives back in power. But the Tory party, as King and others saw it, was almost as bad as Labour. In 1968 the party turned its back on the one person King thought capable of leading the Conservatives and the country through the crisis – Enoch Powell, the Conservative right-winger. Powell had ruined his chances by emerging as a dedicated racist, making a speech in which he said the streets of Britain would turn into "rivers of blood" as a result of black and Asian immigration into Britain.

King now decided to look for a "third force" – an independent strong man who could take charge. At first, he turned to exactly the same "strong man" as Rothermere – the former British Union of Fascists leader Oswald Mosley, now an old man living in splendid exile in a mansion just outside Paris. King went to visit him to seek advice and – incredible but true from the evidence of his diaries – sound him out as the head of a military-backed government in Britain.

The King-Mosley dinner took place on April 23, 1968. Stephens was not invited, but the following day tried to find out what had happened, and reported: "For once Cecil did not talk – except to say that Mosley was 'a most fascinating man, we had a most interesting evening'." Stephens added: "It must have been a fascinating evening because I later found out that King [who was famous for going to bed by 9.30 p.m. at the latest] did not leave until 11.30 p.m." Stephens reported that King had continued by saying Mosley was "by far the cleverest politician of the 1930s. He just chose the wrong side during the war. He was an extremely brilliant man and he could still make a useful contribution." Stephens, astonished, had asked: "You are surely not thinking of including him in your replacement government?" and King replied: "Why not? People have forgotten about his past."

Evidently King decided that Mosley was too old or otherwise not quite right for the role of *Daily Mirror* dictator of Britain. Lord Louis Mountbatten, a relative of the Queen and the highest-ranking military officer in the country, was his next choice. King's French tour had convinced him that the Paris street riots could happen in London and intensify the economic crisis already gripping the country.

"The world is heading for another 1929," Stephens reported King as saying. "We are obviously going to have another recession, and Britain will not be able to survive it. There may be two or three million unemployed and the workers will never stand for it. We may well have serious riots on the streets and if that happens the military could step in and seize power. When I say the military, I mean the navy, because naval officers would be far more acceptable to the British public than army officers. Lord Mountbatten is being groomed for some possible role. The Royal Family are pushing him forward constantly."

Preparations for a coup began to take more shape at the end of April, 1968 when King returned from his tour of France. And it was Mountbatten, and not King, who made the running.

Mountbatten discovered that Cudlipp was sailing his motor cruiser around the Isle of Wight and asked to see him at his Broadlands estate near Romsey. Cudlipp and Mountbatten were close. All through the 1950s and 1960s the *Mirror* had promoted Mountbatten's Burma Star Association, a welfare network for veterans of the war against Japan. Since the mid-1950s the *Mirror* had also organised reunions of men who had served in submarines during the war – an extension of the secret work done by Bartholomew in editing *Good Morning* – a newspaper for submariners produced by the *Mirror* during the war.[36]

Cudlipp produced a report of what happened at the Romsey meeting, which he forwarded to King. Cudlipp wrote:

"Mountbatten said important people, leaders of industry and others approach him increasingly saying something 'must be done'. Of course I tell them that we can't go on like this. But [he said] I'm 67 and a relative of the Queen: my usefulness is limited. This is a job for younger men and obviously talent and administrative ability – which does not exist in parliament – must be harnessed. Perhaps there should be something like the emergency committee I ran in India – Nehru and others said they had just come out of prison and knew nothing about administration. I didn't want the job for obvious reasons and agreed to do it only if there was no publicity..."

Mountbatten named various people who might be willing to serve on such a committee or who, otherwise, would definitely be needed. Top of the list was Solly Zuckerman, the government's advisor on nuclear matters and the man, in effect, with his finger on the trigger that could launch Britain's nuclear weapons. For any new "regime" to gain international recognition, its control of the country's nuclear missiles would be crucial. Finally, Mountbatten stressed to Cudlipp that the work of any such emergency committee would depend on editorial support from the *Mirror,* "the most important and influential newspaper in the country". A date was set for a further meeting to take place at Mountbatten's Kinnerton Street flat in central London.[37]

King agreed at once to attend the meeting which took place on May 8 at Kinnerton Street. The idea was to discuss things in more detail and to sound out Zuckerman.

The Kinnerton Street meeting took place, though it remained secret for many years afterwards and what was said and planned there remains controversial to this day. It consisted of King, Cudlipp, Mountbatten and Solly Zuckerman.[38] Accounts of what happened were published by all those present. Those of Cudlipp, Mountbatten and Zuckerman tally. Indeed, papers in Cudlipp's archive show he took great care to corroborate his version of events with Mountbatten and Zuckerman before making it public. Even then it was misleading. The original agreed draft had described Mountbatten saying that he thought that the Queen might not object to the formation of a new government. Mountbatten asked for this reference to be removed from the published "official account", and Cudlipp did so.[39]

According to Cudlipp's "approved" version of what happened at the meeting, King raged against the Wilson government and asked Mountbatten to form a new government immediately. Mountbatten supposedly turned to Zuckerman and asked what he thought about the proposal. Zuckerman reportedly replied: "This is all treachery. All this talk of machine guns at street corners is appalling. I am a public servant and will have nothing to do with it. Nor should you, Dickie." Then he stormed out. Mountbatten had courteously but firmly turned down King's invitation to make himself Britain's temporary military dictator, saying that he could not even contemplate such a course of action.

For reasons best known to himself, Zuckerman, if this account is true, did not report Cudlipp or King to the authorities or otherwise make the attempted "treachery" public. It also stuck some as odd that King made no mention of the meeting in his otherwise extremely detailed diaries, published in 1972.[40]

King's account of the meeting, when he finally gave one many years later, was entirely different to that of Cudlipp and Zuckerman. But by that time he had retired from official life. According to the *Mirror* chairman, the meeting took place at Mountbatten's request. Solly Zuckerman left early, apparently embarrassed by Mountbatten's description of him as one of the "greatest brains in the world" and never made his statement about "treachery". Mountbatten made all the running at the meeting, emphasising the great anxiety felt by the Queen herself at the parlous state of the nation and her willingness to sanction urgent action. When King suggested a time might come when somebody might have to head a national government Mountbatten had said "nothing to indicate that he would find the role unattractive". There was no talk of treason, and no indignant retreat by Solly Zuckerman.

Details of the Kinnerton Street meeting were kept secret for seven years. In 1975 dark hints about what had happened there were made in the columns of *Private Eye* magazine – then a favourite outlet for intelligence service gossip and the grinding of axes by one faction within the secret establishment against another. Once the *Eye's* garbled account had had been published, Cudlipp rushed out a book called *Walking on the Water* with remarkable speed. It was supposedly his autobiography but was largely devoted to Cecil King and the 1968 "coup that never was".

Cudlipp confirmed that the Kinnerton Street meeting had taken place and even supplied a selective account of his previous meeting with Mountbatten at Romsey. But Cudlipp said there was nothing to the "coup" other than King's vanity, ego and desire to play as large a role in British public life as his illustrious uncles. Much amateur psychoanalysis of King was provided to show that he was a strange and twisted individual, who could not be relied upon to tell the truth. The important thing, and Cudlipp emphasised this over and over, was that there was little or no substance to the "coup". He did not even mention the role of the intelligence services at the time.

A couple of years later two freelance journalists – Barry Penrose and Roger Courtiour – opened up the case again. Working under the joint by-line Pencourt, they produced a dossier on the attempted coup and a supposed dirty tricks campaign by MI5 against Wilson, based on briefings by Marcia Williams and the retired Wilson himself. Harold Wilson gave them a version of the official account, saying: "two people high up in the press had approached Lord Mountbatten to discuss their plan for a coup, but that Mountbatten and Solly Zuckerman had sent them packing".

But through the 1970s and 1980s more evidence began to emerge showing that a group of about 30 intelligence officers, tending towards the extreme right in their politics, had indeed decided that the Wilson government was a threat to national security and – in addition – were somehow secretly plotting with the IRA to create a united Ireland. These mavericks had run an operation called "Operation Clockwork Orange" which had peaked in 1968 and was designed to both undermine or remove the Labour government from power and replace the Tory leader Edward Heath (also incorrectly suspected by renegade MI5 officers of being both homosexual and therefore possibly under the influence of KGB blackmail) with a more reliable figure.

During the 1986 Spycatcher affair, the former high-ranking MI5 officer Peter Wright said King had been a "long-term agent" of MI5. Cudlipp again instantly popped up, though he was retired, to deny everything – just as he had done when the original story of the Kinnerton Street meeting had come to light. It was highly unlikely that King had ever been an intelligence "agent", Cudlipp said, because he could not keep a secret.

The reality was that King's dealings with the intelligence services went back at least to 1947 when, according to his diaries, he had been urged by a "senior Whitehall official" to set up "pro-British" popular newspapers in Nigeria to quell African nationalism. According to King's biographer Ruth Dudley Edwards, his own son Michael worked for MI5, using the post of foreign editor of the *Daily Mirror* as "cover" for his secret service work. This was a common enough arrangement. Kim Philby, the most famous MI6 agent of all time, had been given cover as "foreign editor" of the *Observer* and, before that, as a senior journalist on *The Economist* and *The Times*. Chapman Pincher, the *Daily Express*'s intelligence and security expert – who had his own contacts within MI5 and MI6 – said the relationship between the intelligence services and the proprietors and senior managers was close, and that by the 1950s "every newspaper in Fleet Street" had its quota of intelligence officers. Some journalists at the *Mirror* said you could spot the "spooks" on the foreign desk by their unnatural interest in Eastern Europe and complete inability to write tabloidese.

Cudlipp had worked on army internal propaganda during the war, being promoted to the rank of colonel. A fascinating letter from King in Cudlipp's personal archive refers to Cudlipp joining the intelligence service as "an excellent idea". But nothing more is recorded, or mentioned again. At the end of the war, when Bartholomew was still chairman, there were repeated "purges" of the *Mirror* staff aimed at rooting out Communists. Through the 1950s and 1960s the *Mirror* had fought the Cold War with real venom, with Cudlipp penning anti-communist propaganda of such ferocity that it would have put the American senator Joe McCarthy to shame. In the 1990s, declassified cabinet documents showed that in the 1970s King had worked for British intelligence in Ireland, setting up secret meetings between the government and IRA leaders.

Most extraordinarily of all it was revealed in the 1980s that Percy Roberts, the Mirror Group's managing director from 1966 until his retirement in 1980, had been a British intelligence officer and MI6 informant and contact for many years. Roberts had joined British military intelligence in Palestine in 1945 and they had set him up with a job as a journalist on a paper called the *Middle East Mail* in Palestine. In 1949 he was appointed editor of the *Nigerian Citizen* – "his secret service record was almost certainly a help" said his old friend, the *Mirror* industrial correspondent – and then became the main editorial advisor to the chain of West African newspapers Cecil King had set up "with the encouragement of Whitehall". Roberts returned to the Mirror group to become managing director, working closely with Cecil King.[41]

And Percy Roberts was to be the only senior figure at the *Mirror* who defended King when – after his publication of ENOUGH IS ENOUGH – he was sacked from the *Mirror* and IPC.

17 THE COUP THAT DIDN'T FAIL

A month after Cecil King put his name to the ENOUGH IS ENOUGH article, the board of IPC sacked him from his position as chairman.

The dismissal came as a shock to King, who believed he had the support of his protégé Cudlipp and that, between them, they held absolute sway over the IPC board. King had created IPC in a series of mergers and had hand-picked the board. None of the directors represented an especially large block of shareholders or otherwise had a power base from which to attack him.

The letter requesting King's departure came from Cudlipp, who had individually lobbied each board member, gaining their support for the action to remove the chairman. This was an exact copy of the way in which King had disposed of Bartholomew seventeen years earlier.

King received the thin white envelope at his home at 8.15 a.m. on a Saturday morning while he was in his dressing gown, shaving. It was delivered by John Chandler, the company secretary. "I was met at the door by Cecil King's valet and shown into the drawing room," Chandler later wrote. "Cecil was in a long dressing gown. He stayed in the doorway at first to read the letter and then moved over to the window so that he could read it in the lighter place."

"I have been instructed to inform you by letter of some decisions which have been reached by all your IPC colleagues," Cudlipp wrote.

"The feeling is that your increasing preoccupation with and intervention in national affairs in a personal sense, rather than in a more objective publishing sense, has created a situation between you and your colleagues which is detrimental to the future conduct of the business of IPC.

"The decisions were unanimous and I enclose a formal request for your resignation."

King said he would not resign. If they wanted him out, they would have to sack him. Cudlipp and the others disappeared to consult all the members of the board and reappeared at 3 p.m. with a letter sacking him.

King jumped into his Rolls Royce and went round the TV studios giving live interviews. It was a big story. ITN even interrupted coverage of the Epsom races with a newsflash.

Members of the board went on the record, describing why King had to go. The ENOUGH IS ENOUGH article was only part of it. At that time none of them knew of any "coup" plan, unless Cudlipp had let them in on the secret. Board member Edward "Pick" Pickering said that King's management style was "too patriarchal and feudal" and that a change was needed. King had started interfering, Pick said, and that had led to fears that Cudlipp – his natural successor – might leave. Pickering had spoken to four or five other board members earlier in the year and all had thought that he was getting on and it was time for him to go.

Another director and the board's senior lawyer, Ellis Birk, had been angered when he saw ENOUGH IS ENOUGH and remembered thinking: This is end of Cecil as far as I'm concerned. His objection was not so much to the attack on Harold Wilson – that was bad enough in a Labour-supporting paper – but to the printing of privileged information about the state of the Bank of England's gold reserves, gained by King in the course of his work on the board of governors.

"The references to the reserves were outrageous, and it was unforgivable that a director of the Bank should make statements that could only have – and indeed did – deleterious effect on sterling." Veere Sherren, also a director, complained that King had been "an absolute dictator in the fashion of the old days of Fleet Street. As he became older so the megalomania became worse because his desire for power spread well beyond IPC and the consequence was loss of interest in the company of which he was chairman." The board should have got rid of him earlier, but too many were afraid of him. He had lost all interest in running IPC as a business and had allowed the company to go into the red: "My monthly meeting to discuss the profit and loss accounts scarcely lasted five minutes, the rest of the time was devoted to discussing politics and personalities."

Most eloquent was Frank Rogers, director of production at the time. He said that by 1968 IPC and the Mirror Group newspapers were starting to face very serious problems caused by growing trade union power, a much worse general economic background compared with the free-spending 1950s and 1960s and a wasteful, cumbersome, top-heavy management system created by King's mergers and acquisitions spree.

"The day the decline of the *Mirror* company began can be pin-pointed with total accuracy – the day Cecil King walked down Fetter Lane into the *Daily Telegraph* office and told Michael Berry that the *Daily Mirror* wanted to buy his family's shares in the Amalgamated Press," Rogers wrote in a memo to Cudlipp. "This was the start of the expansion of the

Mirror into areas of publishing it did not understand. It was a decision taken by Cecil King without making a single enquiry about the finances and prospects of the Amalgamated Press and with no board discussion as I understood at the time."

Another director, John Dennett, recorded in his diary how King's behaviour was becoming steadily more bizarre. He used to avoid accountability to the board by calling board meetings in his room never earlier than 11.30 a.m., so there would not be enough time to go into detail before lunch. He would then talk all the time about his job at the Bank of England saying, "There you are, gentlemen – gloom I'm afraid. I am now going round to the Bank for more gloom. I bid you good day."

There were those who pointed to the influence of King's wife, the eccentric Ruth Railton, whose behaviour was becoming stranger even than Cecil's. She was a firm believer in extra-sensory perception and believed she had psychic powers. Ruth had persuaded Cecil to use tens of thousands of pounds of IPC money to support research into the paranormal. King himself had given a lecture on ESP to the Royal Institution during which he described how a man suffering from acute pain had seen Ruth and details of her address in a dream. He had then visited Ruth at home and claimed that simply by touching her he felt better. According to King's biographer Ruth Dudley Edwards, under the influence of Ruth, King came to believe that he had the power to make himself literally invisible as he walked along the street. In another dream Ruth saw a great crack appearing in the wall of the Holborn Circus tower block, leading to its collapse and the death of hundreds of employees. According to the *Daily Express*'s gossip column he commissioned a full structural survey for £10,000 – which pronounced the structure safe. It was all very odd or, to use a favourite *Daily Mirror* word – "potty".[42]

Whatever his frame of mind, Cecil King's swansong came at the annual general meeting of IPC held on July 23, 1968 at the Café Royal. He was allowed to speak and described the board's action against him as "a squalid coup". Cudlipp, he said, would have difficulty rising to the job of running IPC – he was "a good first violinist" but would find it difficult to become the conductor.

Cudlipp was in a grim mood as he faced up to steering IPC and the *Daily Mirror* into the future. He was, after all, a journalist and not a businessman.

"They have called the high-wire act down to count the takings," he complained.

Once King had gone, Cudlipp could not psychologically face going into King's office for several weeks. His first act as chairman was to sell off King's antiques, art and silver collections. He then had the room gutted. The chairman's office was completely redesigned in modern minimalist

Northcliffe, the Napoleon of Fleet Street who founded the *Daily Mirror* as a 'paper for ladies' in 1903.

Hannen Swaffer – pioneer of photojournalism and the key creative force in the very early days of the *Mirror*.

ALLIES' DRASTIC ARMISTICE TERMS TO HUNS

The Daily Mirror

CERTIFIED CIRCULATION LARGER THAN THAT OF ANY OTHER DAILY PICTURE PAPER

No. 4,696.   Registered at the G.P.O. as a Newspaper.   TUESDAY, NOVEMBER 12, 1918   One Penny.

HOW LONDON HAILED THE END OF WAR

The King and Queen appeared on the balcony at Buckingham Palace to acknowledge the cheers of the crowd that gathered to congratulate their Majesties on the victory.

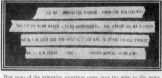

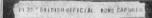

Home on short leave, but now safe for always from the dangers of Hun bullet and steel.

How news of the armistice signature came over the wire to the newspaper offices. A facsimile of it as automatically printed on the tape machine. The cheers which greeted it were the first to be raised.

An historic message as it came over the wire. It is dramatic that the last British war communiqué should proclaim our forces at Mons.

"Now entitled to rejoice" and doing it. Daddy has beaten the Huns and is coming home.

Nothing gave greater satisfaction to all of us than the news that the cessation of hostilities found the British armies once more in possession of Mons, where the immortal | "Contemptibles" first taught the Huns what British valour and steadfastness could do. They left the town as defenders of a forlorn hope; they re-entered it conquerors indeed.

The *Daily Mirror* 1918 edition marking the end of the First World War.
The war boosted the paper to a sale of two million, making it the largest
selling 'picture paper' in the world, inspiring imitators in New York and
boosting the career of Harry Guy Bartholomew.

Rothermere, owner of the Mirror in the 1920s and '30s with his hero, Adolf Hitler.

The snatched picture of Ruth Snyder at the moment of her death which appeared on the front page of the New York *Daily News*, under the headline DEAD! The *Daily News* was the original model for the modern *Daily Mirror*.

Harry Guy Bartholomew (left) – 'Bart' – illiterate, drunkard, bully... and 'the man who made the *Mirror*'.

The Price of Oil... The World War Two cartoon which almost led to the *Mirror* being closed down for subversion.

"*Here you are—don't lose it again*"

Here... don't lose it again. The *Mirror*'s comment on the end of the Second World War.

Hugh Cudlipp, the Welsh wizard of the *Mirror* and, according to many,
the greatest tabloid journalist of the twentieth century.

Cecil Harmsworth King (above centre), nephew of
Northcliffe and Rothermere and chairman of the
Daily Mirror during the 'golden age' of the 1950s
and '60s. He left the *Mirror* after involvement in a
murky campaign against Harold Wilson (below)and
the Labour Government.

David Montgomery. Made chief executive after the ravages of Robert Maxwell, 'Monty' cut back on editorial budgets and made millions through share options doing massive damage to the paper according to his many critics.

Larry Lamb. Passed over as *Mirror* editor, he took his revenge by making Rupert Murdoch's rival *Sun* the UK's biggest selling paper

2003 - *Mirror* editor Piers Morgan. Appointed by Montgomery, many thought Morgan was out of his depth. Sudden changes in editorial direction saw sales fall to under two million for the first time since the 1930s.

Richard Desmond, owner of a string of pornographic magazines, bought the ailing *Daily Express* and the booming soft porn *Daily Star* and associated websites - the end of the line for Britain's tabloid nation?

Scandinavian style. The ceiling was lowered and the fireplace was covered up.

When the work was done, every last trace of King and every association the room or the *Daily Mirror* may have had with him or the Harmsworth family was gone for ever.

18 SALE OF THE CENTURY

Rupert Murdoch was later to say that he was constantly amazed by the ease with which he had entered the British newspaper industry.

Murdoch inherited wealth and newspaper interests in Australia from his father, Sir Keith Murdoch. Despite much egalitarian chest-beating in later years, Murdoch was the living embodiment of the conservative establishment and inherited wealth and privilege. His problem was that he wanted more of both these things and to get them he would have to move from his antipodean backwater to London and then use London as a launch-pad for his ultimate plan of becoming a player in the world of American and global media ownership.

Murdoch's first conquest on his way to World Domination came in 1968 when he bought the *News of the World*. He got the paper cheaply by posing as a white knight, allowing the Carr family to avoid the ignominy of selling to Robert Maxwell, the paper's main suitor. The *News of the World* had been in the Carr family since 1891 and, although they urgently needed money, chairman Sir William Carr was desperate not to sell to Maxwell, recently elected a Labour MP, who was certain to alter the paper's traditional conservative politics.

There was another objection to Maxwell. He was "a foreigner" – which was a euphemism for Jewish. At a time when anti-Semitism was still prevalent in business, selling out to a Jew for money was seen as not the thing to do. Carr wrote a celebrated front-page article about Maxwell's bid, saying that the *News of the World* was "as English as roast beef and Yorkshire pudding". Maxwell, on the other hand, had been born in Czechoslovakia. His original name, the paper stated, was Jan Ludwig Hoch. Murdoch – more genuinely a foreigner as an Australian citizen at the time – saw his chance, played hard-ball over the price, demanded a quick private sale and snatched the paper from under Maxwell's nose for a song. Maxwell stomped off complaining about Murdoch's sharp practice and vowing revenge.

But for now Murdoch was just a somewhat humble proprietor with a tiny stake in the British newspaper scene. When he took possession of the *News of the World* and its dilapidated offices and presses in Bouverie Street he found an incredibly badly managed enterprise which, despite its eight million weekly Sunday sales, was making a loss. Murdoch was able to cut the losses at once by making a few simple changes. But the *News of the World's* main financial problem was that it had no daily counterpart and so the Bouverie Street presses were idle for six days a week. He was thinking about launching a new daily paper to soak up the free printing capacity when in April, 1969 Cudlipp and IPC put the *Sun* up for sale.

The experiment of converting the *Daily Herald* into the *Sun* had failed. Sales were reasonable at over 800,000. But circulation was falling and stood nowhere near what was needed to make it profitable. The obligation to keep the paper going until the end of the decade, given by King and Cudlipp when they bought Odhams press, was coming to an end. Unless a buyer could be found, the paper would close.

Maxwell, still smarting from his failure to get hold of the *News of the World,* immediately made an offer for the paper and had talks with Cudlipp. Maxwell offered to take on the paper's losses and give an undertaking that it would continue to support the Labour party. Ownership would go to a non-profit-making trust, similar to the Scott Trust that owned the *Guardian.* The paper could be kept going on a smaller scale in this way. Naturally, Maxwell would not pay any money for the title. But IPC would be relieved of the losses. Under his leadership, Maxwell explained, the paper would move up-market to become more like the *Guardian.* It would not compete with the *Mirror* or any existing IPC title.

Cudlipp liked the idea. But mainly because he thought Maxwell's plan had no chance of success. When the inevitable closure came, Maxwell would have to deal with the problems and pain of closure and he, instead of IPC, would get all the opprobrium of closing down the paper. So offloading all the responsibilities to Maxwell had an immediate attraction.

But there was a problem. Maxwell's plan depended on agreeing redundancies with the unions, especially the printers, and there was no chance of that. When details of Maxwell's plans became clearer the unions became truculent and threatened secondary strike action against the *Mirror, Sunday Mirror* and the *People* if Maxwell came anywhere near the paper.

Murdoch once again saw an opportunity to get the *Sun* cheaply or for nothing. He saw that the unions could be of immense use to him. If they were on his side he would have a free hand in negotiating for control of the *Sun.* He flew to Rome and met the print union leader Richard Briginshaw, who was on holiday there. Murdoch promised that there would be no redundancies if he got the paper instead of Maxwell.

With the unions signed up on his side Murdoch turned up at IPC asking for the same terms for taking over the *Sun* that the company had offered to Maxwell – that he should be given the paper for free in return for keeping it going. But that had been on condition that the *Sun* should be run as a non-profit trust, as well as an undertaking not to compete directly with the *Mirror*, Cudlipp said. Murdoch wanted none of that and so a purchase price of £50,000 a year for every year the paper stayed in production up to a maximum of £850,000 was agreed. The Fleet Street analyst Charles Wintour later wrote that the price Murdoch had to pay was "astonishingly low".

Cudlipp had replaced King as chairman of IPC halfway through the *Sun* crisis. His dealings with Maxwell and Murdoch were to be the first challenge of his chairmanship. He explained to directors why he had taken the decision to sell the paper to Murdoch – a move that was to be seen in retrospect as suicidal. The option of turning the *Sun* into a "jazzed-up tabloid" under continuing IPC ownership, Cudlipp explained, was closed because it would compete directly with the *Mirror*. "Journalistically, it would have meant turning the *Sun* into a brash sex-mad tabloid aimed at the bottom end of the *Mirror* readership," he said. Such a plan would have been "against the whole trend and recent development" of the *Mirror* as an "intelligent tabloid" which was the only path to the future.

The logical thing was to close the *Sun* and merge it with the *Mirror*. But, at the time of the Odhams takeover, Cudlipp and the *Mirror* board had given solemn undertakings never to merge the paper with the *Mirror*. That was part of the fair price paid to get the profitable Odhams magazines. An undertaking had been given and any attempt to go back on it would be seen as "a shoddy evasion".

Murdoch had the capacity on his *News of the World* presses to produce a daily tabloid and was likely to launch one anyway as a direct down-market competitor to the *Mirror*. They could not stop him. At least by dumping the *Sun* on him, they would keep the unions sweet, honour their obligations and, hopefully, land Murdoch with the problem of dealing with the drunks, dross and union militants Cudlipp had tried to steer on to the IPC *Sun* and who, if the merger option was taken, would be washed back into the *Mirror*.

Cudlipp did not know Rupert Murdoch very well at the time, but he knew his father Sir Keith Murdoch, who ran the highly successful *Sun-Pictorial* Group in Melbourne. In 1957 Cudlipp and King had extensive dealing with Sir Keith when they were closing down the *Melbourne Argus*, a paper launched by Bartholomew when he was chairman and which had been a sales and financial disaster. Cudlipp admired Sir Keith, thinking of him as a decent and cultivated chap – as near as you got to an aristocrat in Australia. He ran conservative, broadsheet newspapers. During their business dealing Sir Keith had mentioned that he was worried about his son Rupert who was at Oxford at the time. Rupert Murdoch had apparently been converted to doctrinaire Marxist socialism and kept a bust of Lenin on his mantelpiece. Cudlipp was more amused than surprised at Sir Keith's colonial parochialism. In unsophisticated Australia, Marxism, if it existed as all, was the real bomb-throwing thing. In London and Oxbridge it was not much more than an undergraduate fashion. Cudlipp assured Sir Keith that Rupert's conversion was just a "fashionable veneer" which he would leave behind at university. Now Rupert – this naive young colonial pup silly enough to flirt with Marxism, the pampered scion of a conservative, broadsheet newspaper empire – had come to London and was amusing himself with the *News of the World*.

Unable to think of Rupert Murdoch as anything other than a younger version of his cape-and-top-hat-wearing Northcliffe-era father, Cudlipp seriously underestimated him. The new owner of the *Sun* certainly believed that IPC had made an immense mistake by letting him have the paper almost as a gift.

During one of their meetings about the proposed sale of the *Sun* Cudlipp had kept Murdoch waiting in an anteroom on the palatial ninth floor of Holborn Circus. The young Australian noticed a graph tracking the upward sales of the *Daily Mirror* and the downward plunge of the *Sun* with pieces of coloured string pinned to a board. Murdoch amused himself by switching the two pieces of string around – the *Sun* was now shown as soaring away and the *Mirror* crashing towards disaster.

To make that vision come true Murdoch decided to make the *Sun* an exact copy of the *Mirror* in its 1950s and 1960s heyday.

The first step was to find a man who knew enough about the *Mirror* to make it happen.

19 WHEN LARRY MET RUPERT

As Larry Lamb saw it, he and not Lee Howard should have been made editor of the *Daily Mirror* in 1961 when Jack Nener retired. Lamb's job at that time was "chief sub" – a vital post on any sort of tabloid newspaper, and especially important at the *Mirror*. Since the days of Bartholomew what really counted was the way the paper looked and how it was actually put together at the last possible minute by the subs under pressure both of the clock and the "bollocking" demands of the editor.

Lamb had been a brilliant *Mirror* chief sub, everyone agreed, sweating over the pages line by line, word by word – a master of the whole business of laying out pages, picking pictures and writing headlines, showing a real flair for language and, at the same time, more than able to hold his drink in the approved Jack Nener "hollow legs" tradition.

But when Nener's job became vacant, Lamb did not even get a look-in. Lamb was only 32 when Nener retired and, having been passed over, gained what he described as "a very large chip on my shoulder". Cudlipp instead went for Howard, who was twenty years older. Instead of bringing on the new generation that Lamb represented, Cudlipp had stuck with the boozy old crowd.

When Lee Howard then led the charge up-market, lavishing attention and money on innovations like Mirrorscope, Lamb started to become disenchanted. The millions being poured in to Cudlipp's up-market *Sun* also dismayed Lamb. The IPC *Sun*, Lamb thought, was "so smooth, so laid-back, so iffy-butty, as to be totally devoid of character." Cudlipp, the man who had passed him over, was getting it wrong over and over again.

In 1968, Lamb hit 40 and decided that he would never make it as editor of the *Daily Mirror*. Tony Miles, the cultured up-market feature-writer and gossip columnist, and then editor of Mirrorscope, had already been lined up to take over from Lee Howard when he retired, according to plan, in 1971. That meant, barring accidents, the job would not become vacant until Lamb was well into his fifties, and therefore well past it. Lamb returned instead to the *Daily Mail* in Manchester, where he had previously worked, with a promotion to the post of editor of the *Mail's* northern edition. Lamb saw it as his last, and fairly slim, chance of becoming a Fleet Street editor.[43]

He had been at the *Mail* for less than a year when he was phoned out of the blue by "a Mr Rupert Murdoch" – as his secretary had put it. He knew of him only as the owner of the *News of the World*. Murdoch asked an intrigued Lamb if he was at all interested in editing the *Sun*. Lamb had no idea that Murdoch was about to buy the paper and was momentarily taken aback. What was the owner of the *News of the World* doing talking about Cudlipp's pet project, the failing IPC *Sun*? He even wondered if the call was a hoax.

But it really was Murdoch and he invited Lamb to come down to London for a "quiet dinner" where they could talk things over. Lamb got straight on the train and, over three bottles of Pouilly Fumé and lobster, Murdoch explained how he wanted to completely transform the IPC *Sun* into a paper much more like the *Mirror* under Nener, the all-conquering, five-million-selling tabloid that Lamb, as chief sub, had fashioned line by line every night for so many years and for so little ultimate reward. Murdoch, it turned out, shared Lamb's low opinion of Cudlipp: "He's just a pamphleteer," Murdoch had said, and was, anyway, well past his sell-by date and hopelessly out of his depth as chairman of a major company like IPC. In the phrase Cecil King had once used about John Cowley and the pre-war *Mirror* board, Cudlipp and the cronies and time-servers he had gathered around him at the *Mirror* "no longer had the stomach for popular journalism".

They discussed how the *Sun*, now set free from IPC control, could compete against the *Mirror*. Lamb said he thought Cudlipp had badly misjudged the younger readers it needed to recruit. That was not surprising – they were both approaching sixty and their ideas had been shaped by the hungry 1930s and the war. It was all summed up by Mirrorscope – Cudlipp and Lee Howard's pet project. It was patronising and it irritated the readers, as though they were being told: "This is the important bit – the rest, all the things you are actually interested in, is rubbish." Mirrorscope was a "pull-out" all right, Lamb said, readers pulled it out and threw it away. The top decks of London buses were ankle-deep in copies. The only reliable measure of a newspaper's quality was how many copies it sold, not the opinion of other journalists or critics. Jack Nener had known that. Bart had known that. Cudlipp had once known that, too. Which was how they had created the *Mirror's* tremendous success.

Murdoch was impressed. He had found Pommie journalists a stuck-up bunch, but here was one who talked sense. The two men continued rubbishing the contemporary *Mirror* and sketching out plans to ensure the new *Sun* captured the spirit of the *Mirror* in its glory years – strident, campaigning, radical, anti-establishment and full of sexy seaside postcard fun.

The meal went on until 2 a.m. in the morning. Murdoch then dropped Lamb back at his hotel. A few minutes later, Lamb's bedside phone rang. It was Murdoch, offering him the editorship of the *Sun*. Lamb accepted on the spot. The next morning he went round to meet Murdoch and his then wife Anna at their house in Sussex Square. "He doesn't waste much time, does he?" Lamb quipped to Anna.

"No," she replied, smiling. "Not much."

Shortly before the launch of Murdoch and Lamb's version of the *Sun*, Cudlipp hosted a dinner for senior *Mirror* editorial people at the Ivy restaurant in Soho. He had been supplied with details of the reporters and editors Murdoch had hired and his spies had given him a complete rundown of the plans for the contents of the paper.

The gathering represented the top names available to the *Mirror*, a veritable galaxy of talent – Sydney Jacobson, the paper's political expert and former editor of the *Daily Herald*, Lee Howard, Marje Proops, sports editor Peter Wilson – the boozy "man they cannot gag" - Donald Zec - friend to the stars - *Mirror* editor-in-waiting Tony Miles of Mirrorscope and others. The average age of those present was well over fifty.

Lee Howard spoke for a while without, people present thought, much conviction about the enormous mistake Murdoch was about to make. He was planning to produce an old-fashioned, 1930s-style "down-market, gut-bucket tabloid", worse than the risible *Daily Sketch* and worse than anything the *Mirror* had produced since the early 1950s. The important thing, Howard assured everyone, was that the *Mirror* should not be deflected from the strategy of becoming an "intelligent tabloid". The impending launch of the *Mirror*'s own mid-week glossy up-market giveaway magazine – a mid-week answer to the Sunday supplements – would reinforce that. The *Daily Express* was losing sales and was on the retreat. In the dawning decade of the 1970s the *Mirror* would be centre-stage, dominating the mid-market with an audience ranging from *Guardian* and *Times* readers at the "top" end through to Sunday readers of the *News of the World* and the daily readers of the *Sketch* – and now Murdoch's new paper – at "the bottom". Having said all this Lee Howard sat down, squeezing his massive frame into a groaning chair and looking distinctly unwell and unconvinced.

In contrast, Cudlipp was brimming with confidence and gave a vintage performance. He mocked Murdoch – "The Dirty Digger" – reading out a list of regular features planned for the new paper, his voice dripping with sarcasm and contempt. It was as though Murdoch and Larry Lamb – who had never been good enough to make the grade at the *Mirror* – had gone through the dustbins at the back of Holborn Circus like tramps and scavengers, picking scraps of discarded ideas and rubbish rejected by the *Mirror* in its move to modernise. The new *Sun's* letters page was going to be called "liveliest letters" – a straight lift of the *Mirror's* "live letters" which had been running since the 1930s. They were going to have a cartoon called "Scarf", an inferior copy of Garth, the equally venerable *Daily Mirror* cartoon originally brought in by Basil Nicholson, also in the 1930s. Murdoch had gone for all the most ancient and out-of-date bits of the *Mirror*. He had not dared to copy the new *Mirror's* best and most adventurous material, the content that appealed to the young and forward-looking. There was no Mirrorscope in the new *Sun* or anything remotely as good. Instead, they had copied Andy Capp, producing a rip-off version called Wack and – most risible of all – they were planning to use the ancient 1940s and 1950s *Mirror* "forward with the people" slogan on the masthead, without even bothering to rewrite it.

The new *Sun's* politics, Cudlipp said, were hard to work out. They were planning to run hardly any politics at all. The new *Sun's* news operation was shot full of holes and, as far as he could work out, would just be a rag-bag of court stories, bought-in agency material and other cheap and nasty sensationalist stuff. Lamb had found it predictably difficult to find people willing to work on "Rupert's Shit Sheet", as the risky new venture was being called in the pubs and bars of Fleet Street. All the good people from the old IPC *Sun* had returned to the *Mirror*. This, Cudlipp assured everyone, was where it had been clever to sell the old *Sun* to Murdoch, rather than simply close it down. Poor old Larry had inherited the duds – and even then he had been seen trawling the depths just to find enough people to form a basic staff. Cudlipp triumphantly informed his top team that the *Sun* would have less than one hundred journalists – many of them useless. The *Mirror* at the time had more than four hundred – all of them the pick of the crop. That fact alone, surely, meant the *Sun* could not possibly do them any damage.

In terms of popular journalism, Cudlipp concluded, Murdoch was trying to "put the clock back fifteen or twenty years". Yes, Larry and Rupert were going to catch a cold with this. It was going to be a bigger mess than even the *Sketch*. If the *Mirror* had to respond to Murdoch's travesty – which it would not – it could just put a line in small type on page one: "BEWARE OF CHEAP IMITATIONS". But instead of laughter at this brilliant stroke of wit there was hardly a murmur, just mumbling and general foreboding.

All eyes turned to Lee Howard. He was wriggling uncomfortably in his chair, had turned deathly white and looked as if he might be about to have a heart attack.

20 A CROCODILE ON MOGADON

The *Mirror* threw a party at the Royal Festival Hall to mark the its official "re-launch" as "Britain's first quality tabloid". Some of the older (and more popular) features were being done away with, others – like the lively letters page – were updated. There was to be a new, softer design style with more rounded type and smaller headlines. Coverage of subjects like fashion would become more "with it" and avant-garde, the Marje Proops advice page more permissive and daring. Mirrorscope was enshrined in the paper, and "puffed" more prominently on the front page.

But the jewel in the crown of the new "Qualoid" *Mirror* was the entirely new, expensively printed, glossy, give-away *Mirror* magazine. The venture was a self-conscious copy of the colour supplements developed by the up-market Sunday broadsheets during the 1960s as vehicles for hard-hitting photojournalism, art-school graphic design and lengthy slabs of "fine writing" in the tradition not of the New York *Daily News* but that of the *New Yorker* or *New York Review of Books*.

The magazine was the secret weapon the *Mirror* would use to see off the threat of new competition from Rupert Murdoch. It had been put together by what was, by the standards of the *Mirror* at the time, a young team of journalists led by Mike Molloy, the long-haired and Zapata-moustached art-school graduate and rising star of the *Mirror*'s production department. One of his models was the ultra-fashionable new-wave women's magazine *Nova* (slogan: "a new kind of magazine for the new kind of woman") then published by the *Mirror*'s parent company IPC and source of all things groovy in newspaper and magazine journalism for the next two decades. The *Mirror Magazine* was to be distributed with the paper every Wednesday and, according to plan, would not only boost circulation but bring in a fortune in the form of up-market colour advertising.

The magazine was heavily promoted before launch as "the publishing innovation of the decade". It was all very Zeitgeist – very much the *Mirror*'s entrée to the photographers, writers, cartoonists and models of "Swinging London". But the *Mirror Magazine* was to be a publishing catastrophe to rank with Northcliffe's miscalculation in launching the original *Daily Mirror* as a paper for gentlewomen. Reaction from readers was dire and the advertising trade magazine *Campaign* gave a damning verdict: "Agency reaction to the editorial is that IPC has fallen flat on its face. Views were varied, but largely anti. It was, they said, too pop, too up-market, too vulgar, too sexy. They didn't like the colour clash between ads and editorial – they didn't think it was like the *Mirror*."

Within weeks the IPC board was thinking about closing the magazine. The planned-for income from ad sales of £12 million a year had failed to materialise – no bad thing in a way since the advertising was being sold at a loss, as a result of ruinously expensive bonus payments the *Mirror* management had conceded to the printers' union in return for working on the magazine. Had the *Mirror Magazine* sold dozens of pages of ads and therefore had to print another section, the losses would have been even greater. Within weeks the magazine was making projected losses of £5 million for the year.

So, when the *Sun* was launched a few weeks later, the *Mirror* had to face up to its new competitor in the worst possible circumstances. The management was panicking over what to do about the magazine and ordering emergency economies in the main part of the paper to cover the losses. A decision had been taken to close the magazine – so the whole "up-market" strategy of the paper was suddenly thrown into confusion. But closure had been deferred for a year because of threats of strike action against the paper over redundancies, thus dragging out a problem that above all required urgent, decisive action.

Even worse was the reaction to the magazine on the part of the newsagents. They hated it even more than the advertisers and the readers because they were expected to get up earlier in the morning to stuff the magazine into the paper (they were printed and delivered separately), only to see them thrown away again. Their national federation began demanding a "handling charge" which would add massively to the losses and actually provide an incentive for newsagents not to sell the paper.

In contrast, Rupert Murdoch had prepared the way for the launch of *Sun* very carefully, offering the newsagents a bigger share of his paper's cover price than they ever got from the *Mirror* for every copy sold, treating them with respect (rather than taking them for granted as the *Mirror* had done with the magazine launch), offering them bonuses for good sales performance and deals such as sale or return, where they were not charged for unsold copies. It was no wonder that, the newsagents loved Murdoch's paper and tended to shove the *Mirror* to the back of the counter.

On the evening of the "Murdoch *Sun*" launch, Cudlipp held a "sigh of relief" party at the Café Royal, celebrating the end of the IPC *Sun*. The message was that those returning to the *Mirror* faced a much better future now that the millstone of what had once been the *Daily Herald* had been laid to rest. The "Murdoch *Sun*" was at that moment being put together at Murdoch's Bouverie Street *News of the World* building by Larry Lamb's scratched-together team of "*Mirror* rejects". There was no break in production. Cudlipp had ordered the Café Royal tables to be decorated with dead sunflowers to mark the death of one version of the paper and the stillbirth of another. Lamb, when he heard about it, had thought of responding by having a "cracked *Mirror*" party, but he didn't have the time to organise it.

After some heavy drinking at the Café Royal, Cudlipp, Lee Howard and others made their way back some time around midnight to the executive dining club on the ninth floor of the *Mirror* building. Over a glass of champagne, and taking in the magnificent view across the illuminated skyline of London, Cudlipp leafed through the first edition of the Murdoch *Sun* with pity and contempt.

His spies at the *Mirror* had been right. The new paper was abysmal. Editorially it was the "cheap imitation" he had predicted. As foreseen the news coverage was no good at all – the front-page story was headlined HORSE DOPE SENATION and was a very windy kite-flyer about a supposed new horse-racing corruption scandal about to break. What surprised Cudlipp was the very poor technical quality of production. They had expected Larry – a former *Daily Mirror* chief sub – to get at least that right. But the *Sun* was a failure even at that level. The paper was full of spelling errors, layout problems, blotchy pictures and badly fitting headlines, some of which made little sense. Cudlipp threw his copy of the *Sun* into the bin and told Lee Howard, "You've got nothing to worry about."

Within eighteen months the *Sun* was selling 2.5 million copies and the *Mirror* had lost the best part of a million regular readers to the new paper. Larry Lamb could not believe his luck. He had expected his old paper to fight fire with fire, repositioning itself down-market and out-tabloiding him blow for blow, at least until the new competitive threat was seen off and their monopoly protected. They could then have resumed their Magical Mystery Tour up-market as signified by the sub-psychedelic approach of the *Mirror Magazine*. Instead, they had allowed him to get a foothold.

"Had the *Mirror* gone for us, all guns blazing in 1970, I think we might have found it difficult to survive," Larry Lamb later wrote, "but instead they reacted like the proverbial crocodile on Mogadon."

After the production problems which had dogged the first few editions of the (Murdoch) *Sun* had been ironed out, the paper began to take on a fresh, hot-off-the-press look compared to the *Mirror's* smaller headlines and more studied design. The *Sun's* pages also often looked like better value for money because the *Mirror* was carrying far more advertising to pay for its bloated costs. Even the quality of the paper used by the *Sun* was better than that available to the *Mirror*, which in the years of monopoly IPC had grown used to using as a way of getting rid of substandard paper from its Canadian mills.

The *Sun* was performing far better than most people expected – certainly better than Cudlipp had believed possible. That was bad enough. Worse was the fact that there appeared to be no "Plan B" – even after the *Mirror Magazine* was finally closed. Sales lost to the *Sun* had a devastating and immediate effect on revenue that was sharply down. Cudlipp and the board reacted by increasing still further the number of adverts, economising and generally trying to squeeze more money out of the paper, making it an even worse product and creating what started to look like a vicious circle. As the *Sun* started to be seen as a success – and not a one-hit wonder – Lamb found it easier to recruit more experienced staff. Murdoch's personal control of the paper meant he had no board of directors to consult, and so he could raid the *Mirror* any time and get a yes or no answer to wage demands in a matters of hours, if not minutes.

As for content, the *Sun* displayed vulgarity on a scale to rival the Golden Mile and Pleasure Beach that Cudlipp had got to know as a reporter in the 1930s. From day one the paper also had massive sex content. "Mr Murdoch has not invented sex," said *The Times*, "but he does show a remarkable enthusiasm for its benefits to circulation, such as a tired old Fleet Street has not seen for many years." It was a rule that on as many days as possible the *Sun's* front page had to have the words WIN, FREE and SEX (or "LOVE" – to use the more acceptable euphemism of the time) on the front page – possibly giving the bleary-eyed punter rushing to work the impression that he was buying a lottery ticket with an expenses-paid trip to a brothel as the first prize. (Lamb did once literally offer ownership of the celebrity nude model Vivien Neves as a prize in a competition "for a strictly limited period" and, according to Lamb, it was one of the paper's most successful front pages ever in terms of sales.)

Lamb turned out to be a dab hand at turning criticism, particularly of his paper's high sex content, into entertaining free publicity. When the anti-pornography campaigner Lord Longford complained that the *Sun* was "thriving on the uninhibited presentation of Mr Rupert Murdoch's particular Antipodean blend of erotica" Lamb responded by explaining that antipodean meant Australian and printed the Page Three picture upside down, to show how antipodean erotica differed from the British kind. The next day he offered *Sun* readers a competition prize described as "an antipodean erotica kit". This consisted of a musk candle, a bottle of champagne, oysters, a sun-bed, a two month supply of vitamin pills and "much, much more".

Unlike the *Mirror*, the *Sun* was advertised wall to wall on TV, and Murdoch bought a large stake in the London ITV company LWT – the channel which carried the all-important Sunday night ads that flagged up the contents of the *Sun's* feature pages for the coming week – and installed his people on the board and in the key position of advertising director. The strategy was to run the ads cheaply over the weekend on LWT, hooking readers in on Monday and then holding on to them with serialisations of books (for example *The Love Machine*) which had to be read every day, with the material getting steadily more steamy as Friday approached. The *Sun* also had a lot of "themed" weeks – as in IT'S PUSSY WEEK IN THE SUN! The paper also had Romance Week, Pony Week, Dog Week, Bicycle Week, Ooh! La! La! Week, Fishing Week - which were mainly excuses to have pictures of semi-naked girls riding ponies or bicycles or whatever it was - and to try hook in the readers for another five days.

To vary the pace a little the ads would sometimes switch from "love" and "aspiration" (i.e., sex and greed) to majoring on crime and public welfare (i.e., fear and horror). One of the *Sun's* most famous ads was for a feature called THE DAY OF THE MAD DOGS – a supposed investigation into the country's lack of preparation for dealing with an outbreak of rabies. The commercial began sedately with a middle-aged couple relaxing in the drawing room of their elegant country home with their two evidently well-behaved pedigree dogs. Then suddenly the dogs had a fit, leapt up and savagely attacked the defenceless couple. Viewers were shown close-ups of the dogs' foaming mouths (shaving cream was used) and bloodied victims writhing on the floor. The ad attracted a record number of complaints. Lamb was delighted. The following morning his paper "walked off the news stands".

As the *Sun* powered ahead, editorial people at the *Mirror* were like rabbits caught in the headlights. Should they, for example, compete with the *Sun,* copying its Page Three topless feature? Or should the *Mirror* take out whatever titillating pictures the paper already had so as not to be confused with the *Sun*? Having topless girls just didn't "rest easily" on the *Mirror* and in some ways all the problems of the paper came to rest on this small and seemingly irrelevant detail of the paper.

Cudlipp kept quiet in public about the *Sun* once it had been launched. The *Mirror* corporate view was expressed instead in public by Michael Christiansen, editor of the *Sunday Mirror,* son of a famous *Daily Express* editor and the man Cudlipp was at the time grooming to become editor of the *Daily Mirror*. In 1970 Christiansen said:

I think Murdoch's arrival in Fleet Street was the worst thing that could have happened. The clock of journalistic standards has been put back ten to fifteen years, and it now seems that what has happened on my paper is that one's major consideration every week is whether you should have a picture that shows pubic hair.

Missing the point, Larry Lamb reacted furiously, saying there had never been a wisp of public hair pictured in the *Sun*.

But Larry Lamb and the *Sun* did not have it all their own way all the time, or across all of the country. Unlike the *Sun*, the *Mirror* was produced in Manchester and this gave Derek Jameson, the *Mirror*'s northern editor at the time, a huge advantage. The *Sun*'s first edition had to be printed by 7.30 p.m. so that copies would be ready by midnight to go on trains to the north and be in the shops the next morning. Jameson in Manchester could wait until 10 p.m. or midnight before printing, and so could include more up to date news and, importantly, midweek football results and match reports. Jameson would get the London news-desk to phone through any stories or features running in the *Sun*. He would then "lift" – the jargon for copying – the rival paper's best material, print it and get it out on the street while the bundles of the *Sun* were still on the train.44

At the same time Jameson, an intelligent man who some were apt to underestimate because of his thick Gorblimey cockney accent, had decided to follow a more down-market, *Sun*-like agenda whenever possible, making the northern editions of the *Mirror* sometimes look very different to those produced by Holborn Circus. Ignoring the move up-market signalled by Mirrorscope and *Mirror Magazine*, Jameson delighted in printing cheerful tosh such as a competition to find the country's oldest budgie. It was won by a sad creature Jameson described as "Bald, plucked and indignant, the most evil-looking brute this side of the Timor Sea". Thousands had entered the competition, circulation had increased and, all in all, the ugly budgie contest was one of the most successful features in the history of the *Mirror*'s northern edition. Jameson had also solved the Page Three dilemma by purchasing rejected Page Three pictures cheaply from the *Sun*'s freelance photographers and printing them in late editions of the paper, hoping that there would not be too much fuss.

While the circulation of the *Mirror* was falling across the country as a whole, it held up and even increased in the north where it had the printing advantage and a more *Sun*-like approach to content. The *Sun* was selling best in London and the south, and the circulation battle between the two papers was to have this regional bias for the next thirty years.

Jameson continued to get away with printing the occasional Page Three reject in the northern *Mirror*, especially in the last couple of years of Lee Howard's easy-going editorship. But in 1971 Cudlipp's protégé Tony Miles took over and told Jameson that the topless girls had to go.

"Those papers of yours," Miles reportedly told Jameson, "I am ashamed to think they will be put into museums as a permanent record of the *Daily Mirror* during those days." Miles was more interested in countering the *Sun* by reviving the old Cudlipp device of the Shock Issue. But, up against the *Sun* and serving a generation brought up on new-wave film violence and shock-horror television, it was hard to achieve the same impact. Even John Pilger's famous 1970s SHOCK ISSUE on the "Killing Fields" of Cambodia was tied in to a TV documentary. More run-of-the-mill material – a look at housing problems or the education system – no longer worked. Thus, in the middle of Lamb's PUSSY WEEK attack, the *Mirror* hit back with a SHOCK ISSUE on the voguish 1970s problem of environmental pollution entitled OUR GREEN AND POISONED LAND. Within was a very average discussion of pollution, overlaid with pressure group agit-prop, brought to life with a silly front-page picture of a girl in a mini-skirt going to work in a gas-mask ("this could happen before the end of the decade"). Jameson got the message. He believed the *Mirror* had become too "establishment-minded" in craving respectability at a time when it needed to fight fire with down-market fire to see off the *Sun*. He soon left the *Mirror* to briefly edit the *Daily Express* before launching the ultra-down-market *Daily Star* in 1978.

By that time the *Sun* had already overtaken the *Mirror* as the best-selling newspaper in the known universe.

21 AN UNPARDONABLE VANITY

Hugh Cudlipp left the *Daily Mirror* on January 1, 1974. There had been a whole series of farewell parties after he announced his intention to go fifteen months earlier, but the final "party to end all parties" was spectacular, even by *Mirror* standards. It was reckoned to have cost more than £50,000 and had been factored into IPC's business plan as a specific overhead, like the rates or the electricity bill, and spread over a number of years.

The celebrations began with hundreds of merry-makers making their way down the Thames from Charing Cross pier in a river steamer surrounded by a small armada of pleasure boats. Many were drunk before they set foot on land at their destination − the huge Trafalgar pub overlooking the impressive bend of the Thames at Greenwich. The customary vast quantities of champagne had been laid on. After a few hours of good, solid drinking the throng moved on to the seventeenth century Painted Hall at Greenwich Naval College. Here, under a huge domed roof decorated with paintings of goddesses representing the four continents in submission to British naval power, 100 guests gathered around the 150ft long solid oak dining table.

There had already been an "office" party at which Cudlipp had been presented with an antique barrel organ, presented by night editor Mike Taylor dressed in parrot costume. Taylor said that the instrument would come in handy if Cudlipp ever had to go begging on the streets to make a living. In the meantime, Taylor added, it would replace the piano in Cudlipp's private Cheyne Walk ground floor pub that had been wrecked when, during the Jack Nener Welsh sing-song era, somebody had been sick in it.

Then everyone rolled the few hundred yards down Farringdon Road to the embankment of the river Thames near Blackfriars where they got on a series of boats - each laden down with yet more booze - for the hour long journey down the river to Greenwich. There, surrounded by priceless paintings, deep leather furnishings, oak panels and glittering gilt, editor Tony Miles made a sentimental speech, full of praise for Cudlipp's achievements, his rags to riches progress, his contributions to politics and the fact, generally, that he had been the greatest popular journalist of the century, creating the model for all others to copy.

A speech by Sir Alex Jarratt, the *Mirror's* newly arrived chief executive was less well received. Jarratt was a former civil servant and not a journalist and therefore seen as a bit of a gatecrasher at the party. As he droned on the drunken hacks started booing and pelting him good-naturedly with bread rolls for being a "boring old sod".

The boozing continued and in the small hours the party began to break up – some groups headed back to the ninth floor at Holborn; others went to the Press Club with its all-night drinking licence. Still others found lock-ins in pubs around Greenwich. There was an apocryphal story that one reporter went on a "bender" around local pubs and was found wandering around Greenwich dazed and confused two days later. Reporter Richard Stott, who was present, remembered it as being a bit like Dunkirk – with earnest discussions of last sightings, stories of men lost at sea and groups of bedraggled "survivors" finding their way back up the river and arriving back on dry land near Holborn Circus at irregular intervals.

Cudlipp had announced his retirement during a cocktail party at a hotel in Manchester in October, 1972. The news came as a bolt out of the blue and some, at first, wondered if he was serious. He was still in vigorous good health, was not yet 60 and had recently handed over the chore – which he hated – of running the business side of the IPC conglomerate to others, becoming once again editorial director – the job he loved and had made his own. (In 1970 IPC had been merged with its former paper-making subsidiary Reed to create Reed International. The move was in fact a "reverse takeover" of IPC by Reed.)

Cudlipp told his stunned listeners he had been an editor since he was 24 years old and had several times had to readjust his thinking so as to remain "sympathetic to the ever-changing outlook on life of the younger generation". Then, in his familiar way, he delivered the punch line: "Anyone attempting to substantiate such claims after the age of 60 would in my view be a charlatan." Cudlipp said he wanted to leave just before his sixtieth birthday. It would be "an unpardonable vanity", he said, to stay on in charge of the editorial side of newspapers designed to appeal to a younger generation after his sixtieth birthday.

There were loyal pleas for him to reconsider over the massed gin and tonics. But Cudlipp would not be moved. He had even lined up his successor – a journalist of immense stature and the perfect man to lead them all to the next stage in the *Mirror's* history. He could not reveal the name at the time as there were still details to be sorted out. But he was sure he would get his man and that they would all be delighted.

Cudlipp's choice was Harold "Harry" Evans, the former editor of the *Yorkshire Post* who had turned the *Sunday Times* into the biggest-selling "quality" Sunday newspaper in the country, turning it into a model of the sort of modern "quality-popular" newspapers Cudlipp still believed were the path to the future. But Cudlipp was to be disappointed. Evans refused to come to the *Mirror,* so the editorial director's job went instead to the mild-mannered Tony Miles, Lee Howard's successor as editor in 1971, a Cudlipp protégé and a former editor of Mirroscope.

Miles was famous in Fleet Street for two things. The first was his unconvincing affectation of peppering any conversation with the trademark word "cock" (as in "How are you today then, cock?") and secondly as the man who had his marriage ruined by the rival medium of television. Miles's already troubled marriage fell apart when TV cameras repeatedly captured him with his arm round his mistress sitting in the best seats just under the scoreboard on centre court, Wimbledon. His wife saw the pictures and divorced him. Miles's bad luck continued as editor of the *Mirror*, where he was cursed with the problem of being reasonably – but not spectacularly – successful. He was called "the editor whose indecision is final" – mainly because of dithering within senior editorial ranks over whether or not to try and compete with the *Sun,* as people like Derek Jameson in the Manchester operation wanted, or whether to stick to Cudlipp's strategy of officially ignoring the new paper. When Miles took over the *Mirror* in 1971 the paper had already lost the best part of half a million daily sales in the wake of the launch of the *Sun*. At that rate the *Sun* was scheduled to overtake the *Mirror* by the end of 1973. Tracing the graph forward the *Mirror* would have precisely zero readers by about 1977.

But Miles kept his nerve. The dramatic fall in the *Mirror's* circulation was stemmed, and settled at around four and a half million – by no means a disaster. The *Sun* was increasing its sales at a much faster rate than the *Mirror* was losing them, which meant the new Murdoch paper was stealing readers from the *Daily Sketch* – or, just as likely, was expanding the market, attracting people who had never regularly read a newspaper before. But the circulation war was even more complicated than that. The *Express* was losing readers much more quickly than the *Mirror*. Some of these readers were probably coming over to the *Mirror*, replacing some of those who had defected to the *Sun*. All this presented Miles with a nightmare of an editing problem. Before the launch of the *Sun*, the strategy had been simple. All the down-market readers were "in the bag" because they had no other paper to buy. So it made sense for the *Mirror* to move steadily up-market, capturing new readers from the *Express*. But now the "down-market" readers were being offered the *Sun*.

Yet Miles lost only 300,000 sales by the time he became editorial director in 1975 and handed over the day-to-day editorship of the *Mirror* to acting editor Mike Molloy. Over the same period the *Sun* had added over 1.5 million to its circulation. (Miles's designated successor, Michael Christiansen, had a serious heart attack after just a few weeks in the editor's chair. Molloy stood in for Christiansen and was confirmed in the job when it became clear that Christiansen was not fit enough to stay.)

Mike Molloy was the first *Mirror* editor to have been born after the outbreak of the Second World War and therefore was a representative of the "baby boomer" generation the *Mirror* was struggling to come to terms with. He had a background not in local newspaper journalism but – like Harry Guy Bartholomew – was a graphic designer who had spent time at art school. Molloy however was charm personified, an affable man with an impeccable Cudlippian pedigree (co-creator of the Shock Issues, associate editor of Mirrorscope, editor of the *Mirror Magazine*) who seemed to get on with everybody and was already a sort of *Mirror* institution before he became editor. He had started as a messenger boy in the 1950s, graduated to drawing illustrations for the fashion pages and, apart from a short spell at the *Daily Sketch* in the early 1960s, had never worked for any paper other than the *Mirror*. Molloy was an undoubted talent on the visual side, credited with improving and modernising the *Mirror's* look, softening the original 1930s New York design with smaller, less raucous, more *Express*-like rounded typefaces designed to appeal to the more female, design-conscious mid-market readership the *Mirror* was after, according to the Cudlipp plan.

Molloy's editorship began badly with a big year-on-year drop in sales that took the paper's circulation to under four million for the first time since the early 1950s. But after that he held sales remarkably steady – helped by a sudden collapse of sales of the *Daily Express*. In the first two years of Molloy's editorship, the *Express* lost almost a million readers after a series of internal ructions that made the *Mirror's* troubles look slight by comparison. The *Sun* had nevertheless continued its "soar-away" circulation rise and so the gap closed. For the first half of Molloy's editorship the *Mirror* and the *Sun* were neck and neck in circulation terms, both with sales in the region of 3.75 to 4 million until the end of the decade.

Molloy finally addressed the issue of Page Three, which had caused huge dissension at the *Mirror*. Molloy held out until 1975 before printing his first bare nipple – it belonged to "holiday girl Jilly Johnson", whose naked breasts were shown in tasteful profile. The picture was printed as much to test the reaction of other *Mirror* executives and staff in Holborn Circus as the readers. The internal outrage was led by Marje Proops and plans to continue the feature were dropped.

In return for the Page Three ban Proops agreed to support Molloy's plans to get some more "wholesome" sex into the paper as often as possible, providing him with a SHOCK ISSUE-type edition called THE *MIRROR* GUIDE TO SEXUAL KNOWLEDGE illustrated with a tasteful picture of a naked young mum cuddling a baby. This was supposed to be so steamy that it carried the warning "Parents Please Note: This issue of the *Daily Mirror* contains a guide to sexual knowledge: allow your children to read it at your discretion." Sadly the edition only succeeded in showing that Marje Proops was stuck in the past.

After that, Molloy experimented with nudes on pages five or seven. But then the feature was dropped without warning. Molloy told *The Times* he had got rid of the nudes "to see whether there was something more interesting to put in the paper… the girls can always reappear if the demand is there." The reality was that there had been a second and even more serious staff revolt. Molloy responded with a Page Three-type feature called "The Next to Nothing Girls" which only succeeded in falling between two stools.

Once the fuss died down, Molloy brought nudes back under the heading of *MIRROR* GIRLS. But he was overwhelmed once again by reported defections of former *Express* readers and internal feminist revolt. When the *MIRROR* GIRLS disappeared from the *Mirror* without explanation Larry Lamb at the *Sun* gleefully arranged for his Page Three girls to pose in front of full-length wardrobe mirrors for a week, running the slogan: "Remember the best *MIRROR* GIRLS are in the *Sun*." But Molloy still did not give up. While the *Sun* was running its straightforward daily Page Three – take it or leave it – Molloy was tying himself in knots furtively and sporadically reinstating the nudes in the form of patently hypocritical series like "The Raw Material" (supposedly about the art of photography) "Britain's loveliest girls, a photographic beauty parade", updated to become topless, but which otherwise would have looked like an old-fashioned idea even in the failing 1920s *Mirror,* which had placed heavy reliance on exactly the same stunt.

While trying to fight the circulation war on the *Sun* front, Molloy attacked the declining *Express*'s readership, downplaying as much as he could the *Mirror*'s support for the unpopular 1974–79 Labour government (anathema to *Express* readers), placing more emphasis on features and material designed to attract women readers. There was a more chatty approach, led by the whimsical gossip columnist Peter Tory. Molloy balanced all the lightweight fluff by giving a full page to former "IPC *Sun*" investigative reporter and left-wing activist Paul Foot who tackled such unpopular causes as getting wrongly convicted murderers released from jail.

Molloy's more graphic and feature-led approach seemed to work. The fall in the *Mirror's* circulation slowed and in some months, when Murdoch took his foot off the pedal of TV advertising, it even went up. Most importantly, Molloy felt, he was producing a paper which had "heart", one which he and his journalists and maybe the readers felt proud of producing and reading.

In 1977 circulation nudged back up above four million helped by a series of investigative scoops about corruption in football and Molloy's discovery that – against all conventional newspaper wisdom – the "serialisation" of extracts from best-selling books could boost the circulation of daily as well as Sunday newspapers. Molloy, feeling extremely pleased with himself, set off for a business meeting in New York, leaving his deputy Peter Thompson to look after the shop. No sooner had Molloy arrived at his Manhattan hotel than he received a panicky phone call from Thompson back at Holborn Circus. The paper's journalists had been goaded into going on strike after finding that they were being paid less than the cleaners and, worst of all, the unskilled "casual" staff who were hired to tie up bundles of printed papers ready for distribution.

The journalists' protests had started when the "FoC" (Father of the Chapel, meaning branch secretary) representing the string-tiers had been boasting in the pub to a bunch of *Mirror* subs, telling them that the unions representing the admin and labouring staff – NATSOPA and SOGAT – were so strong and the journalists' union, the NUJ, was so useless that some casuals earned "twice as much" as journalists. It was already known and accepted as a fact of life that skilled printers earned far more than journalists as members of the mightiest of all print unions, the NGA and SLADE. But this was too much – now the bloke who cleaned out the bogs was getting more than the hacks who produced the paper.

A few days after the end of the strike, when the *Mirror* reappeared on the streets, Molloy attended a board meeting with all 17 directors present. Managing Director Percy Roberts asked circulation director Tony Griffin for the latest sales figures. Griffin replied: "Three point one million." There was complete pin-drop silence as this sank in. Molloy felt the atmosphere in the room chill by several degrees as he thought to himself, "Oh shit! That's it." His paper had lost almost a million readers in the space of a few weeks. Percy Roberts broke the silence by asking Griffin what he was going to do about it. Griffin not unreasonably said sarcastically, "Well... it would of course help if the unions would allow us to print a newspaper which we could then sell." He then forlornly asked Molloy if he had any more big book serialisations up his sleeve. Some of the damage was repaired but the crash pulled the average sales figures for 1977 down well below the four million mark.

The *Sun* overtook *Mirror* circulation for the first time in March 1978 with sales of 3.8 million. Ron Cotton, circulation director of the *Mirror* Group, phoned his opposite number at the *Sun*, Brian Horwite, to offer congratulations. In June 1978, the sales of the *Sun* went over four million for the first time, helped by a series of features commemorating the death of Elvis.

Critics later said that Molloy made too much of the 1977 strike as the cause of the loss of the top spot to the *Mirror*, claiming that the *Sun* too had suffered similar problems with strike action around the same time. A report by the Economist Intelligence Unit had found that right across Fleet Street manning levels were set by "horse-trading" and they often bore no relationship to the work that needed doing. Wage bargaining, the same report found, was "a jungle". Take-home pay was made up of all kinds of bonus payments that had built up over the years. The basic rate of pay meant little and was seen by the unions as "a starting point for negotiation" over what their members would actually get.

But in Molloy's mind the journalists' strike in 1977 was a turning point. He did not so much blame the unions – and least of all the journalists – but he did blame the management style of Reed International who had bought IPC in 1970, making the *Mirror* and its sister papers a small and not much-loved subsidiary of a huge and troubled multinational corporation. Reed was best known for making wallpaper, Crown emulsion, Polycell wallpaper paste and Twyford toilet fittings.

News of the Reed takeover had come as a complete surprise to almost everyone connected with the *Mirror*. When the news broke it hit Holborn Circus like a "shock wave". Without warning the editors, senior journalists and managers were called into managing director Ted Pickering's office on the fourth floor. He was seen in shirt-sleeves, sweating, and struck people as a man under tremendous pressure. He told them that everybody would continue to work on the same contracts, wages and conditions. One of those present, Bob Edwards, noticed Percy Roberts, the sometime MI6 officer, on the far side of the massive office hurriedly destroying a huge pile of documents by putting them through a shredder.

As Molloy saw it, the new management installed by Reed was the cause of most of the *Mirror*'s woes. They showed little interest in the paper, and lacked the understanding or decisiveness of Rupert Murdoch, who could make a circulation-winning move in moments and was prepared to invest and gamble in order to win. Murdoch knew how to compete and was spending four times as much on TV advertising for the *Sun* than Reed was spending on the *Mirror*. At the same time Reed's reluctance to provoke strike action meant the *Mirror* was carrying a salary bill it could afford less and less as circulation dribbled away. The *Mirror* no longer had the biggest cheque-book in Fleet Street. Larry Lamb at the *Sun* now wielded that, meaning he could beat the *Mirror* by signing up any columnist, contributor or book serialisation he wanted.

Writing in the *Guardian* a few years later about the *Mirror*'s loss of the top slot to the *Sun,* Molloy directly criticised what he saw as the inept and laid-back style of the Reed board and nostalgically lamented the passing of the autocratic press lords who had previously run the paper.

"Since Cecil King was deposed and ownership passed into the hands of Reed International," Molloy wrote, "the Mirror Group has lacked the kind of autocratic player who can take his seat in the Fleet Street poker game." The man Reed had put in charge of the *Mirror* was Sir Alex Jarratt, a former civil servant and assistant to Barbara Castle at the Department of Trade. Molloy thought Jarratt and the rest of the *Mirror* board knew little about newspapers and cared less. He publicly yearned for "power to once again return to the ninth floor at Holborn Circus."

The *Mirror* under Molloy remained what it always had been – home to some of the most celebrated and talented lushes in the country. Keith Waterhouse, author of *Billy Liar* and that unrestrained celebration of drinking "Jeffrey Bernard is Unwell", was one of the contingent who was able to combine a level of alcohol consumption which would knock out the average cart horse with the ability to produce some of the finest modern English prose ever written.[45]

The annual high point of Waterhouse's boozing was the Labour party conference. When it was held in Blackpool he would hold court at Yates's Wine Lodge, pressed into service as a sort of temporary field-hospital El Vino's, taking occasional tram rides along the Blackpool front to the Fleetwood kipper shop and Fisherman's Friend factory where he would breath in the fumes in order to sober up and stay in touch with "ooupp North". Anne Robinson was another *Mirror* journalist from the Molloy era who had a ferocious thirst but, in her case, it also became a serious problem. She later claimed that she had spent most of the 1970s drunk and had to get help for the problem before making a complete recovery.

Molloy's own drinking and working habits were the cause of much comment. His successor as editor, Mike Stott, jokingly described Molloy's typical day at the office thus:

"Arrive at office 11 a.m. to 11.30 a.m., bone up for half an hour. Twelve noon break out the champagne cocktails, aperitifs with whomever he was going to dine with, dine in the *Mirror*'s spectacular dining room on the ninth floor or out to the pub and a restaurant, back from lunch at 4 p.m. or thereabouts, dinner until about midnight, on to Tramp nightclub and then driven home by his chauffeur."

According to another colleague Molloy was, like Cudlipp, a man who liked "the trappings of power" that came with senior editorial rank at such an important paper as the *Mirror* – invitations to High Table at Oxford and Cambridge, Royal Ascot, dinner at 10 Downing Street, trips to America. He delegated much of the actual work to subordinates and concentrated instead on his own interest in the minutiae of Westminster party politics, teasing out gossip over long lunches with politicians and celebrities.

Nothing was going to change while Reed remained in charge. And a new owner was starting to eye up the Mirror Group.

His name was Robert Maxwell.

22 IN THE LAND OF THE LEGLESS...

Mike Molloy had been praying for a strong proprietor with "ink in his veins" who understood the newspaper business and was prepared to take risks, even if it meant working for a tyrant. The most likely candidate for the post in the early 1980s was Robert Maxwell and Molloy often wondered what it might be like to have to work for him.

But Molloy did not, at first, get Robert Maxwell. What he got was a small, stocky, bespectacled, unassuming, self-taught Geordie solicitor and building-society manager. Clive Thornton was appointed as chief executive of the *Mirror* in 1983 by the board of Reed International. The idea was that he would prepare the Mirror Group for floatation on the stock market as a separate company, cutting it off from the rest of the crumbling IPC empire created by Cecil King and making it an independent entity once again.

At the time, Thornton was best known for having invented the "Granny Bond" during his spell running the Abbey National building society. Looking on from the sidelines Cudlipp described the latest wearer of the Northcliffe crown as "a fussy little solicitor who goes round tidying up and switching off the lights to save money". Thornton was nevertheless a highly paid business executive. But, whereas King had collected priceless Georgian silverware and antiques from around the world and Cudlipp had indulged himself with champagne, cigars, endless sexual affairs, ocean-going powerboats and by building a pub in his back garden, Thornton's idea of the high life was the purchase of a small herd of prize heifers. He was, in addition, a devout Roman Catholic and worst of all strictly teetotal. Mike Molloy always said the strongest drink Thornton would ever take was a large mug of tea, which he drank while watching "Coronation Street".

There was something else, apart from his stunning ordinariness, which set Clive Thornton apart at the *Mirror*. He had a wooden leg. He had worn it since being involved in an horrendous accident involving a tram when he was 14 years old. Now that the board of Reed International had given Thornton supreme power at *Mirror* the word went round the building:

IN THE LAND OF THE LEGLESS – THE ONE-LEGGED MAN IS KING.

Thornton had been put in place by the Reed International board because they were thoroughly sick of the *Mirror* and its Sunday sister papers and wanted rid of them. The acute problem was the power of print workers and their unions who, not being stupid and having sensed that computers would soon put them out of a job, were having one last splurge of militancy aimed at getting their hands on as much money as they could before, as they correctly suspected, they were to be rendered unemployable, and put out on the street at the first available opportunity. By the early 1980s the unions no longer believed that they had any future. They no longer cared about the long-term interests of the *Mirror*, because they were about to be history.

The idea was that Thornton would deal with the trades unions – reducing costs, increasing efficiency and restoring the profits needed to make the Mirror Group attractive to investors as an independent company in a stock-market floatation. Thornton's credentials for the job of getting the unions and the workforce on-side were excellent. He was a prominent individual supporter of the Labour party (which, in those days, also implied support for trade unionism as a principle). Thornton had pioneered Scandinavian-style worker participation, workforce share ownership and a "democratic" management style (he was very proud of abolishing 51 committees) at Abbey National, one of the largest financial concerns in the country. He had even said, on a TV chat show, that the building society movement represented "the highest form of socialism" to be found in Britain and was very proud of the fact. If the unions wouldn't trust and work with Thornton, Reed reasoned, they wouldn't work with anyone.

Thornton was a puritanical man who practised what he preached: he was horrified by the size and opulence of King's old office and immediately ordered that it should be partitioned into a number of smaller, functional workspaces. There was a problem with this. The unions wanted large numbers of workmen assigned to the job, who then dragged their feet with the barely disguised intention of making it their meal-ticket for as long as possible.

Thornton was also a very thorough man. His first act was to crawl all over the paper's accounts. On his very first day he stood in the corridor near the cashiers' windows watching with his jaw dangling as people came and collected money one after another all day like customers drawing cash just before Christmas in a high-street branch of the Abbey National. But at the *Mirror* it seemed to be Christmas every day – especially for the more senior journalists and executives. Thornton produced a report for the board detailing expenses claims. These amounted to £5 million a year, with £1.3 million spent just on entertaining. He drew up a list of people who had claimed more than £8,000 in a single year in expenses. "I cannot continue to present a bleak picture to the trade unions and ask for restraint against this background," Thornton said. He demanded that the expenses should be at least halved within the financial year.

Thornton's overall strategy was to launch two new papers while keeping the workforce the same size. One would be a London evening paper designed to break the monopoly of the *Evening Standard*, the other an up-market Sunday "quality tabloid" reminiscent in some ways of the plan for the original "IPC *Sun*" and provisionally entitled the *Sunday Globe*. These new titles might not sell very many copies at first, but any revenue they made would go straight on to the bottom line since they would be produced free by the otherwise severely under-employed *Mirror* workforce. Thornton was sure that it was a viable plan, because the unions would see that the only alternative would be the sale of the group to a predator businessman who would arrive and sack them all. Robert Maxwell was in the frame already and Reed were quietly letting it be known they were ready to unload the papers on to anyone if the Thornton plan did not work out.

And so Thornton began meetings with each of the Mirror Group's 57 different chapels, as union branches were called, persuading them to back the plan, offering job security in return for more realistic manning levels on the new titles. Finally, he addressed all the union leaders telling them his main aim was to keep everyone in a job.

Thornton stressed that he understood the lack of trust of the shop-floor in the Fleet Street. But he wanted to win that trust. To guarantee they were not being led up the garden path the *Mirror* would henceforth be "transparent" in its decision-making. Union representatives would be consulted and given all the facts. They would all, for the first time, share in the profits if things went well and thus reap the rewards of their own hard work. He offered them all kinds of industrial democracy – representation on the board of directors, profit-sharing, worker-shareholder schemes, endless consultation with the shop-floor – possibly even a say over the choice of top executives. There would be a "golden share" held by the workforce, which would prevent takeover by a union-busting predator and thus protect their jobs for good. All they had to do was to agree not to keep threatening strike action, so that he could raise enough money in the City to meet Reed International's asking price of around

£80 million. Leaders of the *Mirror's* myriad chapels listened carefully. It was all very interesting. They thought it over.

And then they told him where he could stick it.

Accurate figures were hard to come by, but the *Economist's* resident newspaper industry analyst at the time, Graham Cleverley, claimed that, because of union action and management ineptitude, the *Mirror* had been selling advertising at a loss since at least 1958 when Cudlipp and King were in their prime and the papers suddenly got bigger because of the end of paper rationing. The rate of subsidy fell in the 1970s, but by the early 1980s the *Mirror* was still making a loss on every page of advertising it sold. As early as May 1974 the paper's new Reed-installed advertising director had told an internal conference that because of union and labour costs the *Mirror* paid £514 to produce a column of advertising, which the paper then sold for £475.

All the paper's income was coming from sales, and nothing from advertising – which was fine when the paper was selling over five million. But by the early 1980s sales had fallen to well under four million. Despite putting the price up to compensate for lost sales, revenue had fallen overall, squeezing profits to the point where in some years they were less than the expenses claimed by directors and reporters for entertaining their friends and contacts.

As revenue had tumbled, the wages bill had gone up. Members of the main skilled printers' union, the National Graphical Association, found that their weekly earnings, adjusted for inflation, more than tripled between 1961 and 1981. And those were the official figures – actual take-home pay might have been as much as double again in some cases, once various "Old Spanish Customs" were taken into account.

The Royal Commission on the Press in 1962 reported that the total number of printing staff at the *Mirror* included "39 men surplus to negotiated mechanical publishing staff who do not physically take part in production". The situation had got worse in the 1970s because of the increased demand for printers caused by the arrival of the *Sun*. Murdoch had cleverly given in to many of the printers' demands – which would then be imposed on the basis of parity across all the Fleet Street papers – knowing that, while it would hurt him, it would hurt his even more heavily staffed rivals far more. Staffing levels were inflated by the unions in all sorts of ways. Even those accounted for as actually "taking part in production" rarely did anything like a full day's work. There was the system of what was known as "blow". A "one-for-one" blow system was operated at the *Mirror* and it meant that for every hour worked an hour's rest – or "blow" – would follow. But printers would frequently claim they had worked through their "blow" and claim it as overtime.

Alongside "blow" there was the "fat" system, which meant work paid for but not done. The classic example of "fat" was payment to production workers for producing illustrations that had in fact been supplied to the paper by advertisers. Then there was the well-known practice of "ghosting", meaning that the unions would negotiate a minimum number of printers to be employed – inflating their wages with plenty of fat and blow – and then secretly agree with managers a much higher manning level. The pay of the non-existent extra workforce was then shared between the real workers, with some claiming second pay packets under made-up names. On top of everything else there were *ad hoc* "custom and practice" payments that continued to be made even though nobody could remember what they were for. At the Royal Commission, the *Daily Telegraph* made the classic admission: "We pay workers in the printing department a 'House Extra' of £5 10s a week, but we are far from clear what we get for it."

Many printers regarded themselves as working for their union boss or FoC, rather than the management of the newspaper that paid their wages. There had been a famous test case in the 1950s at the *Mirror* when an FoC in the *Mirror's* press room was grossly insubordinate to the press room manager and was given a week's notice. The following night the men refused to produce the paper unless he was reinstated. The Newspaper Publishers Association at first told the *Mirror* to stick to its guns, but then collapsed in the face of a threatened national newspaper strike.

It later became fashionable to blame the printers for all the *Mirror's* problems. But, as Thornton had told the board, they were no greedier than the journalists and board members who had their own well-known expense account fiddles and "blow" system of reading the papers for half an hour in the morning and then going for lunch until 3 p.m. The printers knew that management cared not one jot for them. The filth and noise of the press hall and production areas – filled with clouds of poisonous chemicals – contrasted with the opulence of the ninth floor and the newsroom floor with its drinks cabinets everywhere and the sight of senior executives ordering multiple bottles of wine and spirits, half of which were known to be immediately filched and taken home in briefcases.

Printers were loyal to their unions because they looked after them on basic things like health and safety – nobody else seemed to be interested. Above all, they knew – and were proved right by events – that at the first technological opportunity they were about be thrown on the street with the minimum level of compensation the company could get away with.

After his failure to get the unions on-side, Thornton's strategy was in tatters. For weeks he presided over one doom-laden board meeting after another. Reed International wanted shot of the papers – now more than ever. The group's problems went all the way back to the 1970s when they had bought IPC and the *Mirror* titles. In 1975–76 Reed's core business of paper and packaging was badly hit by the world economic recession and the weak pound. Profits for the group as a whole dropped to less than £40 million on a turnover of more than £1 billion. Reed started on a massive programme of cost-cutting, cutting the total workforce across the board from 86,000 to 60,000. But in the end they did not have the stomach for making mass redundancies and then handling the huge and possibly violent response of printers throughout Fleet Street and the whole of their printing empire. The only other thing to do was get rid of the papers and make the unions somebody else's headache.

The problem was that there were few likely buyers for such a can of worms. No normal company or consortium of banks simply looking for a profit would be interested. Another press group might be interested in buying the *Mirror*. But most of them were as unprofitable and cash-strapped as Reed. One exception was Rupert Murdoch who doubtless would have been delighted to take on the *Mirror*, probably merging it with the *Sun*. But he had recently had to call in political favours (so it was widely believed) to prevent the monopoly authorities blocking his purchase of *The Times* and *Sunday Times*. Purchase of the Mirror Group by Murdoch was a non-starter, politically.

That left Robert Maxwell with a free run at the paper if Reed were prepared to sell out to him. Maxwell had wanted control of a national newspaper since challenging Rupert Murdoch for ownership of the *News of the World* and the *Sun* in 1968. Twice Murdoch had out-foxed him. This time Murdoch, chained by the monopoly regulators, could not interfere. Maxwell had already taken on the print unions at his Pergamon Press business and seemed keen to do the same at the *Mirror*. He was circling around the *Mirror* during the entire period when Thornton was attempting to negotiate with the unions and prepare for a stock market floatation. Thornton planned a "protective structure" for the new independent Mirror Group Newspapers company, which would prevent any single investor such as Maxwell obtaining complete control of the company.

Using the threat of a Maxwell takeover, Thornton made one last effort to get the unions to co-operate with his expansion and floatation plans. He was not getting much help and support from some of the senior editorial people at the paper but one exception was Joe Haines, a Labour party political hack and former speechwriter for Harold Wilson who had joined the *Mirror* as a leader-writer and linkman to the Labour party hierarchy.

At Thornton's prompting Haines gave a *tour de force* speech to the massed chapel leaders. According to those who were there Haines's face was red with passion as he ferociously denounced Maxwell as a union-buster and a fundamentally corrupt man. He told of how Maxwell had tried to buy influence by making big donations to the Labour party, and of how Haines had told Harold Wilson: "Do not touch this man with a barge pole." Shaking his fists Haines said that, personally, he would have to be "dragged through the door" to work for a crook and a monster like Robert Maxwell. Swayed by all this the unions promised a year of industrial peace and "active goodwill".

But by then it was too late. Reed had been in secret talks with Maxwell after Alex Jarratt had received an unsolicited offer for the company. Maxwell had phoned Jarratt to propose takeover talks and was told Reed were not interested. "You can't stop me sending you a letter," Maxwell said. "You can't refuse that." A letter arrived within the hour, containing an offer that meant Reed would clear at least £90 million. Since earnings that year from the *Mirror* were about £1 million Jarratt felt that, in law, he could not afford to deprive his shareholders of such a huge windfall.

A few days later, the board of Reed International sold the paper to Robert Maxwell who, within a few hours, was installed on the ninth floor, lavishing the booze, ordering arrangements to be made for the parking of his private helicopter on the roof, booming about returning the *Mirror* to the great days of the 1960s, promising to make all the top editors millionaires in short order, boasting about the vast pots of money his success as a businessman had made available for him to invest in the paper's future greatness and – generally – lying through his teeth.[46]

But his first job was a simple one. He had Thornton's office partition demolished. The work that had taken Thornton six months to achieve was undone in a matter of minutes, thanks to Robert Maxwell's judicious use of the old system. The work was commissioned with a cash-in-hand, tax-free, off-the-books, Spanish Customs bonus payment made with the approval of *Mirror* cashiers and the appropriate union officials.

PART FOUR:
Tabloid Nation

23 THE EGO HAS LANDED

It is just after 4 p.m. on Friday, July 13, 1984. Robert Maxwell is sweltering under the lights of TV cameras at a press conference called to announce his acquisition of Mirror Group Newspapers. Despite having slept for only a few hours during the past week of intensive and secretive takeover negotiations, Maxwell is looking relaxed and extremely pleased with himself. He is flanked by stony-faced Mike Molloy on one side and the editors or senior journalists of his newly acquired Mirror Group titles.

Maxwell looks extraordinary. Already massively obese, he has dyed his hair jet black – so dark and oily that it has reflective properties under the lights. His thickly applied theatrical make-up is starting to run in the heat. His head nods this way and that – seemingly under the sheer weight of its fleshy immensity – a vacant smile on his face, the occasional growl causing layers of jowls to wobble above the newly adopted trade mark of a bright red bow-tie. Maxwell bats away questions from the rat-pack of journalists who have turned up to record the historic scene and keeps repeating his clichéd, pre-prepared speech over and over.

"Under *my management* editors will be free to produce their newspapers without interference with their journalistic skills and judgements…" he says slowly, pausing to smile and draw breath before proceeding, graciously: "I shall place only *two* strictures on those who have editorial responsibilities… One, the papers must retain their *broadly sympathetic approach* to the Labour movement…" He stops to take a sip from his glass of water.

"*Two*… the papers must and will have a *Britain First* policy. I want to *inform* Britain, *entertain* Britain and *boost* Britain."

In the early hours of that morning Robert Maxwell had entered the *Mirror* building for the first time as its owner. He had bought the paper from Reed for a "headline" figure of £113 million. But with arrangements for the transfer of *Mirror* debt to Reed the real cost was £90 million. Maxwell had paid in cash, with a loan from the National Westminster Bank. In fact, the bank had been prepared to lend Maxwell only £84 million in cash. But Reed's directors were so keen to sell that they loaned Maxwell the extra £6 million he needed, without any security. For once, Maxwell quickly repaid the Reed loan and became undisputed sole owner of the *Mirror*. It was his personal fiefdom. He had more formal control over the paper and its controlling companies than anybody since Rothermere's original floatation of the paper in 1920.

Maxwell's people later claimed that they had hired private detectives to bug the *Mirror* and Reed boardrooms. He claimed he knew in advance that Reed and Thornton's private forecast was that the maximum that could be raised by floatation was £40 million – half their original target. He found out they would accept a bid of around £80 million presented in such a way that Reed board could tell the financial world that they had really got the impressively round figure of £100 million.

Maxwell and Alex Jarratt, for the Reed board, signed the papers just before midnight. Like a child with a wonderful new toy Maxwell drove straight round to *Mirror* building. He pushed past the doorman and bumped into the startled figure of Molloy as he was searching for the chief executive Douglas Long's office. Maxwell did not seem to be entirely sure who he was. Highly agitated and sweating profusely Maxwell practically dragged the editor of the *Daily Mirror* along the corridors. Molloy later remembered the scene as being like the stage arrival of a demon prince in full make-up at a pantomime: "A puff of smoke, and there he was."

Once they reached their destination, Maxwell dived into Long's drinks cabinet and without asking permission poured himself a massive Scotch: "Whose fucking whisky is it, anyway?" Maxwell now owned everything and – as he saw it – everyone connected with the paper and he was beside himself. He had captured the *Daily Mirror* – a far greater prize than the either the *News of the World* or the *Sun*, which had previously eluded him. Maxwell composed himself, a *Mirror* photographer was found in the newsroom and the first of many *Mirror* "picture exclusives" featuring Robert Maxwell was born. Then, like a scene from a movie, Maxwell walked over to the window of the ninth-floor office to admire the magnificent view, his face illuminated from time to time by lightning flashes as an unusually violent thunderstorm suddenly broke over London and raged all around the Holborn Tower.

Maxwell then called a board meeting. Long and Molloy were joined by various other directors who struggled in to the Holborn building in the early hours. Thornton could not be contacted, but Maxwell nevertheless held the meeting and as sole proprietor he appointed himself both chairman and chief executive. To celebrate he opened a box of expensive Cuban cigars and asked everyone present to light up in celebration. Tony Miles, the editorial director, refused on the grounds that he recently given up the evil habit and did not want to start again. Maxwell took the cigar and stuffed it into Miles's top pocket growling: "Mark my words, you will smoke that…" Miles had already decided he was off. Two weeks later, he cleared his desk and was careful to leave the cigar symbolically lying in the middle of his empty desktop.

The meeting broke up at dawn and, as was Maxwell's way, after stuffing himself with whatever food could be rustled up in the executive dining room, he met Thornton at 8 a.m. and sacked him on the spot. Reporters on the doorstep asked Thornton: "Did you see Mr Maxwell?" Thornton replied: "I could hardly miss him. He was sitting at my desk."

The next day the Maxwell became the third *Mirror* proprietor to purloin the front page of the paper to make a signed, personal statement. First Northcliffe, then Cecil King and now the headline was FORWARD WITH BRITAIN above a flattering picture of Maxwell's beaming, bow-tie-framed, arch-eyebrowed face. The *Mirror*'s new sole owner wrote: "I am proud to be the proprietor of this group which holds such an important place in the life of the nation. The *Daily Mirror* and I already have one thing in common. We have supported the Labour Party in every General Election since 1945. That support will continue. But it will not become a Labour Party organ now. We treasure our independence."

The article was signed by Maxwell himself. Thereafter, the old *Mirror* slogan "Forward with the People" – so recently stolen by the *Sun* – was brought back and printed every day under the front-page logo in the updated and more nationalistic form of "Forward with Britain".

Before Maxwell's arrival things had been starting to look a little better for the *Mirror*. Sales of the *Daily Express* had collapsed and, although the *Daily Mail* was once again on the way up, Molloy had been able to turn his guns much more on direct competition with the *Sun*, which had its own problems competing with the newly launched, ultra-down-market *Daily Star*. In 1980, Rupert Murdoch had increased the price of the *Sun*, thinking that he could afford to do so now sales were ahead of the *Mirror*'s. But the move proved almost disastrously premature. The *Mirror* used the *Sun* price rise to make a renewed circulation push. The *Mirror* competed well, closed the sales gap and in some weeks was within an ace of going ahead again. Murdoch reacted with more decisiveness than Reed could ever have managed. He flew into London, sacked Larry Lamb as editor and replaced him with the much more aggressively competitive Jack Nener-like figure of Kelvin McKenzie. Murdoch also cut the price and introduced newspaper "Bingo" – with huge cash giveaway prizes. Molloy could only watch in frustration as this lightning attack restored the *Sun*'s lead.

When the sales gap between the *Sun* and *Mirror* widened to half a million, Molloy, deeply sickened, heard that Murdoch had said to his new editor MacKenzie: "How does it feel to be editor of a paper that puts on 600,000 readers and know it has got fuck all to do with you?"

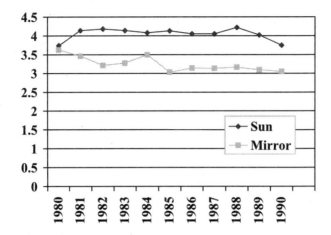

Above: sales of the *Mirror* and the *Sun* in 1980s. Figures in millions of sales. Nb the sharp rise in 1981 in *Sun* sales following the introduction of newspaper Bingo, and the *Mirror's* slight recovery followed by a sharp fall in 1984 after the arrival of Robert Maxwell.

Under MacKenzie, the *Sun* dived down-market to see off the threat of the *Daily Star*, adding a hard right-wing edge to the paper, making the *Sun* the mouthpiece of the new "Thatcherite" working class – the "loadsa-money" generation who had bought their own council houses under the Thatcher government's "right to buy" legislation. The *Mirror* and the *Sun* were to come to blows in editorial terms over the 1982 Falklands War. The *Sun* supported the war effort in a bid both to support Mrs Thatcher and to win from the *Mirror* the reputation of being the forces' paper.

The *Sun* celebrated the sinking of the obsolete sitting-duck Argentinean battleship *General Belgrano* and the death of 300 mostly reluctant raw teenage conscripts with probably the most cold-blooded, gloating headline since the New York *Daily News* Ruth Snyder DEAD! headline fifty years earlier: GOTCHA. At another point during the war the *Sun* raised money to sponsor a Sidewinder missile aboard a British warship. The *Sun's* reporter with the British taskforce claimed to have chalked the words STICK IT UP YOUR JUNTA (Argentina at the time was being ruled by a military junta). But after the sinking of the British warship *Sheffield* with many deaths and horrific injuries the reporting took on a more serious tone. The *Mirror* began to doubt the purpose of fighting on and called on the Thatcher government to look again at terms being offered by Argentina for the settlement of the dispute. The paper ran an editorial entitled MIGHT ISN'T RIGHT and warned against mounting hysteria and the mounting cost of the war in lives. The *Mirror* concluded: "The killing has got to stop... If that means Britain and

Argentina need to compromise, then compromise they must."

The *Sun* responded by trying to send the circulation equivalent of a high-explosive torpedo into the side of the Holborn Tower. Under the headline DARE TO CALL IT TREASON the *Sun* wrote of the *Mirror*: "What is it but treason for this timorous, whining publication to plead day after day for appeasing the Argentinian dictators... We are truly sorry for the *Daily Mirror*'s readers. They are buying a paper which again and again demonstrates it has no faith in its country and no respect for her people."

Molloy considered suing for libel. The *Sun*'s attack went far beyond mere comment. It more or less said that Molloy and others at the paper were traitors, involved in somehow helping the Argentines conquer the Falklands and kill British citizens and soldiers. But instead he ordered Joe Haines to write an article denouncing the *Sun* as THE HARLOT OF FLEET STREET.

The *Sun*, Haines wrote, had become a "coarse and demented newspaper" which had "fallen from the gutter to sewer". The paper's journalists had "broken all records for telling lies" and were cowards who called for war and killing "from behind the safety of their typewriters". The *Sun* had become to journalism "what Dr Joseph Goebbels was to truth". After the incident the *Sun* came to be really hated by a section of journalists for the way in which it had smeared fellow hacks as traitors just for expressing their honest opinion. In a profession where "dog does not bite dog", the *Sun* – and its still new editor the "coarse and demented" Kelvin McKenzie – were seen as having passed beyond the pale.

It was a lower moment for the *Mirror* than the *Sun*, nevertheless. There was a war on and it was the *Sun* which was making all the noise and was the centre of attention, with the *Mirror* essentially relegated to the sidelines along with the highly unpopular anti-war opposition Labour party it still loyally supported. At the end of 1982, the year of the war, the *Sun* had opened a lead of exactly one million in the circulation war. Its potent mixture of "Jingo and Bingo" was satirised with a famous *Private Eye* spoof *Sun* front page: KILL AN ARGIE AND WIN A MINI-METRO.

Maxwell and his advisors were watching all this from afar. They were still preparing their bid for the paper. He persuaded himself that the *Mirror* could win back its number one position fairly easily. First, it had to copy the *Sun*'s bingo campaign – but with bigger prizes. That move alone should bring them back neck and neck. But Maxwell also believed that the *Sun*'s new love affair with Margaret Thatcher was a weakness. The "Iron Lady" was tremendously popular – especially after her Falklands win – with one part of the mass audience. But she was loathed with equal passion by another and probably larger part of the audience. The problem was the negative one of the Labour party leadership in the early 1980s which Maxwell thought was too left wing. He was already hoping that the Labour "modernisers" Neil Kinnock and Roy Hattersley would take over the party, making it – and therefore the *Mirror* – much more popular.

After he got control of the paper, Maxwell took Molloy and Tony Miles, the editorial director, out for a celebration lunch at Claridge's. A great deal of optimistic talk took place, with Maxwell rubbishing Jarratt and Reed – the "committee of wallpaper manufacturers" - demanding anecdotes about Murdoch and this new editor Kelvin MacKenzie – with whom Maxwell was rapidly becoming obsessed – and boasting about his plans to outwit The Dirty Digger, his old Aussie rival. Everything was going just famously until the group got up to leave. At that point the hotel manager came scampering after them waving a piece of paper.

"Mr Maxwell, sir, I am afraid you have to pay."

Maxwell waved him away in irritated fashion, telling him to send the bill to his office.

"But, Mr Maxwell," the manager insisted, trying to make light of the situation, "you always say that, Mr Maxwell, sir. And you *never* pay…"

With his guests shuffling their feet in embarrassment Maxwell got out his wallet in Claridge's lobby and paid off the manager.

It was just about the last time anyone ever saw him pay hard cash for anything.

24 THE DAILY MAXWELL

With the arrival of Robert Maxwell on the ninth floor, Mike Molloy had got what he had asked for in his *Guardian* article a couple of years earlier – a powerful proprietor able to make decisions in seconds and willing to take risks in order to reap massive rewards.

What he had not bargained for was the scale of his new boss's hidden corruption, combined with a degree of megalomania, deviousness and paranoia which, Molloy finally decided, probably meant that Maxwell had succumbed to some form of fairly serious psychiatric illness.

Some of Maxwell's behaviour was certainly crazy from day one. Despite all the promises he had made about editorial independence Molloy sound found out that Swaffer's Law still applied – Molloy was totally free to print articles which appealed to Maxwell's prejudices, so long as they did not upset the advertisers too much. Maxwell interfered with every aspect of the production of the paper – from delaying the payment of bills to writing headlines and changing the layout and graphic design of pages. The problem was that he did this in an apparently random way – suddenly delaying a vital multi-million pound decision over distribution to delivered an ill-informed hour-long lecture on politics in the Middle East, or get involved with long discussions about what typefaces the paper should be using, even though he knew next to nothing about the subject.

Within a few days of arriving at the paper Maxwell began on his master plan to launch a *Daily Mirror* version of newspaper bingo. At first the *Mirror* went in for "honest bingo" with a series of celebrities called upon to pick balls out of a bag just like the real game. The problem was that this method did not produce a winner every time, unlike the "fixed" bingo operated by the *Sun, Star* and other papers. "Fixed" bingo produced a winner every week because it was basically a mendacious piece of marketing and was nothing like the real game. In fact, the only similarity was the process of ticking off numbers on a pre-printed card. Unlike the real game, the numbers were not randomly generated. They were simply picked by the marketing department to match or (much more often) not match the cards that had been distributed in advance. Most days the chance of winning any money was pure illusion. But, as part of a marketing campaign usually tied into TV advertising, a decision could be made to activate one of the cards by printing matching numbers in the paper and give away the jackpot.

After a few weeks of "honest bingo", Stott changed to the fixed version, which proved far more popular with readers because it produced a regular weekly winner. Maxwell loved everything about fixed bingo, once it was explained to him. His eyes would twinkle whenever it was discussed. He seemed to like its essential deviousness. But above all it involved him being on the front page of the *Mirror* (circulation 3.5 million; readership 12 million) day after day appearing as the man "giving away a million" and – even better – appearing on prime-time ITV (audience 12 million) in TV ads, talking directly to the country: "I absolutely guarantee that I am going to make one of our readers a millionaire," he would smarm directly into the camera in the style of the Prime Minister giving a state of the nation broadcast. It was the behaviour, the *Mirror*'s amateur psychologists decided, of a man who desperately wanted to be loved. But it was unlikely to do the paper much good.

The last outbreak of the bingo virus, which had erupted three years earlier during a short, nasty and ruinously expensive circulation battle between the *Sun* and *Daily Star,* had shown that less committed readers switched to whichever paper was lacerating its finances the most that day with prize money and TV advertising, returning to their usual paper, or the one with the best front-page story, as soon as all the fuss was over. The larger, possibly more intelligent segment of the readership had either worked out that it was a scam, or couldn't be bothered and so ignored bingo altogether.

The TV ads may have had the most appeal for Maxwell, but his face was all over the front of the *Mirror,* advertising the bingo game. The *Mirror* front page on the first day of the promotion swept aside the news and instead proclaimed:

ONLY IN THE MIRROR
THE REAL £1 MILLION
HERE IT IS – THE *MIRROR*'S REAL £1 MILLION.
IN CASH

Dominating the front page was a huge picture of "Mirror Group Newspapers publisher Robert Maxwell" leaning on a trolley loaded with great wads of cash in various denominations. It was all written up in a pastiche of a news story. "Maxwell told of how this was the first time he had ever seen £1 million in cash. He admitted he was impressed and beamed. 'I'm itching to give this lot to one of our readers.' He went on:

'This is it – one million in cash which will make someone a millionaire'."

On the day the first "Bingo *Mirror*" was published Maxwell happened to be on a train with John Pilger, on a mission to visit Arthur Scargill, leader of strikers in that year's national coal mining strike – one of the most violent, bitter and expensive in British industrial history. The idea was to generate "stories" (meaning publicity for Maxwell) because the big man was presenting himself as mediator in the strike. They were taking the train to Scargill's Yorkshire headquarters because Maxwell's helicopter – which he had taken to parking on the roof of the Holborn tower – was grounded by fog.

On the train journey Pilger remembered seeing Maxwell read the simple bingo blurb over and over again, beside himself that the *Mirror* featured only pictures of himself surrounded by great piles of money. When the waiter serving breakfast showed an interest in the front page, Maxwell was triumphant. "Do you want us to sign it?" Maxwell demanded of the waiter. "Yes, of course you do. It will be a collector's item." The waiter seemed grateful but perplexed – especially when Maxwell opened his attaché case, took out one of the bundles of £50 notes used in the picture, invited everyone to hold it then pass it back. Then he went back to his obsessive reading and re-reading of the few dozen words of blurb.

The next massive blast of Maxwell on the front page came when the competition's "winner" was announced. This turned out to be an appropriately charming and deserving old lady called Maudie who even had a photogenic pet dog called Thumper. The coverage went on for days and at one point Maxwell had an outline of his face made into a sort of logo on the front page. Yet more *Mirror* money was spent on TV advertising featuring Maxwell, Maudie, Thumper, champagne girls, giant novelty cheques and piles of ready cash.

Maxwell began to demand that he feature in the paper on as many days as possible. He told Molloy and others that this was a massive advantage for the *Mirror* over the *Sun*. The paper had its very own A-list celebrity – him. It was just like having Princess Diana or any other top-ten celebrity on board – he was famous, admired and anything he did was news. And so Maxwell set off on an amazing non-stop tour, visiting world leaders and especially eastern bloc Communist dictators – where he claimed a special affinity because of his own Eastern European roots and academic publishing interests. Over a matter of a few months he was seen intervening in the "Live Aid" famine in Ethiopia, flying in at the head of a *Mirror* relief effort with a plane full of donated food. He was then seen making the news by visiting the Presidents of Sudan and Bulgaria and meeting with the Chinese leader Deng Xiaoping.

When Maxwell met the Russian leader Mikhail Gorbachev – who was engaged in trying to peacefully dismantle the Communist system and was therefore plausibly the most important man on earth at the time – the *Mirror* ran a picture of the two men with the caption "Robert Maxwell meets Gorbachev". The publisher rewrote the caption himself - the corrected version: "Gorbachev meets Robert Maxwell".

Maxwell the world statesman vied with Big-Hearted Bob the charity fund-raiser, Robert Maxwell the millionaire give-away bingo man and Robert Maxwell the top socialist who was single-handedly modernising the Labour party. That was on the news pages. But Maxwell increasingly invaded the sports pages at the back where his antics in "rescuing" and buying control of ailing football clubs such as Oxford United and Derby County, his bids for control or stakes in Manchester United, Arsenal and Tottenham Hotspur, together with Maxwell's role as media advisor to the football league management committee, provided the paper's sports writers with an endless series of similar "exclusives". The former *Mirror* football writer Harry Harris, a particular confidant of Maxwell's, tells the story of how Maxwell had heard that Bobby Robson, the England football manager, had held up the wrong number when he was trying to substitute a player during a friendly. Maxwell immediately ordered a huge, continuing and – in circulation terms – disastrous back page ROBSON MUST GO campaign. At the time the England football team was doing reasonably well and Robson was one of the most popular men in the country.

Maxwell piled into the features department as well as news, sport, marketing and production, demanding the revival of "Jane" – the mildly pornographic material provided for soldiers away from female company during the war. It was realised with mild revulsion that Maxwell himself must have taken advantage of this public-spirited *Mirror* contribution to morale many times during his famous war service. It was of course hopelessly out of date by the mid-1980s. Cudlipp, who had been involved in the cartoon the first time around, wrote in his memoirs that Jane had started under the title of "Diary of a Bright Young Thing" but she had become a "dull old thing" and had to go. And that was in 1958.

On the remaining pages where Maxwell was not mentioned by name the process of surreptitiously hyping companies and products in which he had invested began to take place on a scale not seen since Rothermere's secret share-hyping PR in the 1930s. The worst example was a *Mirror* exclusive extolling the wonders of "intelligence pills" for children, a product which (and this was not mentioned) he had invested in. The consensus was that the pills were at best a complete rip-off and even potentially dangerous. After a few years, Maxwell, with increasing desperation, tried to use the paper to support the image and share price of companies he had invested in and run down those he was targeting for takeover.

Eventually, a *Mirror* staff photographer, Mike Maloney, became the nucleus of what amounted to Maxwell's Private Reporting Unit, including a personal photographer, rewarded with the use of a company Rolls Royce. "Are you ready, Mr Snapper?" Maxwell would say to Maloney, as he was heading off for another photo opportunity, which, as the editor Molloy knew to his dread, Maxwell would insist on putting in the paper, preferably on the front page. The publisher was slowly turning the paper into a family photo album. There were days when *Mirror* staff photographers were unavailable for news because they were working on "a Captain Bob special"– code for one of Maxwell's ego-trips. The journalists' trade paper, the *Press Gazette,* reported that the name Robert Maxwell appeared 231 times in the *Daily Mirror* in just three days. Molloy was starting to get sacks full of letters complaining about Maxwell and asking the paper to cut down on the number of reports devoted to his activities. One of the letter-writers asked with genuine bafflement: "Why can't you sack this awful man?" The satirical magazine *Private Eye* gave the paper the nickname The Daily Maxwell. It stuck at once. Even reporters working for the paper would talk about how things were going at "The Daily Maxwell".

Maxwell's egomania had a devastating effect on the paper's sales. Circulation had been starting to recover before Maxwell arrived. In June 1984 the *Mirror* had been selling 3,487,721 copies. The launch of a £1-million bingo competition supported by heavy TV advertising might have been expected to put on (albeit temporarily and at huge cost) a lot of circulation, even though the *Sun* had counter-attacked with a similar competition. Instead, the paper had lost 450,000 sales – the biggest year-on-year drop since the launch of the *Sun.* As Maxwell mania continued to fill the paper the sales slide started to accelerate, dropping to 2,900,000 – a new post-war low. The advertising industry magazine *Marketing Week* noted: "It takes something close to genius to lose so much circulation so quickly."

The egomania slowly spread to every aspect of the *Mirror,* including the way the Holborn building was decorated. Maxwell naturally installed himself in Cecil King's old office on the ninth floor, but in contrast to the Old Wykhamist's tasteful classicism and walls full of rare books, Maxwell had the place done up as a cross between an Ottoman Sultan's palace and a cheap executive-style airport hotel – stuccoed ceiling, heavy curtains, outsized sofas, ottomans and bronze glass-topped coffee tables.

The doors of three lifts opened on to a long, narrow hall. The carpet was royal blue with Maxwell's corporate logo – a big letter "M" superimposed over the entire surface of planet earth. A long corridor laid with this carpet, led through double doors that opened into a reception-within-a-reception kept in near-darkness. In the centre a gigantic image of the Maxwell globe mounted high on the wall above a huge reception desk. Elsewhere, the décor featured the logo Maxwell had dreamed up for the Mirror Group Newspapers' operating company. Since the initials were MGN – the same as the famous Hollywood movie studios – he simply stole their logo of a roaring lion and waited to see if they did anything about it. They never did.

Maxwell quickly moved into the building, establishing his personal quarters and treating the *Mirror* as his home. He came and went by helicopter, which landed on the roof of the *Mirror* building – the gigantic insurance payments being met by the paper itself. Normally, he would take the helicopter direct to Farnborough airfield where his private jet was waiting. The Gulfstream 4 executive jet and flying restaurant-cum-playpen registered as VR-BOB (it stood for Very Rich Bob) was ready to take him wherever he wanted to go in the world.

Because he lived in the building, various *Mirror* people got to know about his revolting personal habits. He was reputed to masturbate constantly when he was in his private rooms – the evidence was detected and dealt with by members of his domestic staff interviewed by Tom Bower, Maxwell's unauthorised biographer. Bower was told that Maxwell's obesity and bachelor lifestyle had led to some disgusting episodes. No longer able to use the lavatory properly, Bower reported, Maxwell had taken to messing the bathroom and wiping himself with expensive hand-made towels and face flannels and leaving them around his apartment like so many soiled nappies for the Philippine maids to pick up and place in plastic bags for disposal. Often in the night he would raid the enormous kitchen he had in his penthouse flat next door to the *Mirror* and in the morning the kitchen staff would open the door to a mass of empty packets and tins and food littered all over the floor.

Maxwell's egotism extended to the hiring and humiliation of senior executives, especially those who were clearly better educated or informed than himself. There was general amazement when Peter Jay, the former *Times* economics editor and chief executive of the failed TVAM breakfast-TV channel and a man with impeccable personal and family contacts in the higher reaches of Whitehall and the Labour party, accepted the job as Maxwell's "chief of staff" and general advisor. Jay later explained the move by saying that after the collapse of TVAM he had basically been on his uppers and needed a job. Maxwell was prepared to pay such a respected establishment figure and celebrity intellectual richly.

Jay gulped when he saw how big a job it was going to be to keep track of Maxwell's business dealings and paperwork. The *Mirror* publisher was completely chaotic in the way he operated. He would never finish anything and was always surrounded by great piles of paper. Documents were jumbled and scattered everywhere across the floor, through multiple desks in several rooms, in various safes dotted about the place and, in all probability, stuffed behind the radiators in his luxury toilet on the tenth floor.

Both Molloy and Jay quickly realised that, if they gave Maxwell an important document, it would be lost immediately and so they always kept copies. One problem was that he was difficult to approach because he was constantly surrounded by a gaggle of unknown suitors, debtors, creditors, givers or requesters of favours and services, hired sycophants, relatives and servants ladling soup into a large cup with I AM THE BOSS written on it, which was kept full all the time.

At first all Jay could do was toss an important document into this maelstrom and hope for the best. Then he came up with the masterstroke of having a number of "Black Boxes" made for Maxwell, similar to the Red Boxes used by ministers in Whitehall. For a while the system worked as Maxwell was told he had to work through his black boxes every night just like the Prime Minister or Chancellor of the Exchequer. But then Maxwell got bored with the gimmick and reverted to his old system of phoning or asking Jay for some vital piece of paperwork any time day or night. Jay would tell him that it was in his black box and Maxwell would erupt and kick it furiously across the room.

Maxwell would humiliate Jay and others. Once he called him up in the middle of the night, just to ask him the time. Another time he sent a finance director on a 14-hour flight to Hong Kong – then summoned him back to ask trivial questions which the man had already answered on the phone. One of Maxwell's financial assistants who had a direct line to Maxwell would sometimes get a Murdoch-style "telephone terrorism" call along the lines of a growled and threatening: "You have not spoken to me recently. That is not right. Why haven't you spoken to me recently?" Then the line would go dead before any reply was given.

Above all, he loved forcing people into the position of supplicant so that he could appear magnanimous if he was in the mood. Maxwell insisted on personally signing even the smallest cheque. As a result there was always a long queue of people sitting in chairs along the corridor waiting to see him. But journalists could always walk past the queue and get in to see him, because bored by business Maxwell actually liked talking to journalists. Molloy found that he could go to him and get even big cheques signed by playing the role of co-conspirator in the "we are all journalistic rogues" movie which evidently was playing in Maxwell's head. "Come on, Bob, just sign the fucking thing, will you?" Molloy would say. Maxwell would be flattered and sign the cheque at once.

At first, as Molloy later freely admitted, he had been taken in by Maxwell, hoping against hope that the combination of egomania and total control of the company might give the *Mirror* the strategic direction it had so conspicuously lacked during the years of drift under Reed's ownership.

The new publisher could turn on the charm like a million-watt bulb when he wanted to. And he played the card of the Jewish socialist who was being discriminated against and smeared by the establishment. One of Maxwell's sayings was "I'm only here to help" and he would beam like a cuddly bear and turn up his palms in a gesture of innocence.

Molloy had nevertheless expected a rough ride from Maxwell, interference and the occasional bit of irrational, obsessive tyrannical behaviour. It was the price you paid for having the backing of someone mad enough to put millions into something as risky as a newspaper. Northcliffe, Rothermere, King and even Cudlipp had been like that. That was what newspaper proprietors were like. If you wanted a normal boss, the argument ran, why not go and work for a bank or a building society? Beaverbrook had been a complete tartar when he wanted to be and was reputed to have sent 147 instructions to the editor of the *Daily Express* in a single day. Murdoch was a bit like that too – phoning his editors day and night and using a technique of "telephone terrorism". This meant being put through to one of his editors, saying in a slow and deeply sinister, threatening way: "You are losing your touch... losing your touch," then hanging up and not phoning again for a week.

The obvious problem with Maxwell was the sheer scale with which he was interfering with the front page. Molloy struggled to moderate Maxwell's activities but editing the paper had become near impossible.

Molloy accepted promotion to the position of editorial director of the whole *Mirror* group in 1985 and gave way to Richard Stott, the much more aggressive former star investigative reporter and features editor of the paper. Stott later wrote that, when he was offered the editorship, he said to Maxwell: "Look, I've got to have control of it, otherwise it won't work. You should know before I start, if I don't have control we'll fight and things are going to go further downhill." After that, Maxwell's picture appeared less frequently in the paper, sales stabilised and the gap with the *Sun* began to close – mainly because the Murdoch paper lost a lot of readers the minute it stopped running its bingo competition.[47]

Stott re-positioned the *Mirror*, giving it a harder competitive edge against the *Sun*. His arrival in the editor's chair coincided with the height of the tabloid "soap wars" which came in the wake of the launch of 'EastEnders' by the BBC. In the days before the weekly celebrity and soap magazines the *Sun* led the way in turning itself into a "Daily "EastEnders" supplement" according to a complaint by the BBC. Stott hit back by targeting "Coronation Street" for the *Mirror's* endless supply of soap exclusives. The blurring of fact and fiction that inevitably followed such huge concentration on the soaps seemed to give the *Sun's* agenda a decisive push towards fantasy journalism. This was the era when Kelvin MacKenzie's *Sun* became famous for page three "celebrities" like Sam Fox; front page headlines like FREDDIE STARR ATE MY HAMSTER; endless "kiss'n' tell" exposés of the mild sexual peccadilloes of vast numbers of people vaguely in public life or in the public eye; over-the-top flag-waving campaigns like HOP OFF YOU FROGS against the French and THE *SUN* DECLARES WAR ON GERMANY (because they monopolise the sun-loungers on Spanish beaches) and massive libel battles against the likes of Elton John.

Politics was another complicating factor. MacKenzie and his news editor Tom Petrie had brilliantly worked out a way of turning the terminally dull subject of politics and elections into a source of irresistible tabloid fun by creating the genre of the "loony left" local government story. The *Sun's* greatest hits included a story headlined BAA BAA WHITE SHEEP – describing how a Labour local council had supposedly banned the "Baa Baa Black Sheep" nursery rhyme from local crèches because it was racist, and BARMY BERNIE HAS GONE COFFEE POTTY – STAFF MUST DRINK MARXIST BREW – about London labour politician Bernie Grant's policy of introducing "fair trade" coffee instead of Nescafé into the canteen at Tottenham Town Hall.

Stott, in contrast, had inherited the job of supporting the relatively unpopular Neil Kinnock and his still strife-torn party through the 1987 general election. On election day Stott self-consciously tried to revive the old Cudlipp tradition of the SHOCK ISSUE. The paper ran a front-page picture of two children standing on a rubble-strewn street in front of bricked-up houses against the headline: WHOSE LIFE? WHOSE FUTURE? On the same page there was a smaller picture of Margaret Thatcher with the headline: SHE DOESN'T CARE FOR THEM. DO YOU? Standing behind the insistence on a "serious" political news agenda was Maxwell, now fortified by Hugh Cudlipp who Maxwell had hired as an editorial consultant on "token" wages of about £10,000 a year. Cudlipp provided Maxwell with a huge amount of advice during Molloy's editorship and the first couple of years of Stott's. He was not slow in telling Maxwell where he was going wrong. As part of the usual *Mirror* discussion about how to get younger readers, Maxwell had proposed his own plan called "Operation Rejuvenation" but Cudlipp was dead against it. It was more important to get behind Stott's more modest, step-by-step plan to improve the content of the paper across the board. The deeper problem. Cudlipp advised, was that serious political content had disappeared in the attempt to compete with the *Sun*.

"*Mirror* newspapers are now rarely mentioned in any significant sense," Cudlipp wrote, "and are even more rarely quoted. The *Daily Mirror* must and can regain its position among the world's most quoted and influential newspapers in its own spheres. Popularity isn't enough."

25 NEW BOSS! NEW IDEAS!

Roy Greenslade is lying in bed at home at 7.50 a.m. on Boxing Day 1989. The phone rings. Still bleary, the current managing editor of the *Sunday Times* and former deputy editor of the *Sun* tries to focus on the growling voice at the other end of the line.

"Good morning. It's Bob Maxwell here. Could I speak to Roy Greenslade…?"

Greenslade thinks it is a wind-up… the man at the other end of the line is most probably Paul Callan, TV personality, practical joker and *Mirror* feature-writer. Callan is an expert at mimicking Maxwell's voice. Greenslade considers telling "Callan" to get lost. But what if *it really is* Maxwell? Greenslade's wife works at the *Mirror* and Maxwell has evidently taken a shine to her, professionally speaking. Maybe it has got something to do with that.

Greenslade thinks quickly and says he can't really speak at the moment. He asks for the caller's number and says he will call back – a standard journalistic method of getting an idea of whether calls are hoaxes or not and, also, if the call seems interesting enough, buying time to slot a tape into a recording device.

Greenslade notes the number and the line goes dead. His wife confirms that the number must link to a phone in an office in the *Mirror* building at least somewhere near Maxwell. They decide the call is probably genuine. Greenslade rings back. Maxwell answers, but all he will say was is that he wants to discuss some important business – far too important to discuss over the phone. The two men agree to meet in Maxwell's office on the ninth floor of the *Mirror* building at 4 p.m. that day. Greenslade then spends the rest of the day wondering what the old monster wants.

Greenslade arrived at Holborn Circus on time and, in the normal way, was kept waiting, goggling at the opulent vulgarity of Maxwell's ninth-floor waiting room. He still wondered what it was all about. At the time he was happily employed at the *Sunday Times*, having given up tabloid journalism for good when he reached his fortieth birthday.

Eventually, Maxwell appeared from behind the heavy drapes. Greenslade and others later found out that the waiting room was bugged and it was common for Maxwell to sit in the next room listening to the people he was going to meet chatting and sometimes disclosing their real position in business negotiations. Maxwell turned his charm factor up to maximum and ushered Greenslade into his private office. He poured himself and Greenslade drinks and announced he wanted to get straight to the point. He told Greenslade: "You are here because I have the honour of offering you the editorship of the *Daily Mirror*."

Greenslade was staggered and immediately thought of Stott, who he thought was doing well at the paper. He and MacKenzie had regarded him as a man with weaknesses – more of a reporter than an editor – but one who had done well at the *Mirror* by its recent standards. All Greenslade could say was, "Is it on offer?" Maxwell beamed at full wattage, eyebrows arched, and confirmed that yes, it was. Richard Stott, he confided, was going to take over at the *Sunday People*, where there were plans for a management buy-out. There was no question of Stott having been removed against his will, or Greenslade taking his job from him or anything like that. This was a lie – or at least misleading – because Maxwell had no intention of allowing the buy-out to go ahead. It was the first of an almost unending series of fibs about matters large and small that Maxwell was to tell to Greenslade during his short tenure as editor. Greenslade said that, of course, he was interested. But he would need to think about it. Maxwell, charm itself, said that was perfectly understand-able and he should take his time making his mind up.

It was not really a tough decision. The editorship of the *Daily Mirror* would put Greenslade right at the top of his profession. It would be a fantastic experience, even with all the problems likely to flow from working for Maxwell. Greenslade already knew that Maxwell was "not a man of his word" because at the *Sunday Times* Greenslade had published a series of stories reporting how various sums of money Maxwell had promised to give to charity never turned up once he had got publicity for himself by making the announcements. On the other hand, there did seem to be some sense in the offer from Maxwell's point of view. He had been deputy editor of the *Sun* for many years and – without breaching any sort of business confidentiality – knew the editorial game plan for the *Sun* and Murdoch's operating methods, as well as the strengths and weak-nesses of its editor Kelvin MacKenzie. So Maxwell was at least being rational in making the offer. He decided to take the job. Greenslade might have had second thoughts if he had known at the time about the way in which Stott had been pushed out of the *Mirror* editor's chair.

Stott had led the *Mirror* through a relatively good spell, with the paper's sales holding up and Maxwell – increasingly preoccupied with business affairs beyond the *Mirror* itself – less of a presence on the editorial side. That all changed one night when Stott got a call from Maxwell at home at 11 p.m. The publisher was complaining that the set of the next morning's newspapers that were customarily delivered to his private rooms in Holborn Circus had not arrived. "What sort of bloody circus do you run, mister? I don't interfere and you treat me like shit," Maxwell raved. "Well, fuck you, I'll get an editor who can get me papers on time." Stott, bewildered, suggested that the news desk might have been too busy. "Don't you defend those c★★★s," Maxwell raged. "They're worse than fucking useless and I've fired them. Sort it out!"

Stott felt "soiled, furious and demeaned". He wearily phoned the news desk and asked what had happened about the papers. Somebody discovered that, despite what Maxwell was saying, they had in fact been delivered to his door – but had been left outside because it was locked and nobody was allowed to have the key. The blood rushed to Stott's head. In a fury he punched the numbers on his phone and connected directly to Maxwell, calling him most of the names Maxwell had himself used and finishing up by saying: "You make this job a misery… you don't deserve the loyalty of the staff you have."

Stott thought that was the end of him. But to his surprise the next morning Maxwell had switched back to charm mode, even apologising to Stott, imploring him not to take the incident too seriously. Stott was at first dumbfounded, but then worked out that Maxwell would look pretty stupid if he sacked the editor of the *Daily Mirror* for failing to deliver the newspapers when in fact they had been delivered all along, but Maxwell had been too stupid, lazy or fat to pick them up. Maxwell by this time was planning the market floatation of the *Mirror* group and, since he had so totally identified himself with the business, the floatation's success would rest to a large extent on his personal reputation for good judgement. At the same time, Stott knew that he was on borrowed time. Maxwell would take the first chance, he reckoned, to get rid of him in an apparently more reasonable way.

The knife went into Stott in just before Christmas 1989 and the reason was the fall of the Ceausescu regime in Romania. The dictator, who Maxwell once claimed as a personal friend, was lined up against a wall and shot. The moment – which set off a chain of events leading to the end of Russian control throughout eastern Europe – had been caught on film and the pictures were some of the most dramatic and historic of the decade. Stott naturally wanted to put the execution pictures on the front page. But Maxwell intervened directly. He told Stott editorially the pictures were "a load of shit" and insisted that the *Mirror* should instead run a page one appeal for readers to send money to a Romanian relief fund. The "disagreement" led to Stott's removal, opening the way for Greenslade.

The former *Sun* deputy was a far from universally popular choice as editor. Every previous editor of the paper since the war had come through the ranks of the *Mirror* itself and some of the hacks baulked at being led by a man who had made his name on the filthy *Sun* – Greenslade had been a senior figure at the paper during the Falklands War. In addition, the way that he had stepped into Stott's shoes (innocently though it might have been) after the outgoing editor had been sacked for opposing Maxwell's bullying and censorship was held against him by some.

There were other and more personal reasons for Greenslade's unpopularity at the paper. In 1971, when he had been working as a lowly sub-editor at the *Mirror,* he had run off with Noreen, the wife of the paper's popular chief sub-editor. This act of treachery, as it was seen, meant that Greenslade was personally ostracised. He had to leave the *Mirror* and went over to the *Sun,* where he was tolerated but still so disliked that people would speak to him only with great reluctance. He stayed for two years at the *Sun* before going to Sussex University as a mature student to get a social science degree. It was at this time he gave up an earlier religious-style commitment to doctrinaire Maoist Marxism-Leninism which, anyway, by the mid-1970s, was as out of date as the waist-length hair and Afghan coat he used to sport.

Greenslade finished his studies by writing a Cudlippian-style thesis on why the old working class (which had read the old *Daily Mirror* in the 1940s and 1950s) was changing and disappearing, to be replaced sociologically speaking by what amounted to... *Sun* readers. After making this important discovery – made evident to him by the changes among the car workers of his native Dagenham – Greenslade furtively went back to work as a part-time sub-editor at the *Sunday Mirror* (he believed himself to still be on a blacklist because of the jilting episode). By the time anyone realised it was him, Greenslade had served the 13 weeks he needed under union rules to be unsackable. Only then did the management of the *Sunday Mirror* discover they had clasped this particular adder to their bosom. Greenslade became a print-union-type super-militant, at one point demanding a "hot weather payment" for everyone just because, well, the weather was unseasonably warm and everyone was talking about it. Later, when Greenslade went back to the *Sun* – the epitome of right-wing Thatcherite union-busting – and played a role in the paper's union-crushing move to Wapping, the charge of turncoat was added to that of traitor and adulterer and he picked up the nickname Roy "Green-Slime".

Greenslade had enjoyed his time at the *Sun*. He and MacKenzie had been amazed by how weakly their main rival had performed throughout the 1980s as it went through its twists and turns, first under Reed, then Thornton and finally Maxwell. For most of the time, they had been facing an open goal in competition terms. They were also scathing about the booze culture at the paper that, they knew, was still in full flow.

In 1985, when he was deputy editor of the *Sun*, Greenslade and Noreen had accepted an invitation to lunch with Maxwell and Mike Molloy at the Savoy. It had been a long and indulgent affair with caviar and champagne, which went on all afternoon. Then they all went back to the ninth floor where Molloy mixed champagne cocktails while Maxwell invited the half-cut Greenslade, in his capacity of deputy editor of the *Sun*, to pass judgement on the strengths and weaknesses of that day's edition of the *Mirror*. Greenslade was completely drunk by that stage and never remembered making much sense. But the next day, head throbbing, he was able to report that Maxwell's boast that he had "cleaned up" the *Mirror* didn't appear to mean very much. Maxwell had become "a hostage of the style he had inherited" was how Greenslade charitably put it at the time.

Now that he was editor of the *Mirror* Greenslade found that the drinking culture was almost as bad as ever. One of his first acts was to ban the practice of each executive filling in a weekly order form for booze. His tactic of leading by example had mixed results, however. He mused to Marje Proops that if a drinking ban came in, as it had in Wapping and in many offices in the City, some people might turn to using cocaine instead. "Oh, no, my dear," Marje drawled. "We gave up doing that in the '20s. Terribly boring."[48]

Greenslade once went into the notorious (and now defunct) Vagabonds bar, a round-the-clock drinking club next to the *Mirror*, looking for somebody on the off-chance, and found half his senior staff sitting there in the middle of the day.

As Greenslade arrived, the story was still being told of how alcohol had led *Mirror* journalist John Penrose, the partner of ex-*Mirror* lush Anne Robinson, into an unfortunate incident which resulted in Stott's office being vandalised. It happened after Maxwell sued and won a libel case against *Private Eye*. The magazine claimed Maxwell had demanded a peerage in return for donations he had made to the Labour party. *Private Eye*'s publisher Peter Cook was forced to pay Maxwell £50,000 in damages, but took the setback with good humour. After the case finished he managed to persuade Penrose to go to pub. The two men got drunk and went back to the *Mirror* offices after closing time with the idea of raiding Molloy's famously well-stocked drinks cabinet. Once they were there – both completely drunk – Penrose fell asleep, presenting Cook with the opportunity to spray graffiti on the walls and windows. Cook then placed a direct call to Maxwell in New York via the *Mirror*'s own switchboard and told him he was stealing back some of the £50,000 he had paid out by drinking his way through the *Mirror's* booze lake. Maxwell phoned security – but by the time they arrived, Cook had run away.[49]

Greenslade set about making as many of the editorial changes he thought the paper needed as he could. Maxwell had assured Greenslade that he had backing "to get rid of the dead wood" but, in the end, staff changes amounted to blanket sacking of anybody over 55. They were all shown the door as part of Maxwell's revived "Operation Rejuvenation", regardless of how good they were. Many took their large pay-off cheques and went straight to work for other papers.

One area where Greenslade wanted to make changes was the vital one, for a tabloid, of sport. The department had always been a relative backwater at the *Mirror* because Cudlipp had never been much interested in the subject. Now Greenslade called in sports editor Keith Fisher and complained that in his opinion the back page was "fucking awful" – the headlines were too big, the choice of lead stories was poor and there was not enough of substance to read. Fisher sprang to his feet, stood bolt upright, saluted and barked: "New Boss! New Ideas!" Greenslade broke up laughing.

Beyond this, the wind seemed set fair for the *Mirror* for the first time in many years. Kelvin MacKenzie, Greenslade's old boss, having judged the public mood perfectly for nearly a decade, seemed to be losing some of his touch. The public and parliament were getting sick of the paper's intrusion into privates lives and, especially, into the grief of the recently bereaved. After boosting sales by "exposing" and destroying the private lives of the semi-famous, there was the real threat of a statutory privacy law. Cudlipp himself had made speeches about the problem in the House of Lords and elsewhere. Because of competition, the country had entered "the dark ages of the tabloids" he said, later adding that the popular papers had reached a point where nothing "however personal, was any longer secret or sacred, and the basic human right to privacy was banished in the interest of publishing profit". Murdoch gave his backing to a campaign to "clean up" the tabloids, in order to avoid legislation. This was great news for the *Mirror*. The Great and Good were talking about depriving the *Sun* of the material that it had used to win the battle with the *Mirror*. If the tabloids were forced to head back in the direction of "proper" journalism then, of the two, the *Mirror* was in the better position to prosper.

But against this promising background, many of Greenslade's plans for changes at the paper – designed to exploit what he believed to be the *Sun's* weaknesses – immediately ran into the problem of Maxwell's interference and moods. Greenslade found that Maxwell wanted to be involved in everything from writing advertising blurb to changing the headline on the edition marking the release of Nelson Mandela from jail. The publisher had sanctioned huge spending on a *Mirror*-sponsored pop concert at Wembley in April 1990 at which the recently released Mandela spoke to his supporters in the UK, the anti-apartheid campaigners. The concert was a success and Maxwell briefly met Mandela and was give the full "Mandela meets Maxwell" treatment as though it was the main thing the South African leader had been looking forward to during his 30 years in jail.[50]

Greenslade nevertheless set out to modernise the paper. He got rid of the Old Codgers column, the Jane strip cartoon (which Maxwell had reintroduced) and replaced a column by wrinkly Michael Parkinson with young John Diamond. To target the increasingly important and affluent audience of young women he introduced a new weekly women's supplement, killed off the idea of a *Mirror* "Page Three", or anything like it, for good, and did what he could to promote women at the paper and make them more prominent in its columns. Her ordered populist political campaigns against the Conservative government's much-hated Poll Tax. Sales began to creep up so long as he managed to keep Maxwell off the news pages and, especially, if the *Sun* continued to falter.

But rows with Maxwell began to mount, just as they had done with Stott before him. The inevitable sacking came more quickly in Greenslade's case. The ostensible reason was an interview the editor gave to the *Press Gazette* saying, in a very general way, that the market for tabloid newspapers would decline in the future because of the spread of multi-channel TV. The interview also contained phrases that could have been construed as critical of Maxwell and the *Mirror*. Maxwell was moved to fury by the interview. At the time he was preparing for the market floatation of the *Mirror*, the success of which depended largely on convincing the City – flying in the face of all the evidence – that popular newspapers in general and the *Mirror* in particular would have larger sales in the future.

There had been other many other disagreements – including Greenslade's direct refusal to print a front-page headline saying WAR TO END IN 24 HOURS after the January 1991 Gulf War began, on the basis of nothing other than Maxwell's hope that the headline would stop the crash in stock-market prices triggered by the start of the fighting. The end for Greenslade as editor of the *Mirror* came when Maxwell summoned him to his rooms and said: "Mister Greenslade, you and I are not getting on... our relationship isn't working. That may be 50 per cent your fault, it may be 50 per cent my fault."

Greenslade left the paper.

And within a few months Robert Maxwell was dead.

26 GOING OVERBOARD

On the late afternoon of October 30, 1991, Robert Maxwell was skulking around his headquarters in the *Mirror* wondering what to do about a demand from his consortium of bankers to repay hundreds of millions he had borrowed to finance the acquisition of dozens of companies around the world.

So far he had been able to fob them off with shares in his various companies as a form of payment. But some of the banks had now decided that the shares were at best overvalued and more probably worthless. Maxwell had been forced to promise repayment in hard cash within a few days. The problem was that he did not have the money and had no way of getting hold of it. The next day he faced a meeting with the Mirror Group board when it seemed likely that the whole pack of cards would fall apart revealing that Maxwell's financial empire was based on nothing more than a labyrinthine structure of IOUs.

To everyone's surprise Maxwell announced he was going to take a holiday. He said he had a bad cold and needed some sunshine to get better. It seemed odd. Maxwell was so physically unfit he always had a cold. He put through a call to Gus Rankin, the captain of his luxury yacht, the *Lady Ghislaine*, anchored in Gibraltar. He told Rankin he would be arriving the next morning and wanted to take in the sun off the coast of Spain for a few days. Maxwell said he would be completely alone on the trip, which was unusual. At the very least he would normally have had his photographer Mike "Mr Snapper" Malloney for company. (On a previous occasion the two men had danced to the theme of *Zorba the Greek* alone together on the polished floor of *Lady Ghislaine*'s on-board disco.)

At 6.30 a.m. the following day, Maxwell took off in his helicopter from the helipad he had built on the top of the *Mirror*. It took him to Luton airport where his Gulfstream-4 jet was waiting. Four hours later, he was on board the *Lady Ghislaine*. The plan was to sail some 600 miles to Madeira where, two days later, the private jet would pick him up and take him back to London. Maxwell's mood had unaccountably improved, even though he had to deal with phone calls that made it clear that the banks were closing in. Goldman Sachs, he was told, had just dumped £2.2-million worth of Maxwell Communications Corporation stock on the market and others were sure to follow. The glut of unwanted shares would drive down the share price. Since Maxwell's mountain of debt was secured by the share price this potential turn of events would trigger the banks to demand their cash back. He simply did not have it. He was staring bankruptcy in the face.

Two days later, the *Lady Ghislaine* arrived as planned at Madeira. Maxwell wandered about like a tourist and, in the evening, went gambling in the local casino. The next morning, after taking more financial phone calls and sleeping on the boat, Maxwell changed his plans. Instead of flying back, he told the captain he wanted to go to the Canary Islands. The yacht put ashore in Tenerife, Maxwell did some more wandering about, took some more phone calls and then and went back on board for the last time. As the yacht was heading for Gran Canaria, Maxwell fell off the back of the boat at about 5 a.m. and died soon afterwards. The crew did not realise he was missing until the middle of the following morning. After a search by Air-Sea rescue, the naked, floating corpse of Robert Maxwell was fished out of the water at 6.15 p.m. in the evening. The body was flown ashore, where an autopsy ruled out drowning because there was so little water in the lungs. It was decided he had probably died of natural causes, such as a heart attack, before the body hit the water.

The exact circumstances of Maxwell's fall from the boat were to remain a mystery. Explanations ranged from a simple accident, thought unlikely given the very high safety railings on the yacht and the perfect weather, through suicide on account of his mounting financial worries, to murder, possibly by spies. Maxwell, it was thought, had always been very thick with both the feared Israeli secret service Mossad (and, in fact the *Mirror's* own foreign editor had named him as a Mossad agent) and the KGB, on account of his extensive business dealings with the Eastern Bloc over four decades.

Whatever the reason for his death, there were plenty of people who were delighted. Former *Mirror* editor Roy Greenslade, who had migrated to Murdoch's mid-market *Mirror* "spoiler" *Today*, was delighted when he heard the news, and punched the air to celebrate. At the *Mirror* the reaction was entirely different – terror all round. Maxwell was such a survivor. What if there had been some sort of mistake? Paranoia increased a couple of weeks later when the *Guardian* printed a story suggesting, in all seriousness, that Maxwell somehow faked his own death and had gone into hiding until the debt crisis had passed. Added to that was the normal journalistic fear of jumping the gun, or missing the real news, when a big story was breaking.

Richard Stott, the reinstated *Mirror* editor, opted for caution. The paper reported Maxwell's death under the respectful headline THE MAN WHO SAVED THE DAILY MIRROR next to a beaming posed picture of Maxwell at his most charming. The accompanying story and signed obituary by Joe Haines, the paper's political correspondent, was later denounced as "hagiography". Haines, the man who had threatened to walk out of the paper if Maxwell ever set foot in it, now praised him as "a giant with vision" who had "ploughed enormous sums into the latest newspaper technology" at the *Mirror*. Haines wrote: "His death removes a colossus from the scene."

After striving to keep Maxwell out of the paper for so long Stott now went abruptly into reverse gear. In death, the *Mirror* gave Maxwell the megastar treatment he always believed he deserved in life. Stott devoted a total of eleven pages to Maxwell tributes. "Bob," the paper said, had left the *Mirror* "financially strong" and "strong on integrity". There was even a tribute-laden profile of his £12-million yacht which, *Mirror* readers were told, "business or pleasure, Bob loved".

Most of the other papers were equally respectful in the first days after Maxwell's death. Tributes flowed in from around the world and from political leaders in Britain. Almost all were fulsome, if carefully worded. The *Sun* did not give the story much space, believing that nobody much cared about Robert Maxwell. MacKenzie however used the event as the peg for an advertising campaign based around a picture of Maxwell looking grossly fat and using the slogan:

DON'T GO OVERBOARD TO BUY THE MIRROR.

The first paper to break ranks was the *Independent on Sunday,* which a couple of days later denounced Maxwell as "a liar, a cheat and a bully". But the *Sindie* was a basically lone voice until the full scale of Maxwell's multiple financial deceits became clear. Maxwell was so badly in debt because, after buying the *Mirror*, he had used all the publicity to produce an inflated impression of his size, importance and creditworthiness as a businessman. This, together with the very cheap price at which he had been able to buy the *Mirror* and its highly mortgageable assets such as the buildings and the pension fund (which in the end he simply stole), had enabled him to set off on an astonishing corporate shopping spree – mortgaging genuinely valuable assets like Pergamon Press, his Watford printing business and, eventually, the *Mirror* itself to buy large stakes or outright control of over 60 companies before he was forced to start selling them again at a loss shortly before his death.

Maxwell's shopping list had seemed credible enough at first in the City.

He was breaking the power of the unions at the time – reducing the number of printers employed by 2,000 in a single year. As far as the banks knew, this pleasing anti-union activity would make both the *Mirror* and his other printing companies suddenly and violently profitable. The stock market was rising, the whole business of mergers and acquisitions was fashionable.

At first Maxwell bought modestly into areas he already knew about – printing, publishing, newspapers – and then into fields where there was obvious cross-over which could help the *Mirror* or other existing businesses – "synergy" in City speak. But after the first two or three years, his moves seemed to be increasingly barmy or whimsical. They included several English football clubs, two more football clubs in Israel, an up-market classical music publisher, unrelated scientific instrument and computer manufacturers, a drugs company and a large slice of the Parisian fashion house Christian Dior. The stock market crash that followed the start of the first Gulf War had brought the whole rickety house of cards down.

For the time being, the job of running the empire fell to Maxwell's sons Kevin and Ian. Kevin announced that it would be business as usual and tried to maintain the fiction that the empire's plummeting share price was a temporary difficulty. Kevin was first rumbled by Bronwen Maddox, then a *Financial Times* media finance analyst. Meticulous cross-referencing and checking of some 40 inter-connecting Maxwell companies led her to the conclusion that the empire was at least £750 million in the red and possibly as much as £1 billion in debt. In an interview with Maddox, Kevin confirmed that this might well be the case. An investigation started by Stott himself provided the first convincing evidence that Maxwell had looted the paper, illegally using assets in the paper's pension fund in a desperate attempt to plug the gaps and shore up his crumbling empire.

Under the headline MILLIONS MISSING FROM THE *MIRROR* the paper carried the news that Maxwell had stolen around £350 million from the pension fund and otherwise loaded the *Mirror* down with his personal debts, pushing the stolen or "missing millions" total to £526 million. The MAN WHO SAVED THE *MIRROR* and all his family were now vilified. The *Mirror's* art department knocked up a picture showing what Maxwell "would really have looked like" if he had not dyed his hair and used cosmetics. The result made him look like a hideous, dribbling, B-movie Martian monster.

The *Sun* which, like almost everyone else, had cowered before Maxwell's threats of libel writs while he was alive, now felt no such inhibitions and joined the queue to put the boot in. The paper joined in the campaign, straying dangerously close to anti-Semitism. "Maxwell's last resting place is close by the Garden of Gethsemane where Judas Iscariot betrayed Jesus Christ for thirty pieces of silver," the paper noted, adding:

"he should feel at home there". Paul Foot, the upper-class *Mirror* investigative columnist, coolly told a meeting of *Mirror* journalists that he was delighted that his former patron was dead. He was roundly cheered. A manager of a Maxwell company in Scotland was quoted as saying: "I feel like digging him up and hanging him."

A month after Maxwell's death the estimated figure for the "missing millions" had stabilised at around £800 million, including the £350 million filched from the pension fund. Businesses on the periphery of the worldwide empire started to close at once. Baffled waiters in a Bulgarian hotel bought from the communist regime by Maxwell rioted when their wages suddenly went unpaid. In a desperate attempt to raise cash, Maxwell-owned titles as diverse as *The Times* of Kenya and *Architects Journal* (plus a string of other valuable trade and technical magazines) were sold off. So, too, were the contents of Maxwell's office at the *Mirror* and the family mansion in Oxfordshire, which went under the auction hammer. There was a brisk trade in Maxwell's collection of baseball caps, vulgar furniture and vile trinkets (many were gifts from the likes of the late Nicolae Ceausescu of Romania), raising almost £500,000. Maxwell's personal wine cellar went for another £93,000. A Cheltenham boutique-owner bought Betty Maxwell's raspberry-coloured Rolls Royce for the knockdown price of £40,000. But none of this did much good. The total was less than the fees being charged by the lawyers engaged in trying to come to terms with the mess. Legal fees had soaked up £900,000 before the end of the year.

The main dread was that the *Mirror* would close or, more likely, be sold off to hostile, cost-cutting businessmen to help pay off Maxwell's creditors. Instead, the paper was in effect "bought" by an unwilling and panic-stricken gaggle of banks who converted the *Mirror*'s debts into shares in the company. They were left holding more than half of all the *Mirror*'s shares, giving them control of the board of directors. The bankers appointed a temporary management team and made it very clear that they were keen to sell their unwanted shares, and get their money back, as soon as possible.

Various potential buyers swam in to view, some sensing a Murdoch-style opportunity to buy a wounded (but potentially still very profitable) newspaper group cheap in its hour of weakness. But first into the ring was *Mirror* editor Richard Stott, who was proposing a management buy-out backed by the venture capital group Electra. Unfortunately, Stott was working mainly with junior members of the management team and the only well-known businessman he could turn up was Sir Peter Parker, the retired head of British Rail who had not been seen as any sort of financial or business force since the 1970s. Sir Robert Clarke, who had been installed by Nat West as chairman, also seemed reluctant to deal with

Stott, the man who had recently caused him so much grief by high-lighting in the *Mirror* how he and other directors failed to stop Maxwell. Sir Robert later claimed that there was little he could have done about it, but Stott blasted him anyway.

Rival bids were in the offing from Tony O'Reilly, the Dublin-based chairman and chief executive of Heinz, the baked beans empire; from Conrad Black, the Napoleon-worshipping owner of the *Daily Telegraph*; and the DC Thomson group, of Dundee, owners of the *Sunday Post* and the *Beano*. Murdoch was not allowed to bid because of monopoly restrictions and none of the others were offering enough to interest the bankers. Instead, the banks decided to hang on until a new and more effective management team could be brought in to cut costs, boost profits, pay off the debts and re-finance the pension fund and therefore make the shares saleable once again to institutional investors on the open market.

The Nat West bank took the lead role in trying to sort out the management, since they had loaned the most money to Maxwell and so now had the largest block of shares in the *Mirror*. The bank was now in a position similar to that of Reed when they had wanted rid of the papers ten years earlier. They had to find a chief executive who could "groom" the *Mirror* to make it look like a profitable business so that they could find buyers for the *Mirror* shares they needed to sell in order to get back the cash they had originally loaned to Maxwell.

Despite the terrible financial image the *Mirror* now endured, its fundamentals as a business were actually not too bad. Maxwell had at least been successful in introducing colour printing to the paper and this had led to strong circulation increases. The effect of colour was to make the *Mirror* stand out, tempting readers who had drifted away to pick it up, sample it and start buying again. Conventional wisdom at the time was that colour put people off, its introduction could make a tabloid paper look like a comic. According to the sages – including Rupert Murdoch who refused to introduce colour at the *Sun* – it might be all right for football and fashion, it would be no good for hard news, especially for pictures of disasters. People did not want to see blood in colour. In practice, the exact opposite proved to be the case. Murdoch had been proved wrong about colour in exactly the same way Northcliffe had been proved wrong by Hannen Swaffer about the mass appeal of photographs in papers. The introduction of colour at the *Mirror* had coincided with a run of disasters starting with the Hillsborough football catastrophe and ending up with the Lockerbie plane crash. Stott used colour to maximum effect in each case, out-stripping the black and white *Sun* with circulation increases each time.

Moreover, Maxwell's removal of printers' jobs and Greenslade's cuts in the number of journalists and costs on the editorial side meant that the company was strongly profitable for the first time in decades. The pension fund had been stolen and it would be expensive to replenish. But, apart from that, the business and the share price would doubtless slowly recover as memories of the Maxwell disaster began to fade.

But Nat West was impatient. The bank's first move as *de facto* owner of the *Mirror* was to remove chairman Ernie Burrington and finance director Lawrence Guest. They were replaced by Sir Robert Clarke, a former banker who had done a lot of business with Maxwell. He was put into the position of chairman, even though he had relatively little experience of the newspaper business. Sir Robert's first move was the unfortunate one of putting up the *Mirror's* cover price, hoping this would boost profits and the share price quickly. But the only result was a sharp drop in sales, which meant the paper got in less money overall than before. The blunder over the cover price convinced the board of bankers that they needed to bring in some newspaper expertise at once. At the same time they did not want Stott, Burrington, Guest or anyone else who had been "tainted" by association with Maxwell or even the old Mirror Group before that. The trouble was all the top non-Mirror Group executive talent was already employed at rival newspaper groups.

The main exception was the austere and widely disliked figure of David "Monty" Montgomery, once a humble *Daily Mirror* sub-editor, who had moved over to work for Rupert Murdoch with ambitions to become a media mogul in his own right. As it happened, Montgomery was on the float at the time, having recently been pushed out of the editor's chair at the *Today* newspaper after failing to persuade Murdoch to allow him to buy the newspaper and set himself up as a proprietor in his own right.

Montgomery had been working for a year from the offices of the ad agency Saatchi and Saatchi on a plan to launch a chain of American-style local "City TV" cable news stations in the UK. The plan had not come to very much, but meant Montgomery had made contact with various media finance people, including Clive Hollick, the Labour peer who ran the financial-services group MAI and who shared Montgomery's ambition of becoming the proprietor of a newspaper or TV group or both. When the new *Mirror* board began asking around the City about the availability of newspaper management talent Hollick had recommended Monty. That was good enough for the board – and, with a puff of smoke to rival the arrival of Maxwell himself, Montgomery was installed as *Mirror* chief executive. Hollick joined the board of directors at the same time.

On October 22, 1992 news of Monty's appointment to the throne of Northcliffe, Rothermere, Bartholomew, King and Cudlipp reached the *Mirror's* staff via the wires in the paper's "tape room" – a special department where teams of men monitored and summarised what the news agencies were reporting. A messenger arrived at the news desk bringing the "tape" report of a statement issued by *Mirror* board member Joe Haines. Haines, who had a way with words, announced that he was resigning from the *Mirror* with immediate effect because of the decision to appoint Montgomery as chief executive. Previously, Haines had written a celebrated editorial in the *Mirror*, accusing Monty of being "a liar, a thief, a hypocrite, a bigot and a pornographer". Haines had issued similar strongly worded warning prior to the arrival of Maxwell, but had then adjusted to the new regime, eventually becoming Maxwell's official and enthusiastic biographer. There was to be no such U-turn a second time. Haines was gone and gone for good.

Haines's statement and resignation triggered an immediate storm inside the *Mirror* building, with threats of non-cooperation and strike action. Many of the people at the *Mirror* – at all levels – had worked with Montgomery at the *Mirror* itself or at the *News of the World* and *Today*, where he had also been editor, and hated his guts. For Haines and others the objection was political. Montgomery was no apparent friend of the Labour party. His personal politics were something of a mystery – some thought him, as an Ulsterman of "traditional" right-wing views, to be a supporter of extreme Protestant unionism. What was clear was that Montgomery had loyally banged the drum for the Tory party and Mrs Thatcher while he had been working for Murdoch as editor of the *News of the World*. Montgomery had also led anti-*Daily Mirror* boycott campaign because of the paper's stance in favour of a united Irish republic. Hollick had persuaded the bankers that he was the man to put professional management in place, although as a key New Labour figure Hollick was the custodian of the *Mirror*'s Labour party connection. Montgomery then persuaded Hollick and the board that, as an outsider, a "Murdoch man", he was the only one who could bring to an end the *Mirror*'s wasteful culture of drinking, indulgence and decline.

But first Montgomery would have to face the *Mirror* workforce that was almost universally hostile to him. When Montgomery walked into a room, people joked, the temperature dropped by 10 degrees. He was said to be a fish so cold he kept his brain in the refrigerator overnight – a man who made Genghis Khan look like a socialist.

"I can't understand it," Montgomery would complain in his thick Ulster accent.

"Anyone would think I bite the heads off babies."

27 CORPORAL MONTY'S MULTI-COLOURED KALEIDOSCOPIC UPCHUCK

On the floor of the *Mirror* newsroom the revelation that David Montgomery was going to be the new overall boss was at first greeted with disbelief. Few had much faith in the collection of rhyming-slang merchant bankers now in charge of the paper. The new board's first act had been to put up the price of the *Mirror* as the quickest way to start paying off the paper's debts. That had been turned out to be a huge blunder, allowing the *Sun* to truthfully claim that *Mirror* readers were being asked to pay the cost of Maxwell's villainy, hitting sales and therefore reducing income overall.

But now the same board had dropped an even bigger clanger by falling for "Monty" – a man best known to them as the recently sacked editor of the *Today* newspaper, a short-lived and failed poor-quality Murdoch-owned competitor to the *Mirror*.

The consensus from Stott, as editor, down to the most junior journalist who knew anything at all about "Monty", was that he was a "failed editor", a "Murdoch reject" who simply was not up to the job. Monty's *Today* had been a thumping loss-maker. It was a rubbishy product, worse in every respect and in every department than the *Mirror* and designed more as a yuppie marketing campaign to cash in on ephemeral 1980s consumer fads like "green consumerism" than a newspaper. Stott claimed not to mind honest journalistic competition from *Today*. But Monty's paper, they complained, was just a "spoiler" – which spent a fortune on TV advertising and give-away competitions in an attempt to create confusion in the market and cynically "buy" *Mirror* readers.

Still, it was typical of Monty to have put one over on the collection of newspaper business greenhorns catapulted into control of the *Mirror* by accident as the unexpected result of the brilliant financial *nous* they had displayed in lending vast amounts of their clients' cash to Robert Maxwell. Monty's reputation throughout much of Fleet Street was as a man who put as much effort into his next career move as into doing whatever actual job he had managed to land. The story was told of how one editor at Wapping had gone round accusing another editor of phoning Rupert Murdoch once a week behind his back and asking for his job. "That's nothing," came the reply "Monty's been phoning Murdoch every day to get my job *and* he phones God every week to get Murdoch's job."

When news of Monty's appointment at the *Mirror* was confirmed, a delegation was sent to see the *Mirror* board chairman Sir Robert Clarke asking him to reconsider. Stott simply refused to believe that he and the board had properly checked Montgomery's credentials. Clarke listened carefully, thanked them for the information and then told the delegation that it was too late: the board's vote had been taken. When this bad news was relayed back to the newsroom, the staff took their own vote, deciding by 278 votes to four not to co-operate in any way with Montgomery until he had given assurances that there would be no sackings; that the existing editors – including Stott – would remain in place; that he would not interfere with the day-to-day editing of the group's papers and, in particular, that the *Mirror's* "social stand" and support for the Labour party would continue. Monty at once issued a statement apparently agreeing to all these demands. But his exact words were that "the editorial independence of our newspapers will be preserved and vested in the editors, with continuing support for the left-of-centre traditions of all titles". Monty added: "I have definitely got no plans for job cuts in editorial departments, nor has the board considered any." Finally, Monty said in the statement: "All editors will remain in place."

The talk of "left of centre", it would later be explained, depended on what you meant by centre. If you took Margaret Thatcher as being at the "centre" of British politics, then much of the Tory party including Prime Minister John Major could be considered "left of centre". The statement "I have no plans for job cuts" was almost certainly true, but profoundly misleading. Monty had only been in the job for ten minutes. It would take a few days to refine his ideas for massive downsizing into a "plan". It was also true that Stott and the other *Mirror* editors were to "remain in place". The trick here was not to mention any sort of time-scale. Stott and the others were disposed of within days.

The threat of the strike was lifted, the papers were produced without a hitch and the protest dwindled to a token overnight sit-in. People were suspicious, but later realised they had been naive in accepting the assurances. Stott had even entered the newsroom waving a piece of paper, Munich-style, and played a key role in getting Montgomery accepted. There was a general feeling that after Maxwell it was somehow impossible that they would all be led up the garden path again.

The next morning Monty appeared in person on the editorial floor to begin the process of breaking his promises and stamping his will on every aspect of the paper.

★★★

David Montgomery was born in Bangor, Northern Ireland in 1948 into a family of solidly conservative Presbyterian stock. Young David went to Queen's University, Belfast, in the late 1960s and studied history and politics, intellectual commodities that were not in short supply at the time, since Belfast was in the grip of the civil-rights demonstrations and protests that led to the foundation of the Provisional IRA and the resumption of the "Troubles".

Even as a student Montgomery was a loner with few friends. As in later life he tended to keep himself to himself. Unusually for the time, he was always impeccably dressed, wearing a suit and tie at a time when most of his contemporaries went in for long hair, T-shirts and duffle coats. Montgomery became the editor of the college newspaper, *The Gown*. He was remembered as a moderate opponent of the civil-rights marchers and a staunch but not fanatical unionist, and was quoted in *The Gown*, joking that he was "the last bastion of Protestantism" at the university. But Montgomery was mainly interested in keeping out of trouble and making money. He combined his studies with running a news agency, selling stories about the troubles and students' sexual antics to national newspapers. A long article in *The Gown* described how he had manoeuvred himself into the editor's chair by stitching up rivals at student union meetings. This article was illustrated with a cartoon of Montgomery wearing his suit and playing a typewriter instead of ivories, with the caption "Burning the midnight oil".[51]

At the end of his studies, Montgomery won a place on the *Daily Mirror*'s graduate training scheme where he was later remembered by some as a peripheral figure who hung around the fringes of the crowd at the bar, grimly sipping a half-pint of beer. He passed the course and in 1970 started work in the *Mirror*'s then large Manchester office, when the paper was reeling from the launch of the *Sun* and was about to be thrown into turmoil by the sudden departure of Cudlipp. The main thing the course had taught him was that it was more important to be a production specialist, such as a sub-editor, than a reporter because the production departments had all the power – especially at the *Mirror* where up to that point every single editor since Bartholomew's time had come from the subbing or graphics side. His ambition was to become chief sub – in charge of the whole production side of the paper – at a young enough age to have a chance of becoming editor.

The problem was that the *Mirror* was hopelessly overstaffed with many similarly ambitious people. The competition was intense and it was hard to shine when most subs were allocated probably only an hour's worth of work to be completed in a full eight-hour shift. But Monty always managed to keep himself busy, constantly pestering his superiors for more work to take on, or taking upon himself to re-do and "improve" the work of others. His fellow sub, the much more popular and avuncular David "Banksy" Banks, gave Monty the nickname "Cabin Boy" because of the way he followed around Derek Jameson, the head of the Manchester office, trying to be of service. Jameson found Monty exasperating: "Not you again," he would moan. "Just piss off, will you." Monty was regarded almost universally as an oddball and his tutor on the *Mirror* training scheme, James Dalrymple, said that Monty was the "only guy I've ever known who can walk into a room and reduce the temperature by 10 degrees".

However, Monty had staying power. He stuck it out for ten years in Manchester before making the move to London as a senior sub-editor, during the regime of Mike Molloy (who remembered, "People always found Monty a bit eerie. It was as if he had come from another planet."). Monty left to become deputy editor and then editor of Murdoch's *News of the World* after deciding that his path was blocked at the *Mirror*. The job had been lined up by one of Monty's mentors, the senior *Sun* and *Mirror* journalist Nick Lloyd, who had been editor of the *News of the World*. When Monty took over Lloyd's job, the *News of the World* editor was asked if Monty had stabbed him in the back. Lloyd replied cheerfully, "No, he stabbed me in the front." In fact, the parting was amicable. Murdoch had the job of organising the move of his newspapers from Fleet Street to the new low-cost, union-free plant he had built at Wapping. As Lloyd's number two and a Murdoch editor Monty was a key part of the sensitive plan, the sneakiness of its implementation presumably suiting his operating methods.

In 1987 Murdoch bought the failing *Today* newspaper from Eddie Shah with the idea of opening a new front in the circulation war between the *Sun* and the *Mirror*. At the time Maxwell was in charge of the *Mirror* and – accepting a lower profile in the paper – was encouraging Stott to compete directly with the *Sun*. Murdoch's plan was to target the "top end" of the *Mirror*'s readership, scooping up any *Mirror* readers fed up with content like girly pictures, big, screaming headlines and bingo. *Today*, like the *Mirror* but unlike the *Sun*, was able to print colour pictures and this too, it was reckoned, would harm the *Mirror* in the newsagents, especially if *Today* could be made to look like an up-market version of the newly colourful *Mirror*. Monty badgered Murdoch into giving him the editorship of *Today*.

After the customary mass sackings, Monty gathered his staff at *Today* and told them they were taking on the *Mirror* which was, if not exactly a sitting duck, a paper with no real future. It was not just that the *Mirror* was in the clutches of Maxwell. More serious was the fact that it had failed to modernise. The *Mirror's* latest move was to go head to head with the *Sun* – a battle which they could not win, such was the *Sun's* grip on its working-class, ex-council-house-owning audience. As for the new and younger white-collar working class – which included women as an increasingly important market – the *Mirror* did not understand them at all. These people, Monty told the *Today* hacks, were "the children of the Thatcher revolution". They were "classless" as well as "aspirational and style-conscious". They were interested in making money and above all interested in the lifestyles of the rich, famous and young celebrities they saw during the many hours they spent watching television (including, increasingly, multi-channel satellite and cable TV). They had only the slightest interest in politics and, if they were interested at all, it would be in a soft and main-stream version of the "counter-culture" and alternative politics of the 1960s – anti-racism, women's rights, consumer rights, animal welfare and envi-ronmentalism. Neither the *Sun* nor the *Mirror* understood this kind of stance. But Monty that claimed he did and, at one point, was to briefly make *Today* the first and last national newspaper to support the Green Party.

Struggling to make sense of an agenda that included combining the rampant consumerism of huge, gas-guzzling, yuppie BMWs with support for Friends of the Earth, they decided that *Today* was a paper for "Greedy Green People" or, possibly, "Green Greedy People". In practice, the pursuit of the new "aspirational" working class amounted to an obsession with house-price stories and shopping. One of the paper's best reporters was given the job of scouring estate agents to find examples of ordinary houses that had tripled or quadrupled in price and then getting the story from ecstatic champagne-quaffing householders. At the height of the 1988 house-price boom Monty insisted that there was a house-price story on the front page every day.

Supporting all this was a new and more feminised editorial approach. The *Daily Mail* had begun to really boom away on the back of a direct appeal to the legions of new women readers who had entered the work-force and were slowly progressing towards equal pay and conditions. If the *Mirror* was going to compete with the *Sun*, it would have to fight on the typically blokeish territory of football, Page Three, crime and politics – whereas *Today* could attack the *Mirror's* female readership by means of a women's agenda of family finance, shopping, house prices, health, educa-tion, consumerism and the environment.

The crucial element in a female-friendly newspaper, Monty thought, was to make it as much like a daily version of a weekly woman's magazine as possible, without putting off male readers too much. This meant that the paper's features section was all-important and it was given a magazine feel mainly by wall-to-wall new-wave "celebrity" journalism in the style of *Hello!* magazine. In stark contrast to the scandal-mongering "monstering" of celebrities by the tabloids, *Today*'s celeb coverage was positive and "heart-warming", using the paper's colour printing capabilities to display lavish *Hello!*-style pictures of the much-admired celebs' houses, cars, kitchens and fancy lifestyles. One celeb to be given the fawning treatment was wacky self-mutilating, monkey-loving, American pop-singer and fantasist Michael "Wacko Jacko" Jackson. The paper paid almost half a million pounds to print extracts from his authorised autobiography, supported by massive advertising on TV. This sycophantic approach earned *Today* the nickname "*Toady*".

Under Montgomery, *Today*'s circulation increased by 300,000, but at the vast cost of TV advertising. His problem was that Murdoch had recently launched Sky TV and was trying to cope with set-up costs for the new service, which were so huge that they nearly sank him. Murdoch was thus soon on the look-out for savings, and loss-making *Today* was an obvious target.

Monty's response was to propose a management buy-out of *Today*, which would take the loss-making paper off Murdoch's hands. He secretly prepared a business plan and began to organise finance. This was typical of Monty – who was always pulling rabbits out of the hat in this way – but it was a mistake. Murdoch was furious that the preparations had been made "behind his back", as the mogul thought of it. It was a sensitive time and he did not want bankers at any level to think he was trying to quietly sell off any of his newspaper titles to raise cash, which was one possible interpretation of Monty's unauthorised activities. Monty's presentation was dismissed in minutes. He was relieved of the editorship of *Today* and put in charge of "future projects", investigating, on essentially a consultancy basis, the possibility of starting up a chain of local TV news stations in the UK, to supplement Sky News. The plan came to nothing as far as Murdoch was concerned and there was a parting of the ways. But it was Monty's research into the launch of "local" TV news on satellite and cable that led him, via the merchant bankers, to Hollick and the top job at the *Mirror*.

★★★

Monty's first act at the *Mirror*, after making the statement that bought off the strike threat, was denounce the "culture of waste and inefficiency", which, he said, had come close to ruining the *Mirror* both before and during the reign of Maxwell. As evidence of the moral decadence of the old regime Monty arranged to be photographed in Maxwell's office, pointing at his leather "Mastermind" chair on its plinth, recently refurbished even after the old man's death by his son Ian at a cost of £27,000. Monty then swept into the executive dinning room, announcing that henceforth it would be a canteen open to all staff. The democratic revolution continued with the opening of Cecil King's private executive lift to all comers. Monty said less, at first, about the numbers of journalists employed by the *Mirror*. Getting rid of Maxwell's eccentric extravagance was one thing. Seriously reducing the core costs of producing the *Mirror* and its sister titles was quite another. When Monty arrived, the *Daily Mirror* had about 230 full-time staff – down from a total of about 400 in the mid-1960s. But the paper employed another 100 or so "casuals" – hired on a regular basis to do work that the salaried staff could not do. Most of the sub-editors trained to use computerised page production were, for example, casuals. Montgomery had already promised the board that he would take out hundreds of millions of costs. To do this, he would need to copy the successful example of Murdoch's move to Wapping.

Montgomery began to break the spirit – if not the exact letter – of his promises to the staff almost immediately. The editors of the *Mirror* titles were sacked within a few days. The dismissal of Stott was done in typical sneaky style, with Monty asking to meet him at Claridge's restaurant in order to discuss "matters of national importance". When Stott arrived, Monty explained that he was out. The statement had been carefully worded to prevent a strike while, at the same time, committing him to nothing. There were more threats of strikes and protests when Stott went. But Monty just brazened it out.

Stott's job was given to the unlikely and slightly comical figure of David "Banksy" Banks, a former *Mirror* and *Sun* production expert who at the time was editing a newspaper in Sydney, Australia. Banksy was well known at the paper as a clever and very funny northerner (he came from Warrington, was proud of having been born in a council house) who liked a drink and had been popular as a senior *Mirror* sub-editor in Manchester. He had left-wing political views but, at the same time, could hardly have been thought to be very serious about politics. Ideology, anyhow, had not stopped him working at the *Sun* under its Thatcher-loving editor Kelvin MacKenzie. Kelvin and Banksy had entertained the staff with a non-stop, foul-mouthed political comedy double act. The general feeling was that Bansky was a bit of a comedian who was left wing enough for the *Mirror*, but who had few serious political contacts and none of the gravitas of Stott. Joe Haines, now reduced to shelling Montgomery from the exile of the *Independent*'s media commentary slot, said the appointment of Banks meant "the end of the *Mirror* as a political force". Haines added: "Almost overnight, the *Daily Mirror*, which Hugh Cudlipp built as a political institution in Britain, has been destroyed. The paper that survived, however narrowly, the depredations of Captain Maxwell has fallen to the artillery of the banks, led by Corporal Montgomery."

Banks ignored all this and arrived to announce: "Today, we finally bury Maxwell at the *Daily Mirror*. This is a new beginning." His own appointment, Banks said, was evidence of "a new commercial dynamism at the top of the *Mirror*." Stott went off to work for Murdoch, editing Monty's old paper *Today*, turning it into a "left of centre" competitor to the *Mirror* for a few years before Murdoch finally closed it down.

With Banksy in place, the *Mirror* board announced the immediate dismissal of the *Mirror's* casuals. From now on, Banks said, he as editor and the staff of the paper would produce the paper without any extra outside help. The threat of industrial action fizzled out, the "casuals" remained sacked (though some were taken on as staff) and Monty began importing his own editorial people – some of them from *Today*. Discontent started to brew within the paper through the winter of 1992–93, the main complaint being that Banks was not good enough to do his job and that Monty was filling up the place with yes-men and mediocrities from *Today*. In February 1993, Monty appointed *Today's* political editor David Seymour to Joe Haines's old position as group political editor. Stott went on the record to call Seymour "a lightweight operator but a Montgomery yes-man". Seymour had previously been a fairly junior leader writer at the *Mirror* where he was famous for once having been talked down from the ledge outside Stott's window when, during a messy divorce and the worse for wear for drink, he had threatened to end it all with a single leap. Monty said he wanted a change because the *Mirror's* automatic support for the Labour party had made the paper "stale". The *Mirror's* political reporting in the late 1980s, Monty said, "lacked originality" and too much had been invested in personal contacts with Neil Kinnock, the Labour party leader. In terms of politics, Monty said, the *Mirror* "had no new tunes. It was flogging a dead horse. It was strident, repetitious and boring".

The conspiracy theory speculated that Seymour's appointment was designed to break the *Mirror's* close contacts with the Labour party. The paper's political staff led, after Haines's departure, by Alastair Campbell had been a thorn in the side of Montgomery, reporting back the latest horrors to the Labour leader John Smith and using the threat of political action as a brake on Monty's cost-cutting plans. When Campbell heard that Seymour was being appointed over his head he crashed into Banks's office and began screaming and shouting. According to some reports the argument was so fierce that Banks threw a chair across the room (Banks later reportedly said that he had thrown the chair in order to grab Campbell's attention, Campbell resigned in protest over Seymour's appointment. He then went off to present the TV show "What the Papers Say" and slagged off Banks and the *Mirror* which such vehemence that Monty complained, unsuccessfully, to the Broadcasting Complaints Commission. Campbell was followed out of the *Mirror* by Lord Hollick – the man who had brought in Monty in the first place. The Labour-supporting Hollick, who had been sent to the Lords by Neil Kinnock, issued a statement saying he was resigning because he had been "unable to resolve" some "concerns about a number of governance and policy matters" that had arisen because of the way Monty was running the *Mirror*.

The next high-profile figure to leave the *Mirror* was Paul Foot, the upper-class Socialist Workers Party activist and investigative columnist. Over the years "Footie" had used his column to highlight a series of miscarriages of justice – which had resulted in more than a dozen entirely innocent people serving lifelong prison sentences being set free. He was later voted "journalist of the decade" by fellow members of the profession.

Nobody in the whole of journalism, including Foot himself, thought the column had much effect on the circulation of the paper. Standing up for prisoners' rights or campaigning on behalf of convicted murderers was not exactly the most popular thing to do and it was a good deal more expensive than just printing a picture of a pretty girl, which was how the rival *Sun* was apt to use the space. But the presence of Foot's column was seen as a sign that the *Mirror* was a "decent" paper and not just another soulless money-making media enterprise. The end came when Foot decided to write up the sackings at the *Mirror* and the way the place was being run by Monty, giving the story the same treatment he would dish out to any other group of Fat Cats. When Banks saw the column he immediately declared that Foot had become insane. He ordered him to go home and immediately seek psychiatric help. Foot then had his column printed at his own expense and distributed it as widely as he could. After this, Banks said the column amounted to a "finely turned suicide bullet" and made Foot an offer he could not refuse – either agree that he was sick, take time off and undergo treatment or resign from the paper. Foot chose to resign.

The steady stream of sackings and resignations from the *Mirror* (many, including Alastair Campbell, made their way over to Stott's *Today,* which, for a while, existed as a sort of *Mirror* in exile) led to a wave of criticism, especially after Hollick had gone, breaking the previous umbilical link to the official Labour party leadership. Geoffrey Goodman, the Cudlipp and Molloy-era industrial correspondent and linkman to the trade union leadership, popped up to repeat Joe Haines's comment that the *Mirror* was becoming "increasingly irrelevant as a political force". Molloy, the great design expert whose work had so much to create the basic style of modern popular newspapers around the world, now denounced the *Mirror's* design and use of colour under Montgomery as resembling "an explosion in a paint factory". From the padded-leather comfort of the House of Lords Hugh Cudlipp also criticised the *Mirror*. All the popular newspapers were the same now, he complained, "chasing their tails like hounds with rabies in a breathless Royal gossip hunt. As an encore they savage any randy pop star, wayward football manager, erring priest or two-timing MP they happen to spy in the hedgerows during the chase, and proclaim the sleazy end-product as yet another front page 'world exclusive'."The *Sun*, the *Mirror* and their Sunday equivalents, Cudlipp said, now mostly served up soft porn every day during the week, to be consumed with the cornflakes, with slightly harder porn over the Sunday roast.

A little later, Cudlipp made a speech to a reunion of *Mirror* veterans, to mark his own 81st birthday. Everyone who had been working for the paper when it hit the five and quarter million circulation record in 1964 was invited with Cudlipp, for the very last time, laying on tanker-loads of champagne for those who still had the physical ability to drink it.

"Dammit, we had the best writers and cartoonists, all at the top of their form," Cudlipp told the audience, adding: "Gathered in this room are the real basic Fleet Street whiz-kids." He was withering about the people who had run the *Mirror* since he left: Clive Thornton, a former building society executive, "who went round switching the lights off"; Robert Maxwell (Cudlipp just lifted his eyes to the sky and crossed himself at the mention of his name) and the vampire-like David Montgomery (more crossing of self) who produced a paper which Cudlipp said looked to him like "a multi-coloured kaleidoscopic upchuck". Some days the paper, Cudlipp continued, "looks as though three passers-by have been eating beetroot and been sick over the front page".

Cudlipp ended his speech – uproariously received – by saying that, back in the 1960s, "we were really trying to 'do' something". Then he paused for effect – the spoken equivalent of the technique perfected all those years ago by "Cassandra" and himself before adding the punch line: "I've forgotten now what the bloody hell it was, but nobody's trying to do it now."

More succinctly, Cudlipp answered a letter to ex-*Mirror* columnist John Pilger by signing himself off with two words: "*Fuck Montgomery*".

28 THE DAILY ANDREX

David Montgomery is sitting on a small stage in the main hall of a City conference centre, flanked on one side by Mirror Group Newspapers chairman Sir Robert Clarke and on the other by managing director Charlie Wilson, the former editor of *The Times* brought into the senior management of the group at the end of the Maxwell era. It is April 1994, the end of Monty's second full year in control of the *Mirror*.

Looking exceptionally smug, the chief executive has just reported to the assembled ranks of city analysts, financial journalists, institutional and individual shareholders a surge in profits, mainly the result of sacking 600 people, combined with a move from Holborn Circus to much smaller and cheaper accommodation in the Canary Wharf tower in Docklands. The *Mirror*'s Holborn headquarters, the physical embodiment of the paper's importance and achievements – Cecil King's "Taj Mahal of Journalism", "Cassandra's "Tower of Tosh", Cudlipp's "Gin Palace of Socialism" – had been sold off for £40 million. Only one thing would remain: the *Mirror*'s presses were so heavy and firmly fixed into position in the basement that they could not be removed. The presses that had produced the record print runs and headlines and front pages like FOR ALL OUR TOMORROWS VOTE LABOUR TODAY and ENOUGH IS ENOUGH were to be entombed – buried in concrete and left in place. The rest of the building was to be completely gutted and sold off to property developers. Eventually, it re-emerged as the headquarters of a supermarket chain.

Monty reported that the move had gone off without a hitch, although the hacks were bleating that the building was too crowded. Some realised that it would not be crowded for much longer. Monty was already announcing "firm plans" to reduce the workforce by another 150. The *Mirror* hacks had had 500,000 square feet at their disposal in Holborn. Now they were crammed into 150,000 square feet of call-centre-style, modern, open-plan floor space 800 feet in the air above the soulless concrete ersatz modernist construction site of Docklands where pubs were few and far apart and going out with contacts difficult. But Monty had negotiated a discount lease from the then-bankrupt owners of the tower who, at one point, were so desperate for tenants that they placed shop-front dummies next to the windows to keep up morale. He had also negotiated a cost-effective contract for the printing of the paper (printers would no longer be employed directly or "in-house" as they had been at Holborn). Also, there had been a fortuitous repayment of £30-million worth of missing *Mirror* pension money, previously believed to have been stolen by Maxwell but suddenly found tucked under the metaphorical City equivalent of a mattress. There were plans to pay off the debt the new board had inherited from the old regime. It was true that the circulations of all the Mirror Group's titles were down, thanks in part to a renewed competitive price-cutting "war" launched by the Rupert Murdoch. The *Sun* cut its price by 5p to 20p, but Montgomery held his nerve, keeping the price of the *Mirror* steady at 27p. Sales slipped from just under three million to below 2.5 million for the first time since the war but ad revenue was holding up, Monty reported.

The sales slide meant income was down a little on the previous year. But costs had fallen much more quickly and were set to keep falling quickly. All in all, it meant that the *Mirror* was on course to be making profits again in the near future. The share price had already begun to recover from its post-Maxwell low as the rational expectation of profit began to return. Monty had every reason to look pleased. The rising share price was generating millions in personal profit as part of a share option scheme he had been granted when he came to the *Mirror*. He had been given the right to buy *Mirror* shares at the rock-bottom price of 61p each, in addition to his £350,000-a-year salary as chief executive. Monty was already starting to dip into the share options whenever the price moved up a bit, earning him around £500,000 a year on top of his escalating Fat Cat wages. Sir Robert Clarke was looking pleased too. The share price appeared to be on track to result in a valuation of £200 million for the block of shares controlled by the various bankers on the board. When that price was reached, they would be at last be able to sell *Mirror* shares and get back the money they had lent to Maxwell.

Monty also reported that the Mirror Group was following Murdoch's lead and had plans to get into television. The fashion in the City at the time was for "multi-media" stock – meaning companies that combined newspaper and television interests. The result was to be L!ve TV, the *Mirror*'s answer to Sky, which, as it happened, was to end in disaster, but at the time looked plausible enough to cheer up the investment analysts and share-tippers.

On the editorial front, David Banks was struggling to implement Monty's *Today*-style vision of a feminised, aspirational, new-age, greedy-green, style-conscious, pro-capitalism, suburban, anti-globalisation, inner-city, loft-dwelling, pace-setters' *Mirror,* which, in practice, had meant more emphasis on TV and soap tie-ins, celebrity picture spreads and increased royals coverage, especially of Princess Diana – "The Princess of Sales" – who was riding high on the agenda after her bust-up with the Windsors and her famous "Queen of Hearts" performance on the BBC's "Panorama". All of this meant an increased reliance on arch-celebrity PR-man and wholesale, harmless, made-to-measure story fabricator, Max Clifford.

Max Clifford was to play a role in the story for which Banks's short tenure in the *Mirror* editor's chair would mainly be remembered – close-up pictures of Diana in her exercise leotard taken by secret cameras hidden on exercise machines she used at a health club in west London. Banks and Monty paid £100,000 for the pictures in a deal with the health club's owner, brokered by Clifford. The official po-faced explanation was that the pictures proved that there was a security risk. If the cameras could be planted, then it would be just as easy to plant a bomb – or miniature, automatic, poisoned-tipped blowpipe or something. The *Mirror* thus had a public duty to reveal the security blunder so that such an important person could be properly protected in future.

In reality, everyone knew that, for the 27p asking price, millions of people would want to look at the pictures out of sheer curiosity. It was a direct answer to the *Sun's* scoop in printing sneak pictures of the pregnant Diana sun-bathing in the Caribbean. Max Clifford claimed the *Mirror* had got the gym pics at a bargain price. "With my contacts these pictures will sell for at least a million pounds worldwide," Clifford boasted.

Predictably, the paper sold out the minute it appeared in the shops. Predictably, the public complained about this latest example of intrusion in privacy. The letters columns and radio phone-ins were heavy with denunciations of this latest tabloid intrusion and politicians made routine calls for tougher laws and regulation to protect privacy. After being censured by the Press Complaints Commission – a voluntary self-regulatory body – Monty pulled out of the organisation. He said his editors, including Banks, had not broken the rules on intrusion because the story was a genuine exposé of a security lapse and therefore in the public interest. He even quoted Cudlipp, saying that the *Mirror's* editorial policy had always been "Publish and be Damned". Monty said the *Mirror* titles would "continue to abide" by the Commission's privacy rules in future. Some of the *Mirror's* advertisers decided to boycott the paper in protest and one leading building society said that the paper had become "stupid and sleazy". Banks tried to turn the heat on the owner of the health club, describing him as scoring nine out of ten on a scale of the world's greatest ratbags. (Later, during a radio interview, Banks rated himself a "seven out of ten ratbag", which he claimed was about average for a tabloid journalist.)

After a few days, the fuss blew over, the *Mirror* rejoined the Press Complaints Commission and Banks was ready to do business with Max again. But that was not entirely the end of the matter. Diana sued the gym club, resulting in a huge loss, which the club then attempted to pass on to the *Mirror*. Banks was embroiled in months of legal argument that only ended when the *Mirror* paid the "ratbag" gym club owner an additional and unforeseen fee estimated at £250,000. Banks left the editor's chair at the *Mirror* in April 1994 – first "kicked upstairs" as editorial director and then to become deputy to Bridget "Death" Rowe, editor of the *Sunday Mirror* (Rowe's nickname was in tribute to sharply falling sales during her editorship). Banks's place was taken by Colin Myler, a Monty favourite from *Today*, where he had been news editor before following him to the Mirror Group.

Myler lasted only four months before he was replaced by the head-hunted editor of the *News of the World*, Piers Morgan, a former *Sun* showbiz reporter. In the period from the end of the Second World War to the arrival of Robert Maxwell there had been just five editors, all had lasted for between five and ten years and only one (Silvester "Bish" Bolam) had been sacked (even then it was hushed up and presented as a voluntary resignation). Likewise, the successful *Sun* had only two editors in more than twenty years. After the arrival of Maxwell and Montgomery, the paper had seven editors in ten years and at least four of them were officially sacked.

The latest occupant of the job, Piers Pughe-Morgan, had been born in leafy Newick, East Sussex, in 1965. He dropped the "Pughe" part of his name when he entered journalism, claiming that he needed a shorter by-line with which to sign off his articles. His father was a former publican who had made money in the wholesale meat trade. The infant Piers was sent to a prep school but the family hit a financial crisis and he then had to go to a comprehensive school. There he was sometimes bullied by the local skinheads because of his posh background, his swotty approach to school work and the fact that, as a vocal supporter of the Tory party, he came over as a nerd, interested in politics. After school, he took a job as an insurance clerk in the City where he earned a lot of money but quickly became bored. After less than a year he dropped out of his job, went on a journalism training course and went to work on local newspapers in Wimbledon and Sutton in the leafy south London suburbs. Morgan was later remembered as a "natural", an excellent but arrogant local newspaper reporter, who made it clear that he regarded himself as better than his editor.

After three or four years of births, marriages and deaths Morgan took the well-worn path of working occasional shifts for the national papers, hoping to come to the attention of editors as young, raw talent. His break came when at the age of 23 in 1988 he began working on the *Sun's* pop music section where – after taking further steps to cover up his posh background and despite the fact that he cheerfully claimed to know "nothing" about show-biz – he came to the attention of *Sun* editor Kelvin MacKenzie, who became his mentor. Morgan had been to interview the long-forgotten pop sensation Bros and MacKenzie had been tickled by the very obviously straight, suit-wearing Morgan ligging with the self-consciously hip pop-stars. He picked the shot that made Morgan look most absurd and blew it up to cover most of two pages – giving him the title of the *Sun's* very own "Friend of the Stars". The title stuck and the "Friend of the Stars" was photographed day after day embracing the likes of David Bowie, Madonna, Paul McCartney and others as though they were long-lost friends. In reality, Morgan knew none of these people and the whole thing was organised between the paper, the pop music PR industry and Morgan himself as a running gag.

Morgan did not mind being treated as a clown. He was being paid a fortune and, still in his early twenties, the idea of travelling around the world first class on expenses to be in the presence of pop and movie stars held immense appeal. Another part of his approach was to slag off the man he came to replace as "editor" of the Bizarre page – the much more rock-star-like Rick Sky who had moved to the *Mirror*. When the two of them appeared on "Noel's House Party" (this was the Mr Blobby era) in tribute to their status as minor and slightly famous-for-being-famous celebrities as "enemies" Morgan was delighted to find that the audience voted to throw him and not Sky into the Gunge Tank as the man they most hated.

On the back of the success of the Bizarre column Murdoch personally offered Morgan the temporary editorship of the *News of the World* after the incumbent, Patsy Chapman (a former knitting magazine journalist and Page Three caption writer), fell ill. He was 28 years old – the youngest editor of a national newspaper since Cudlipp took on the *Sunday Pictorial* at the age of 24 in 1937. But, despite his Champagne Charlie image as "Friend of the Stars", Morgan had a most un-Cudlippian attitude to booze. One of his first acts as editor was to put up a sign in the *News of the World* office saying that lunch should be limited to an hour and drinking should be moderate. When Morgan, with the guidance of his old mentor Kelvin MacKenzie, showed an aptitude for the *News of the World's* agenda of "corn and porn" he was confirmed in the post, where he stayed for four years before moving to the *Mirror*. "I owe it all to Kelvin," Morgan said when he got the *News of the World* job. "He's always been there for me."

By this time MacKenzie had left the *Sun* and was working as a senior manager and the "British face" of Murdoch's essentially American domi-nated and Australian-run Sky TV. The two men remained in contact, since they were still both working for Murdoch's News International, with MacKenzie keen to inject some *News of the World*-type scandal into the staid Sky News channel. Morgan was credited with "revitalising" the *News of the World* by moving it away from plain and simple sleaze towards a more celebrity and "glamour-led" approach. "Some of the massage parlour tarts," Morgan said in an interview, "look utterly horrendous. So I have a simple philosophy – make them appealing. It is a sexy newspaper, because that's what people obviously want. But it should be glamorous too." His scoops included Princess Diana's sexy phone calls from Oliver Hoare (justification – the state of the Monarchy), Defence Chief Sir Peter Harding's luxurious high-life affair with the ever so glamorous Bienvenida Buck (hypocrisy – British troops were enduring the horrors of the first Gulf War at the time) and Conservative minister David Mellor's affair with Lady Penelope Cobham (which needed to be exposed because he was a married man and part of the "back to basics" moralising John Major government) plus a whole host of other "world exclusives", many of them purchased off the peg from Max Clifford, who boasted: "Unlike other editors I can get him on the phone any time. There's no question of being put off until tomorrow."

Morgan arrived at the *Mirror* aged 30, planning to turn the paper into a more "aspirational" version of the *Sun*. "It's well known that the *Mirror* used to outsell the *Sun* comfortably," he said at the time, adding: "That has now been reversed and my job is to get back to where we used to be." It was destined to be a tough task. Under Banks, the *Sun* had stretched its lead over the *Mirror* to 1.5 million. The Wapping paper was back over four million and the *Mirror* was stuck under 2.5 million. Morgan's answer was to provide a riot of raucous, screaming, *Sun*-style headlines, acres of bought-in royal and celebrity "exclusives" and horrific shock-tactic front pages illustrating a not-very-sincere-looking campaign against crime. One poster front page featured the smashed-in face of an elderly victim of mugging; another showed a man with a knife sticking out of the back of his head. Morgan renamed the paper the *Mirror*, dropping the "*Daily*" which, he thought, was too up-market. The "*Mirror*" sounded and looked graphically more like the "*Sun*".

Bingo normally accompanied a dive down-market like this. But this time Monty's cuts meant it could not be afforded, and there was no need anyway – the paper instead majored on the recently launched National Lottery. "Readers can't get enough of the lottery," Morgan explained. "Nine out of ten people play it." A *Mirror* reporter was assigned to get a lottery story every day and even had his name changed by deed poll to Lenny Lottery.

With the "aspirational" needs of the readers catered for by the lottery, Morgan turned his attention to upping the paper's Princess Diana content, which was still believed to work sales magic. Morgan printed pictures of her almost daily, becoming one of the best clients of the paparazzi of any national editor. One picture of the princess – showing her in tears after being chased along the street by a group of photographers – broke new ground for the *Mirror*. It was the first known example of the paper printing a picture that the *Sun* had turned down on the grounds of bad taste.

Politics was of course down played, partly because it was reckoned to be a sales turn-off and partly because Morgan was a convinced "Thatcherite" and as such was completely out of sorts with the remains of the paper's attachment to the Labour cause. Politics would feature mainly as a source of rude and funny personal attacks on better-known and more ridiculous Tory personalities. Thus, when the story went round of how a female prisoner in Holloway jail had given birth while wearing handcuffs in the prison bed, Morgan filled the front page showing Prisons' Minister Ann Widdecombe's head montaged on to the body of a pregnant woman in chains.

The *Mirror* old guard looked on with horror. Cudlipp was quoted as saying that he could not read the paper and hated what it had become. *Private Eye* magazine, where Paul Foot had taken a version of his old *Mirror* column, gave Morgan the nicknames "Piers Gormless" and "Piers Moron" – a reference back to his days as the inanely smiling Bizarre "Friend of the Stars" had apparent difficulty in handling political and other serious stories. Some detected the influence of Morgan's old mentor Kelvin MacKenzie, who had been hired by Monty to set up and run the *Mirror*'s television wing based around the faltering L!ve TV cable channel he had set up with yoof TV inventor and rejected BBC culture chief Janet Street-Porter. "The mantra of Kelvin MacKenzie's *Sun* has become the *Mirror*'s creed," Mike Molloy wrote of his old paper's fate under Morgan. "Respect for the truth is regarded simply as the posturing of pompous prats too snobbish to admit that journalism is merely another branch of the entertainment industry." The skill and craft had gone out of the paper's journalism, Molloy continued. "The carefully crafted piece has given way to an assemblage of sound-bites. Each day reality yields to the triumphs and excesses of a sub-world inhabited by Stringfellow celebrities." Morgan's *Mirror* was "mired in sexual trivia" where "hunting for a good article" was an "exhausting task". The paper's design was especially awful, Molloy wrote. It was a jumble of sections resulting "not in excitement, but the kind of chaos children produce at Christmas when they've torn open the presents and left the wrappings all over the floor".

But from the critics' point of view there was worse to come. During the June 1996 "Football's Coming Home" European Football Championship in England, Morgan got behind the England team with a stream of xenophobic taunts aimed at rival national teams. There was much tut-tutting when the *Mirror* marked an England-Spain fixture with a feature entitled "10 Nasties Spain's Given Europe" – a list which included syphilis, flu and the Inquisition. That was bad enough for the critics but then Morgan outdid even the *Sun* when England reached the semi-finals and found themselves up against Germany. The *Mirror* appeared with a poster front page dominated by the headline ACHTUNG! SURRENDER! FOR YOU FRITZ ZE EURO CHAMPIONSHIP IS OVER. The page was illustrated with pictures of Paul Gascoigne and Teddy Sheringham wearing tin helmets. Elsewhere, the paper ran the headline THE *MIRROR* DECLARES FOOTBALL WAR ON GERMANY. The over-the-top approach was supported by a *Mirror*-sponsored army surplus "tank" (actually an armoured car), which was stopped by police on the M25 on its way to the German team's hotel. Morgan later revealed that he had "come within twenty minutes" of also hiring a Spitfire to buzz the German training camp and drop copies of the *Mirror* on the players and ordering a second *Mirror* "tank" to invade the Berlin offices of *Bild*, the leading German tabloid. But he thought better of it.

The cheerful nonsense of ACHTUNG! SURRENDER! had been intended as a joke and was exactly the sort of thing that had brought the *Sun* such sales success under MacKenzie (who had previously used virtually the same headline at the *Sun*). But it was a bad misjudgement to try the same tactics with the *Mirror*. The *Sun* had, anyway, moved on. Instead of going in for national insults it had played the story fairly straight and distributed patriotic paper hats to football fans and called on them to be peaceful. It was a source of patriotic national pride that the far-right hooligan element often associated with the England team had not turned up for Euro '96. The *Mirror* seemed to be inciting them and echoing one of the racists' favourite World War Two-themed chants – IF IT WASN'T FOR THE BRITS YOU'D BE A KRAUT – usually aimed at other European teams. It also meant that Morgan had again placed the *Mirror* in a more down-market position, in this case looking more like the *Daily Star,* which was likewise banging on about the CHEATING KRAUTS.

Morgan also became something of a laughing stock when a *Mirror* reporter got hold of leaked Budget papers. Instead of printing what could have been the political scoop of the decade, Morgan returned them saying sometimes that he thought the papers might have been a hoax and at other times that he did not want to cause panic in the City. Most people simply thought that he had bottled it because he was out of his depth.

To crown all, just before the June 1996 Euro Championship, Morgan had allowed the *Mirror*'s famous red logo and the entire front page to be printed in blue as a full-page advertisement for Pepsi Cola's "It's New. It's Blue. It's for You" campaign. The move must have made a mighty contribution to the *Mirror*'s ad income. But it was a PR disaster – it was impossible to take seriously a newspaper that would change its very identity in return for a cash payment. When he saw the Pepsi Cola issue Cudlipp declared the paper to be close to death.

The *Mirror* had "sold its tortured soul" Cudlipp wrote. After selling its front page to an advertiser, there was only one way to go. Any day now, he predicted, the *Mirror* in the same spirit would be "printed on soft white paper, perforated…

… in homage for a day to Andrex."

29 "FILL YER BOOTS"

It was meant to be the tabloid story of the decade – maybe the century. The hunt was on to find out who Diana Princess of Wales would take as a partner after her separation from Charles, the announcement of their impending divorce and her baring all, emotionally speaking, on "Panorama".

First into the fray was the *Sunday Mirror*, where Monty authorised the payment of £300,000 to paparazzi who had come up with a smudgy telephoto lens picture of Diana kissing Dodi Fayed – son of Harrods' owner Mohammed Fayed – on the deck of his luxury yacht during a Mediterranean cruise. With money like that on the table and a bidding war going between Wapping and Canary Wharf, the photographers went into overdrive, following Diana's every move with even greater intensity. It came therefore as no surprise that plenty of photographers were on the scene instantly on the night of August 30–31, 1997, when a car carrying Dodi and Diana through Paris crashed, killing them both.

The death of the Princess caused a massive outpouring of national grief, whipped up into something like hysteria by non-stop rolling TV news coverage. At the same time, there was widespread disgust that the paparazzi had been there taking pictures when, it was discovered, the Princess was badly injured, but not yet dead. At one point, there was even an (untrue) story circulated that the photographers – now routinely branded "thugs on motorbikes" – delayed the calling of an ambulance so they could take more pictures.

The day after the accident, Diana's brother Earl Spencer made a trenchant speech – watched on TV by almost every single person in the country – saying that tabloid newspapers had made Diana's life a misery and were to a large extent responsible for her death. The editors and owners of the papers, Spencer said, had "blood on their hands" because of the way in which they "hounded" the princess and created a market for paparazzi pictures obtained by any means. Though he did not give names, Spencer must have had in mind Rupert Murdoch, owner of the *Sun* and the *News of the World,* which had started the trend for "intrusive" pictures of the royals in the 1980s. Also on the list would have been Kelvin MacKenzie, the man who had printed sneak beach pictures of Diana when she had been pregnant. MacKenzie was now installed on the board of the Mirror Group as managing director of Mirror Television and L!ve TV. Then there was Piers Morgan who, while still at the *News of the World,* had printed pictures of Diana's ailing mother, showing a degree of insensitivity which led even Murdoch to criticise him, and who had since made the *Mirror* the paparazzi's first port of call. And there was David Montgomery, who authorised the payment for the Dodi yacht pictures, and before that had bought the pictures of Diana in a leotard, exercising in her gym.

Spencer saw to it that all tabloid editors were excluded from Diana's funeral. Looking for somebody to blame for what was basically a pure accident, some of the crowds prompted on to the summer streets of London by the non-stop TV footage of people laying flowers began to turn ugly. Anger was turned toward the Royal family, which had refused to fly the flag above Buckingham Palace at half-mast or, generally, show much sympathy for the dead Princess. On another level, following Spencer's "blood on their hands" speech there were immediate demands for legal controls of some unspecified sort on the paparazzi and "tabloid intrusion". People queued up in large numbers on the endless TV vox pop and radio phone-in shows to denounce the papers and demand a boycott. At one point, a huge, spontaneous fall in tabloid newspaper circulations seemed to be on the cards – a consumer boycott that might do real and lasting damage.

In the event, just the opposite happened, just as it had after the Diana gym pictures affair. The special "Death of Diana" editions rushed out by all the papers sold in huge numbers. Even in death Diana remained the "Princess of Sales". The mention of her name, or the printing of her picture, could be reckoned to put on sales up to three years after her death. Monty, Kelvin and Piers had doubtless been shaken – however temporarily – by the strength of the anti-tabloid feeling in the wake of Diana's funeral. But they had already decided that it was time they "cleaned up their act", tore up the master plan once again and moved back up-market. The *Sun,* under its new editor Stuart Higgins, had been toned down, partly because of Rupert Murdoch's fear of a statutory privacy law, making the printing of confidential information illegal (such a law might have the effect of closing the *News of the World* down overnight), and partly because of his need to protect the image of Sky TV – the pay television system that was beginning to replace newspapers as the cornerstone of his media operations.

Morgan's original plunge down-market had not worked, anyway – it was impossible to "out-*Sun* the *Sun*" and ended up with disasters like ACHTUNG! SURRENDER! – which hit sales, advertising and corporate image all at the same time. Morgan now went on the record to say: "I've learnt over the last three years that *Mirror* readers are very different animals from *Sun* readers. I might have got away with the 'Achtung! Surrender!' stuff on the *Sun,* but you can't get away with it on the *Mirror,* and I've learnt some valuable lessons."

The *Mirror* had loyally supported Blair and the Labour party at the 1997 general election shortly before Diana's death – but so had the *Sun.* Moreover, the *Mirror's* coverage of the election had been very thin and led by the paper's TV critic who treated the campaign like a month-long (and very boring) TV show. The *Mirror's* once massive political staff had been disposed of as a cost-cutting measure by Monty and the damage was now apparent. The game of treating politics like supporting a football team would no longer run once Blair was in power. Political coverage would have to amount to something subtler and more well informed than printing amusing put-downs or rude and funny pictures of Ann Widdecombe.

Monty had realised that he would have to spend more money investing in the content of the *Mirror* before a move back up-market could be contemplated, not least because this would mean competing more directly with the *Daily Mail* – ironically, the *Mirror's* one-time "serious" Northcliffe stable-mate – which was putting on circulation and starting to threaten the *Mirror's* position as the second-best-selling paper in the country. Monty authorised the spending of £16 million to "rejuvenate" the paper. Morgan was allowed to hire 40 journalists – including 22 "big name" columnists such as Tony Parsons, Brian Reade, Victor Lewis-Smith and the comedian Jo Brand (described by Morgan as great writers "in the tradition of Cassandra"). For the next two years, the *Mirror's* circulation stabilised at about 2.5 million, the gap with the *Sun* narrowed, but the *Daily Mail* began to catch up. The paper began to recover some of its reputation and Morgan was seen as a young editor with a lot of energy, whose mistakes in the first years after his arrival could be put down to inexperience. He was obviously getting help from MacKenzie, who had moved over from the disaster of Monty's L!ve TV cable channel (where he had pioneered "news bunny" – the first news bulletins to be presented by a man wearing a bunny rabbit costume) to become editorial director and thus Morgan's boss once again.

One of the innovations made by Morgan and MacKenzie was the introduction of the "City Slickers" share-tipping column – a popular feature given that the stock market was soaring and almost any tip was bound to come good. The two-man slicker team of Anil Bhoyrul and James Hipwell – slogan: "Fill Your Boots!" – appeared in the paper deliberately looking like spivvy barrow boys. In contrast to the boring and solid personal finance advice dished out in many other papers, the slickers tended to ignore the more stable but slow-growing blue-chip stocks and concentrated on the more risky "penny shares" where investment was much more of a gamble and – as it happened – extremely sensitive to newspaper articles… such as their own. The slicker column was to lead Morgan into immense trouble when he bought a large chunk of stock in Viglan, the computer firm set up by Alan Sugar (another new-wave, up-market *Mirror* columnist), which the very next day was hyped in the slickers column as "certain" to rise in price, thus in all probability creating a self-fulfilling prophecy. Morgan was accused of dishonesty and was censured by the Press Complaints Committee (its code of conduct says that journalists should not seek personal profit from financial information that comes their way) but was backed by the *Mirror* board, even though Bhoyrul and Hipwell were shown the door.

But, by then, David Montgomery had left Canary Wharf and the Mirror Group. The board of bankers who put him in charge saw the chance of get their money back and make a considerable profit by selling the company to Trinity, the owners of the *Liverpool Post* and a string of local newspapers throughout the UK. Trinity's chief executive Victor Graf had made it clear that they were not interested in the *Mirror* if Monty was still running it and so Montgomery was dumped by the moneymen as quickly as they had hired him. Monty was described as "an obstacle" to the takeover and so he had to go, comforted only by a pay-off worth about £1.4 million.

During his time in charge Monty was known to have made an additional £750,000 from cashing in share options. All of this was on top of his salary, which had grown with a series of pay rises to over £350,000 a year. All in all, Monty had earned about £5 million in return for his work with the Mirror Group titles. During his time, the *Mirror* had lost about 500,000 sales, the *Sunday Mirror* had lost almost 800,000 – more than one quarter of its total sales and the *People* had lost over 400,000 sales – about a fifth of its total pre-Monty sales. Monty disappeared from the *Mirror*, taking some of his associates with him. With Banks and Bridget "Death" Rowe, lately editor of the *Sunday Mirror* and others, he set up a company that aimed to install internet terminals in pubs. It was not a great success. Thereafter Monty was "on the float" and, as journalists realised, likely to turn up anywhere at any time in the future. The *Guardian* and *Observer* media expert Emily Bell, for example, claimed to have woken up sweating from a nightmare in which Monty had suddenly turned up on the *Observer* newsroom floor in a puff of smoke, announcing he was the new owner.

Monty's passing from the *Mirror* and – at least temporarily – from the national newspaper scene was not greatly mourned. Andrew Marr, who had worked for Monty as editor of the broadsheet *Independent*, which Monty had bought for the Mirror Group during one of the twists and turns in its market strategy, was withering.

"I hope he got a decent payoff," Marr said, "as he will do much less harm to the business counting his money than doing anything else."

And John Pilger spoke for many ex-*Mirror* journalists when he said that Montgomery had "come from obscurity" and had perhaps returned there for good. Montgomery, Pilger said, "was one of those who brought the virus of Murdoch-ism to the *Daily Mirror* and amassed a personal fortune in the process.

"This was an anti-journalism that helped deliver what appears to be the *coup de grâce* to a once great newspaper."

30 WAR ON THE WORLD

Piers Morgan and the *Mirror* were well placed to do a first-class reporting job on the September 11, 2001 terrorist attacks on the World Trade Center and the Pentagon.

Morgan had already been strengthening his news team and had started to move away from the non-stop, TV tie-in and celebrity agenda where he was being heavily beaten by the *Sun*. At a professional level "9/11" presented Morgan and the *Mirror* with chance to get stuck into a massive, visually-led news story that would allow it to recapture some of its old glory as a hard-hitting "picture paper".

There were plenty of issues where Morgan could have slipped up, repeating some the errors of his early years as editor. Instead, he and his team rose to the occasion. The front page was given over to a foldout poster-type design with a picture of the exploding World Trade Center and the words TOTAL WAR. The paper had 23 more pages of pictures and dozens of reports, covering every angle from the confessional human-interest stories of attack survivors to hard news about diplomatic reaction from around the world. A full-page picture of people jumping to their deaths from the windows of burning building carried the headline WE ARE ALL F★★★ING DYING IN HERE. All the time, Morgan and the reporting team were looking out of the windows of their offices in Canary Wharf. At one point it was thought that the building – the tallest in London and a symbol of Western power almost as potent as the World Trade Center – might have to be evacuated as a possible additional terrorist target. Instead, the government grounded all flights over London, lifting the immediate threat.

The *Mirror* resisted the temptation to exaggerate the scale of the attack, speculate too wildly about the likely perpetrators or call for the Western military to lash out. This was in contrast with Murdoch media in particular. Shortly after the attacks, Murdoch's Sky News Channel came back from an ad break to announce: "The whole of the eastern seaboard of the United States of America is under sustained military attack" and speculated wildly about the identity and whereabouts of the terrorists. The *Mirror*, which did have the advantage of a couple of hours to get its act together, moderately reported that Osama bin Laden had been identified "almost certainly" as the mastermind of the attack. A carefully written leading article was headed IT'S TIME FOR REASON NOT RETRIBUTION and warned that any hasty military action could provoke further attacks on the US and Britain.

Former *Mirror* editor Roy Greenslade, who had been withering about Morgan's earlier performance, now said his old paper had handled 9/11 "with an authority and polish that some people doubted was possible under Piers Morgan". Part of this critical success was down to the fact that the *Mirror*, having now drifted away from its close ties with the Labour leadership, was unique in not having to hesitate before squaring the political line with Downing Street and the White House. Murdoch's *Sun*, *Times* and Sky TV did not have this luxury – they were deeply ensnared in close political contacts with the American and British leaderships.

For twelve of the next thirteen days Morgan led the front page with uninhibited news about the "War on Terrorism" promised by George W Bush and Tony Blair in the wake of the Twin Towers attack. The *Mirror* was particularly strong on reporting "bio-terrorist" attacks in the US involving anthrax. As a result, Morgan claimed his paper had sold an extra 2.5 million copies – the biggest rise in sales attributable to a news event since the death of Diana.

Before September 11th the *Mirror* had been struggling to compete with the *Sun* on a tabloid agenda dominated in the summer of 2001 by one thing – the success of the reality-TV game show "Big Brother". The *Sun* had a bigger chequebook with which to buy up the confessional memoirs of game-show winners and losers and beat the *Mirror* every time. The *Sun* had increased its daily sale by almost 200,000 by devoting its front page to "Big Brother" mania – relieved only by the occasional off-the-wall scoop such as a front-page picture of the actual bright yellow rubber duck the Queen supposedly had in her bath. Morgan said that he decided to stop trying to compete in the celebrity stakes when he was asked to pay £300,000 – enough money to employ ten investigative journalists for a year – just for a single interview with a temporary "Big Brother" micro-celebrity called Helen, who was a hairdresser from Swansea. He was also fed up by the growing arrogance of show-business PRs, who now expected the papers to give them money and free *Hello*-style advertising (despite the fact Morgan had personally pioneered exactly these sorts of practices on his notoriously PR-ridden Bizarre column in the *Sun*).

Morgan's Road of Damascus conversion came, he claimed, when an unusually snotty PR working for low-luminosity TV celebs Richard and

Judy had demanded "copy approval" of an article as the price of "access" for a *Mirror* photographer and interviewer. The *Mirror's* 1,000-word piece, Morgan said, had been "pretty positive" but the PR person rewrote 800 words, turning the article into nothing more than a publicity hand-out. Morgan cancelled the deal and announced a new policy – no more "copy approval". Stars would grant interviews on the *Mirror's* terms or they would not take place at all. At the same time, Morgan had launched the "3 a.m. Girls" section of the paper, in the style of "underground" anti-PR websites like PopBitch and designed to be the "scourge of celebs", filled with unauthorised articles about their foibles. The feature was a re-run of Morgan's old Bizarre column, but whereas Morgan had been "Friend of the Stars", 3 a.m.'s three female reporters were officially something more like "enemies of the stars". 3 a.m. girl Jessica Callan claimed in a newspaper interview: "Celebrities fear us. If they are at parties surrounded by PR people and they meet us, something clicks. They're usually drunk or on drugs, and they lose it. It's just brilliant."

Now, after September 11th, even the *Sun* had been forced to fight on the more level playing field of hard news reporting and the *Mirror* was, at least for the moment, starting to win the battle. Morgan was so exhilarated by the *Mirror's* coverage of the Twin Towers that he told a meeting of the Society of Editors that "a change of culture" had taken place among the readers of popular papers, meaning that "the era of Big Brother splash front pages is over". His evidence for the change was that he now heard *Daily Mirror* secretaries "talking about anthrax, not EastEnders; Bin Laden, not Robbie Williams; the terrain of northern Afghanistan, not their next holiday in Crete". Morgan concluded: "There is a sudden and prolonged hunger for serious news and information." He said that journalists at the *Mirror* were "in shock" after discovering that serious news "was not only exhilarating to produce, but sells a lot of newspapers".

But, only one month later, Morgan came down to earth with a thump. The sales increase after September 11th had turned out to be a purely temporary phenomenon as the majority of readers slowly got bored with war news and began to demand the reassuring normality of ordinary TV and celeb trivia news. One consolation was that, as the relentless fall in month-on-month and year-on-year sales figures resumed, the *Sun* was losing readers at a slightly faster rate. This might have meant that at least a few tens or hundreds of thousands of readers – certainly not millions – had been attracted by the new "serious" approach. More ominously, the *Daily Mail* had held on to the 100,000 extra sales it had added to its total in the weeks after September 11th – leading to the theory that these were refugees fleeing the *Mirror*, *Sun* and possibly even broadsheet saturation terrorism news in search of light relief. Once again, the circulation game resembled the alarming process of receiving a blood transfusion while bleeding from the jugular – if you pumped in more readers than you lost, you were OK. If you lost them more quickly than you recruited fresh blood, you were in trouble.

The new "serious" direction taken by the *Mirror* was underlined in March 2002 with the official re-launch of the paper as a "mid-market" paper. The change was symbolised by the replacement of the paper's "red top" logo with a more up-market, tastefully designed, black-and-white *Daily Mirror* standing head. The move was announced by Philip Graf, the man who had replaced Montgomery as head of the merged Trinity-Mirror company, who revealed that management consultants had been recommending a move up-market even before September 11th. Research, Graf said, showed that there was a total of 21 million potential tabloid readers in the country, but only about half a million were ever inclined to switch between papers. Most of the rises and falls in circulation took place when people who already thought of themselves as *Mirror* readers started or stopped buying the paper more regularly.

It therefore made no sense for the *Mirror* to try to make the paper appealing to *Sun* readers, Graf reasoned. Very few of them could be persuaded to abandon the habit of a lifetime and the more likely result would be to irritate existing *Mirror* readers, causing them to buy the paper less frequently or give up reading altogether. "There is a different set of values between *Sun* and *Mirror* readers," Graf claimed. "We are in the same part of the market, but not fighting over the same readers."

Graf then appeared to promptly contradict himself by suggesting Morgan should copy some of the style of the *Daily Mail* – the most successful paper in terms of increased circulation. "We are developing a strong brand of our own," Graf said. "That brand is quite radical and campaigning. I suppose we are a *Daily Mail* with a heart and slightly more compassion." So, after the failed attempt at being a "left-wing *Sun*", the new order of the day was to become a "left-wing *Daily Mail*" – a bizarre and mind-bending idea.

Morgan explained the change in direction in more colourful terms. "I gave up the rampaging *News of the World* for the rotting, dismembered carcass of the stricken *Daily Mirror*," he said, "convinced that turning it around would be a piece of cake. But my early strategy of trying to out-*Sun* the *Sun* was not a brilliant success. In fact it was virtually a total disaster, culminating in Achtung! Surrender! and enough opprobrium to wilt a forest of oak trees." He added that he had at first "served up buckets of trashy, racy, celeb-driven scandal and sleaze". *Mirror* readers had not wanted that. Now the transformation was so complete that the *Mirror*, Morgan insisted, was in many ways a more serious newspaper than the broadsheets and chattering-class journals that had once lambasted him as "Piers Moron".

After September 11th the *Mirror* had deployed the largest number of journalists of any British newspaper – including *The Times* and the *Telegraph* – to cover the War on Terrorism. Left-wing broadsheet columnists like Miranda Sawyer, Jonathan Freeland and Christopher Hitchens were brought in to write great screeds criticising or analysing Western policy and, especially, the bombing of Afghanistan.

Even John Pilger was invited back on board, billed as "the legendary campaigning journalist". A matter of months before, when Monty was still stalking Canary Wharf, Morgan had denounced Pilger scathingly as a has-been who had helped the *Mirror* lose two million readers. Pilger, for his part, had denounced Morgan as the man who delivered the deathblow to the paper. Now Pilger and Morgan were working together again. Pilger was given acres of space in the paper to attack Western policy, creating just the sort of controversy Morgan wanted. After years of trivia and irrelevance, the paper was being talked about again as a serious, if minority and oppositional, player in the national debate.

Meanwhile, the *Mirror*'s front page had been given over to coverage of foreign news for 50 days on the trot and the agenda had expanded from Osama bin Laden and the bombing of Afghanistan to the only comprehensive front page reporting of the famine in Malawi. The first front page to be published without the red logo was an austere affair – a big picture of Osama bin Laden with the hectoring headline: THINK HE'S DEAD – THINK AGAIN. This was followed by two more days of foreign and political front pages before something more like normal service was restored – the 3am team's exposé alongside the *News of the World*, of the affair between England football manager Sven Goran Eriksson and Ulrika Johnson, which jostled schizophrenically on the front page with international terrorism; exposés of domestic British fascism and pictures of bumtastic Kylie Minogue in her underwear advertising free pop CD giveaways.

All the talk of armies of young readers hungry for information and hard news on the big issues reminded those with longer memories of the research that Cudlipp and King had done prior to the launch of Mirroscope and the old IPC *Sun*. The *Mirror* was now targeting the same "steak-eating weekenders" – the illusive mass of upwardly mobile, better-educated and more discriminating, classless "pace-setter" tabloid audience first identified in the early 1960s and then vaguely tracked by Monty at *Today*. But now, instead of steak-eating and enjoyment of package holidays, the year 2000 version pace-setters could, according to Morgan, be identified by their ownership of "DVD players and flashy cars" and their spending on "foreign holidays in far-flung places like Thailand and

Australia, dining out and drinking nice wine". Morgan said that this "new working class" had "nudged ever closer to what their parents would have deemed middle class in the 1960s. "It has been one of the most dramatic shifts in history," Morgan said, "but the *Mirror* really has just sat back and watched it happen".

The winners had been those papers who had catered for these people, including broadsheets like the *Guardian* and the *Times,* which had moved slightly down-market, introducing "Qual-oid" (Quality-Tabloid) or possibly "Tab-sheet" (Tabloid-Broadsheet) sections with odd names like *G2, T2, The Information* and so on. But the main winner had been the *Daily Mail,* which had locked on to the modern pace-setters, especially young female white-collar, New University-educated, DVD-owning, long-haul, wine-drinking car-owners. Morgan said the *Mirror* was going to make itself appealing to thrusting young women (much beloved of advertisers because of their free-spending ways). "We've targeted young feisty career women," Morgan said, "aware that they are now buying papers in massively larger numbers than their mothers' generation."

One result was the launch of *"M"* magazine, a version of a glossy weekly women's magazine, to be given away free with the paper mid-week. Another was the nomination of the *Mirror* as "Newspaper of the Year" at the official industry awards ceremony. After this, former critics like Mike Molloy – who had denounced Morgan's paper as looking and reading like waste wrapping paper – started purring. Molloy, writing in the *Evening Standard*, now placed Morgan in the pantheon of greatest-ever journalists. "Newspapers may achieve many forms of excellence as journalistic products," Molloy wrote. "But there is no substitute for an editor who shares a mystic harmony with his readers. Arthur Christiansen had it with the *Daily Express*; David English with the *Daily Mail*; Harry Evans with *The Sunday Times* and Larry Lamb and Kelvin MacKenzie with the *Sun*. Now, I think Piers Morgan has found it with today's *Mirror*."

The move up-market and the new importance given to politics led the paper to fall out with the New Labour leadership, which had formed a close, if uneasy, alliance with Murdoch's bigger-selling *Sun* – reckoned to be more influential with voters who had switched from the Conservatives and therefore held the key to the party staying in power. Once Montgomery had gone, there was a chance to rebuild bridges with Alastair Campbell, the emotionally charged former *Mirror* political editor who Monty had sacked and who was now the Prime Minister's press officer. But the relationship was not well handled. Morgan was annoyed that Campbell would feed exclusives to the *Sun* first – as the price of maintaining the paper's editorial support – and tended to take the *Mirror* for granted.

When Morgan responded by attacking Labour policy on a range of issues, Campbell complained that Morgan was showing his true colours as an anti-Labour man. The *Mirror* was accused of being "off-message" and "disloyal". Morgan responded by saying that the *Mirror* should have been off-message years before, echoing Monty's old criticism that the paper's support for the party had become "stale" and boring. "Supporting Labour is one thing," Morgan wrote, "but carrying on the almost evangelical arse-licking when they are running the country is totally self-defeating. It had got to the stage where whatever we wrote about Labour was perceived as spoon-fed propaganda from Downing Street. Nobody paid any attention to us, and nobody cared what we had to say. And it had been like that for two decades."

There were further problems troubling the relations between the government and the *Mirror*. The paper's political editor Paul Routledge was aligned with a more "old Labour"-type faction inside the Labour party, gathered around the Chancellor Gordon Brown. His biography and continuing investigations into the activities of Peter Mandelson, the very architect of New Labour and Blair's electoral success, had caused the government enormous embarrassment and that did not make the relationship run smoothly. Before that, Morgan himself, when editor of the *News of the World,* had earned the eternal hostility of the Labour leadership for having "outed" Mandelson as gay, by interviewing a former lover in a classic (horrible) kiss'n' tell sting.

The Conservative-supporting journalist Peter Oborne, Campbell's unofficial biographer, claimed that Campbell had "stitched up" the *Mirror* on at least one occasion as part of a plan to exact revenge. The paper had asked Campbell to get Bill Clinton to put his name to a "ghosted" *Mirror* opinion peace, backing the peace process in Northern Ireland. Campbell told the *Mirror* that the draft article was fine, but he would need 24 hours to make some small changes. The article – cleared with Clinton – was then given as a free gift to the *Sun*. Morgan, apoplectic, went to see Campbell in person, who apologised, claiming there had been an innocent error. According to Oborne, Campbell had said: "I did it for peace." Morgan retorted: "Sure, peace with Murdoch."

Despite all this, the *Mirror* stayed loyal to Labour in the May 2001 general election – the most boring electoral contest in living memory, with a record low turnout and enlivened only by John Prescott's fistfight with a Tory heckler in north Wales. The *Mirror* kicked off its campaign coverage by calling the Tories "bird brains" because of their confused tax-cut policies. Political coverage became mainly a matter of levelling jokey insults at Tory personalities – leader William Hague was transformed into "Bridget Hague" – based on the hit "chick-lit" sensation *Bridget Jones's Diary*. His diary was full of despairing comments like "Blair made good speech about the Euro. V. Bad. Oh My God, feel so crushed". Morgan confirmed their pro-Labour stance. "In the run-up to the election, the *Mirror* will be somewhere north of *Pravda*," he said. "I have told Tony and Alastair that we are absolutely four-square behind them. I am proud to admit that we shall be unashamedly biased and partisan."

But as the world adjusted to permanent war after September 11th, the *Mirror*'s political stance, first against the bombing of Afghanistan and then against the war in Iraq, became increasingly unpopular and sales began to slip. On September 10, 2002, the day before the first anniversary of the Twin Towers attack, Morgan broke his vow that he would never again lead the paper with celebrity "reality TV" news. The edition's front page was devoted entirely to a picture of Tony Blackburn, the star of "I'm a Celebrity Get Me Out of Here", flagging up a "*Mirror* exclusive" interview with the ageing DJ. The day after, the paper was, of course, devoted to the anniversary, with a long and increasingly repetitive tirade against Anglo-American policy.

In February and March 2003, the *Mirror* backed the mass demonstrations against the war in Iraq and when, in the first few days of the war, things seemed to be going badly for British and American forces, the paper announced that Blair had blown it and should resign at once. The headline on Paul Routledge's political column was FACE IT TONY... YOU'RE FINISHED.

"It is over," Routledge wrote. "The Blair decade, which has dominated British politics since the death of John Smith, is moving to a close." The paper called Blair an "American puppet" and a "Yankee Poodle Dandy", likening him to Ferdinand Marcos: "the corrupt US puppet ruler of the Philippines was strong, until people-power dethroned him."

Shooting from the hip, Morgan sanctioned one front page showing Tony Blair's hands dripping with blood and another juxtaposing an idiotic, smiling picture of President Bush next to a bombed-out civilian marketplace in Baghdad with the headline HE LOVES IT. Commentators like Roy Greenslade, who had praised Morgan for his adoption of a "serious" agenda, now queued up to complain that he was out of his depth after all. His anti-war front pages were wildly over the top. They might have been all right as student union posters, but as effective political propaganda or circulation-building sensationalism they did not work at all. Rupert Murdoch – whose entire media empire around the world had been thrown wholeheartedly into the propaganda battle against Iraq – sent Morgan a specially made souvenir "mock" *Sun* front page showing the *Mirror* editor's head superimposed on top of the tumbling statue of Saddam Hussein with the strap-line: "Another Shady Regime is Set to Topple".

After the war, Morgan appeared once again to say that he had got it wrong and to apologise to the nation. It was getting to be a habit – not that readers seemed to be much interested. As Morgan told the *Financial Times*: "I've never seen anything like it. Lots of the public were against the war before it started, but then there was a huge swing during the war – after four or five days of healthy sales, we actually fell off a cliff." The *Mirror's* circulation had fallen to below two million for the first time since the 1930s when Bartholomew, Cudlipp and King had seized control of the paper from Rothermere's placemen.

In March 2003, Morgan appeared before one of the periodic meetings of the Parliamentary select committee dealing with proposals for media regulation. The *Mirror* editor told the MPs that popular newspapers had been "pretty lawless" in the mid-1980s when he had first arrived in Fleet Street. But self-regulation had worked, and they were – if anything – too respectful these days, especially towards "greedy, grasping celebrities on a mission to make a fast buck". Morgan had lately been involved in an expensive legal battle with Naomi Campbell who had sued for invasion of privacy when the paper revealed that she was visiting a drug rehabilitation group.

"Things have moved on so far it is almost impossible to imagine how you could put any more regulations in place to improve it," Morgan said.

For the *Mirror*, at least, the lawless days were well and truly over.

31 TABLOID NATION

Two miles up the River Thames from the Canary Wharf headquarters of the *Mirror,* Richard Desmond is raging at his senior staff in a conference room high up in the office block of the *Daily Express,* nicknamed the Grey Lubyanka in tribute to the former KGB Moscow torture complex.

Desmond's wiry, animated body is framed by the *Express's* multi-million-dollar view over the Thames at Blackfriars. His speech and list of complaints is endless and foul-mouthed – fuck this, fuck that, *fuck you...* The latest in a long line of macho newspaper bullies, Desmond glories in his reputation as a hard-man, famous for once having locked a women employee in a cupboard as a form of punishment after she was late for a meeting.

The tirade stops only when Desmond pauses to draw breath and munch on a banana – one of an unending series brought into the room by his personal waiter and delivered each time on a silver plate. Then he is off again, spraying banana debris all over the boardroom table.

The *Daily Express* never really recovered from the death of Lord Beaverbrook at a crucial moment in 1964. In that year the *Mirror* reached its milestone/millstone of selling more than five million copies every day and – ruling supreme in Tabloid Nation – had started to move out from its circulation heartlands in the north and on the council estates, attempting with some success to attract *Express* readers in the suburbs. At the same time the *Express* started losing even more readers to the steadily improving *Daily Mail,* at last recovering from the damage inflicted upon it by the first Lord Rothermere.

The *Express* of the late 1960s and 1970s was a newspaper out of time, suffering the same problems of ageing readership and a backward-looking "golden age" culture that was to allegedly afflict the *Mirror* in the 1970s and 1980s. But the crisis at the *Express* was even worse. Falls in circulation were relentless and all hope that things could be improved evaporated.

In 1977 the leaderless and enfeebled *Express* was bought by the

Trafalgar House construction and shipping concern – a move that in some ways mirrored the takeover of the *Mirror* by Reed International. Like the *Mirror*, the *Express* suffered the dead hand of arbitrary corporate control combined with half-hearted re-launches, attempted moves up and down market, gimmicks and rapid turnover in the editor's chair. The only consistent thing about the *Express* in the 1970s and 1980s was its slavish support for the Conservative party and Margaret Thatcher. But the *Express* had no monopoly on the delights of "Thatcherism" and its support for the Conservatives was as knee-jerk, stale, unreasonable and uninspired as the *Mirror's* support for Labour sometimes was.

The paper was brilliantly satirised in the 1980s in John Cooper-Clarke's poem "Never Seen a Nipple in the *Daily Express*":

> *This paper's boring, mindless, mean*
> *Full of pornography, the kind that's clean*
> *Where William Hickey meets Michael Caine*
> *Again and Again and Again*
> *I've seen millionaires on the DHSS*
> *But I've never seen a nipple in the Daily Express*

In 1996 the paper was sold to Lord Clive Hollick, the New Labour financier who had left the board of the *Mirror* after first recruiting and then falling out with David Montgomery. The *Express* was turned inside out during the brief period of Hollick's ownership.

The paper's political line was abruptly changed from Conservative to New Labour. More amazingly, the *Express's* "never see a nipple" cultural agenda was transformed by the new editor Rosie Boycott, one of the founders of the *Spare Rib* feminist journalism collective who, at the time, was best known for campaigning for the legalisation of cannabis. Hollick's strategy of bombarding the ancient, Conservative-voting core readership of the *Express* with 100%-proof New Labour propaganda, relieved only by intermittent campaigns for gay rights and the legalisation of soft drugs, did not work. The losses were so large that in 2000 Hollick put the paper up for sale and the only realistic buyer was Richard Desmond, the owner of *OK!* magazine, a string of porn magazines and a porn cable-TV channel.

Desmond had started in publishing selling adverts for *Meat Trades Journal,* which by the early 1970s had provided him with enough money to buy two independent record shops. In 1974 he launched a music magazine called *International Musician.* The title enabled him to learn about the magazine and distributions industries, where he quickly realised the huge profit to be made in porn. In 1982, Desmond acquired the licence to produce the American porn title *Penthouse*. Within a few years, what was to become Desmond's publishing company Northern and Shell was producing a range of magazines with titles like *Asian Babes, Horny Housewives, 40 Plus, Big and Black, Big Ones International, Double Sex Action* and *Spunk-Loving Sluts*.

Much of the profit from these magazines came, not from the cover price, most of which had to be given to the retailer as a sort of bribe for stocking such repellent material, but from advertising for videos and premium-rate phone lines, which contained much "harder" sexual material.

In 1991, Desmond's sales of advertising space in his magazines to phone-line operators led him, according to newspaper reports, to form a business relationship with American sex-industry businessman Richard Martino ("Ricci from the Bronx"), also a New York gangland figure convicted of attempted robbery and assault. Martino bought a block of £1-million worth of ad space in Desmond's UK porn titles for his phone lines. But, according to the *Observer* and the BBC investigative journalist John Sweeney, when the phone ads failed to yield enough money Martino's associates came to London and demanded repayment of the £1 million they had spent on advertising, plus a further million in compensation. Desmond stalled and sent his managing director Philip Bailey to New York to smooth things over. Bailey, entirely innocent himself, claimed that, when he arrived for the meeting, he was abducted, forced into a car, stripped, tortured by means of having a cattle prod applied to his testicles, told to bring Desmond and £2 million in cash to New York and then dumped on the pavement. Eventually, according to the former secretary of Desmond's publishing company James Brown (himself convicted in 1987 for threatening witnesses with a shot gun during a court case), a meeting was held in a London restaurant during which he and Desmond handed over the cash in a collection of sports bags. Desmond himself emphatically denies ever having paid any money to criminals or having had any dealings with them.[52]

Desmond decided to start easing his way out of the sex industry, eventually putting his porn mags (though not his cable channel) up for sale, using the profits and expertise he had amassed in order to launch *OK!* magazine – a new-wave glossy weekly celebrity magazine that remains the cornerstone of his fledgling media empire. *OK!* was designed as a straightforward clone of *Hello!* – the publishing sensation of the early 1990s. *Hello!* had come from nowhere to reach a peak circulation of over half a million a week with a formula of simple posed pictures and sugary interviews with TV stars. After a decade of "bonk journalism" – the endless tabloid hunt led by Kelvin MacKenzie's *Sun* and Piers Morgan's *News of the World* for "kiss'n' tell" scandal – celebs and their increasingly influential PRs loved the 100 per cent positive coverage they got in *Hello!* Readers liked it too, since it used the successful formula of allowing them to think they were part of a big cosy club of successful and aspiring "beautiful people".

Desmond launched *OK!* as a direct competitor to *Hello!*. Suddenly it was raining money for celebs and PR agents as the two magazines battled each week in a series of bidding wars to obtain exclusive rights to such earth-shattering events as the marriage of Anthea Turner. By targeting TV soap stars and a British celebs, rather than the European aristocrats favoured by *Hello!* (because it also sold throughout Europe), *OK!* started to win the circulation war, which was as bitterly fought as any between the tabloids. At one point, as a form of psychological warfare, Desmond even launched a porn magazine called *Posh Wives*, designed and produced to look exactly like *Hello!* magazine, with models made up to look like aristocrats taking their clothes off against the backdrop of stately homes.

Desmond's success with *OK!,* in turn, brought fresh competitors into the field including *Heat* and *Now*, gearing a huge slice of the London media towards "celebrity journalism". The trend was soon followed by television, especially with the development of ultra-cheap "reality TV" shows like "Big Brother", promoted with tie-ins to the celeb magazines and extremely popular with the younger part of the popular audience. Soon the weekly glossy celeb mags had a circulation approaching two million, making them significant players and, eventually, forcing the financially enfeebled *Mirror* out of the celebrity chequebook interview game, hitting circulation and forcing its re-launch as a "serious-popular" or "Qualoid" (i.e., one unable to afford celebrity "buy-ups") newspaper.

Desmond's purchase of the *Express* group fitted perfectly with both his porn interests and with ownership of *OK!*. The *Express* had excellent "fit" with *OK!* – the cost of buying celebrity pictures could be shared and the two titles could be used to advertise each other. One of Desmond's first moves was to offer a "free copy" of *OK!* to anyone buying the *Daily Express* – a clever piece of accounting and a marketing ruse that turned *OK!* purchasers into instant *"Express* readers". It may have been the first case of, in effect, a daily newspaper being given away by a paid-for weekly colour magazine. The *Daily Mail* formed a similar, but unofficial, alliance with *Hello!,* which had the effect of expanding the *OK!* vs *Hello!* struggle to a battle between the *Express* and the *Mail* – with the *Mirror* left bleeding on the sidelines.

Desmond's purchase of the *Express* group brought with it the sex-orientated *Daily Star*. To a large extent, the economics of the *Star* were based on selling advertising space to the sex phone lines and so this was a business Desmond knew well. Whereas the *Daily Star* was way behind the *Sun* and the *Mirror* in circulation terms, the *Star's* online version, *MegaStar,* had by far the biggest audience of any tabloid website. *MegaStar* was launched in 1997 and became an immediate hit at a time when use of the internet was driven by demand for porn. Eventually, all the tabloids had internet versions – but they were ignominious failures, except for *Page Three Dot Com* which, like *MegaStar*, functioned by showing additional and more risqué pictures of the nude girls shown in the "shop front" of the newspapers themselves.

Under Desmond's care, the *Express, Star* and *MegaStar* started to increase circulation – pushed by heavy spending on TV adverts and by price-cutting. A new Sunday edition of the *Daily Star* sold at less than half the price of its obvious rival, the *Mirror* group's down-market *Sunday People*. Desmond paid for the cover price-cuts, continuing big "buy-ups" of celebrity stories and TV adverts by cutting the number of journalists producing his papers by almost a quarter, leaving the *Express* with roughly 100 fewer journalists than the *Mirror, Mail* or *Sun*. Some commentators said that newspapers with so few reporters were bound to fail and, journalistically, the results were often dire by anybody's standards. But, commercially, the picture was different.

There were strong increases in circulation and profits started to rise sharply by 2003 – even in the middle of a deep advertising recession. The sort of people who thought that British journalism had reached the bottom of the barrel with Rupert Murdoch (who had started with a similarly tiny stake in the British media in 1968) began to mentally psych themselves up for the possibility that Desmond was "the next Murdoch", who might end up dominating what remained of the British newspaper industry at some point in the future.

The battle for supremacy between electronic and printing technology in Tabloid Britain began with television. A critical moment was the 1969 moon landing, the first major event to be filmed and broadcast in real-time. Overnight, newspapers lost what had, since the invention of the telegraph machine a century earlier, been their unique selling point – that they were first with the news.

The tragedy for the *Mirror* was that this basic fact was either ignored by those in charge of the paper, or their response was muddled, or too late… or all of these things.

Murdoch's new *Sun,* in contrast, launched in the UK just a year after the moon landing, responded by carrying relatively little "conventional" news, realising that any readers who were interested could get their fill from the more or less non-stop series of news and current affairs programmes run every evening by the BBC-ITV duopoly.

While the *Mirror* and *Express* continued to quixotically concentrate on providing news to a saturated market, the *Sun* concentrated on providing the things that the highly regulated British TV system could not, or chose not, to provide – namely, soft porn (illegal on TV except very late at night), entertainingly extreme political bias (completely forbidden on TV by regulation), gambling (also forbidden), Royal Family gossip and insults (out of the question for the BBC and ITV), a huge amount of comment, criticism and leaks of plot lines from the soaps (impossible/suicidal for TV to do itself), endless TV comment, chat and criticism (not credible on TV itself), astrology (banned by regulators) and wall-to-wall coverage of sport, especially football (there was no live English league football on TV until the late 1980s).

By concentrating on these – to the exclusion of almost all else – the new and successful *Sun* formula slowly spread to all newspapers (including, to varying but increasing degrees, the broadsheets), which re-moulded themselves to live in the gaps and niches in national life that for one reason or another could not be dominated by television. All the papers became structured around the section that Murdoch and Lamb had long known was the tabloid reader's first port of call – the daily TV listings guide. Cudlipp, Molloy and Tony Miles had created the first tabloid pull-out in the form of Mirrorscope. Now pull-outs and supplements were everywhere, each devoted to a particularly popular TV show such as Premier League football (which spawned the Sun's *Goals* supplement and the Mirror's *Mania* section). Soaps or the 9/11 pictures of the Twin Towers were given their own sections.

By the 1990s, with the belated arrival of deregulation and multi-channel TV in the UK, the prospects for the tabloids looked bleak. The Unique Selling Points – porn, football – were lost one by one to cable, satellite or even to newly populist mainstream television channels. Murdoch transferred most of his new investment and his best editorial and corporate talent into "tabloid television" – Fox in the unregulated USA and the tamer Sky in the UK. Maxwell had attempted to get a toehold in TV as well – with his big stake-holding in ITV and plans to get into cable TV production as well, but that was all lost in the crisis following his death. After the collapse of the risible L!ve TV cable channel, the *Mirror* was left as the only significant newspaper group that did not also have increasingly dominant TV interests.

Some in the industry pointed to the fact that the combined circulation of the *Sun, Mirror* and *Star* in 2003 was about seven million, almost exactly the same number of sales as the *Mirror* and the defunct *Daily Sketch* in 1964 – the year of the *Mirror's* all-time highest sales. This was true, but misleading. In 1964, the *Daily Mirror* sold for 3d (three old pennies). That was the equivalent of 20p in 2003 terms and about 70p in terms of purchasing power parity (taking into account both price inflation and increased disposable income). The *Mirror* in 1964 had only 24 pages in a standard edition. The tabloids in 2003 had sixty or more pages, with additional supplements and give-away magazines. In rough terms, people in 1964 were prepared to pay four times as much money for newspapers that had only a quarter of the content. In terms of value for money today papers are sixteen times more valuable, but have only the same number of customers. Put another way, the tabloid industry has to work sixteen times harder just to keep the same number of customers. And the reality is that huge numbers of copies are given away for free on many days. No other major consumer product – from chocolate bars to motorcars – has performed so badly over the same period.

By 2003 young people in Tabloid Britain were starting to turn their backs on the tabloid newspapers. With expanding access to higher education some of the sons and daughters of *Sun* readers (and the grandchildren of Cudlipp-era *Mirror* readers) were bound to grow up into *Guardian* or *Telegraph* readers. Far more were content with television, the burgeoning weekly and monthly glossy celeb, lifestyle and consumer magazines and the internet. They were reluctant to buy newspapers – though they might read one that was given away free (such the *Mail* Group's virtually news-free *Metro* giveaway free sheet). It was widely recognised in the industry that the popular audience would always prefer to watch television than read a newspaper and that tabloids lingered on as adjuncts to TV to be read in the odd moment – at work or on the train – when it was not possible to watch TV.

Cudlipp's last word on the *Mirror* was that it had become little more than the "Daily Andrex".

Piers Morgan, editor of the *Mirror*, said that one thing guaranteed the future of his and all other tabloid newspapers... the fact that in 2003 nobody was in the habit of watching television while they were sitting on the toilet.

NOTES

(1) Another great circulation booster to spring from young Alfred's fertile mind was a simple "guess the missing words" competition. In this piece of hokum, readers had to complete a simple sentence, fill in a coupon and send in a shilling entrance money in order to win a massive cash prize. The competition pushed *Answers'* circulation to half a million before it was banned as an unlicensed lottery – and a bent one at that. Alfred himself could choose the words after the entries had come in, thus making sure there was never a winner. After this setback Alfred's quest for gullibility took on a religious aspect. *Answers* began to offer free bottles of "genuine water from the River Jordan" for use in christening babies.

(2) At the close of the Boer War in 1902 the *Daily Mail* had become the first paper in the world to regularly sell more than a million copies every day. Launched with a capital of £15,000 it was to make average profits of half a million pounds a year until the Second World War.

(3) The term "yellow press" came from the late 19th-century New York newspaper circulation war between William Randolph Hearst's newly launched New York *Journal* and Joseph Pulitzer's more established *New York World*, the model for the *Daily Planet* in the Superman comic strip. Hearst's circulation rose from 77,000 to almost 1,000,000 in a few years. Pulitzer responded by launching a colour supplement full of cartoon strips. One strip was called The Yellow Kid and, since Hearst "poached" the artist by offering more money (prompting Pulitzer to hire a different artist to draw exactly the same cartoon), the circulation war became known as the "Yellow War" fought between the "Yellow Papers".

(4) Swaffer had a sideline in writing comic verse for weekly papers like *Tit-Bits*. He also wrote lyrics for music-hall ballads. In 1904 he had a hit with "The Blind Coon" – which was sung by G H Chirgwin, a leading "blacked up" music-hall singer of his day. This commercial success was followed by yet more "Coon" songs, including "You are a White Little Girl", about a black man regretting the fact there was no point in lusting after a white girl because he would never be able to marry her. Other songs – shocking today but apparently sung without much comment at the time – included the lines "just a simple coon, who's sighin' for the

moon" and "(I'm) mad with passion, nigger fashion, Sambo sings forlorn".

(5) The re-launch depended on a technical breakthrough made by a Hungarian émigré called Arkas Sapt, a printer and editor of a corny Northcliffe magazine called *Home Sweet Home*. Sapt perfected the process of making half-tone blocks and introduced the new art of "re-touching" photographs. The effect was to greatly reduce the number of dots within a photo, creating what was sometimes a hybrid between a photo and a woodcut. As a result the presses could run ten times faster and, armed with three machines, the *Mirror* could at a push produce a million "picture papers" overnight.

(6) Fyfe later had a brilliant career as a front-line reporter in the First World War. The experience converted him from the caring "One Nation" High Toryism to pacifism and socialism. He served for many years as editor of the Labour-supporting and Trade Union-owned mass circulation paper, the *Daily Herald*.

(7) There was an attempt to climb Mont Blanc (the photographic team nearly died) and a more successful crossing of the Alps in a balloon. Some of the photos were to prove historic – a front-page picture showing the cairn marking the collective last resting place of Scott's Antarctic expedition, their skis sticking upright in a mound of snow, was to be remembered as one of the greatest news photographs of the twentieth century. Swaffer also pioneered war photography. During the 1911 Italian-Turkish war in North Africa, the *Mirror* became the first paper to print war atrocity pictures – harrowing images of Muslim women being forced at bayonet point to walk past the piled-up corpses of their husbands.

(8) After the launch of the *Daily Sketch* as a direct but distinctly inferior rip-off of the *Mirror*, the *Mirror* became even more competitive, pushing the formula of pictures towards its logical conclusion in "fashion parades" and "swim-suit beauty contests", which were little more than vaguely acceptable levels of soft-porn.

(9) But in the end Northcliffe could not dispute the success and importance of photojournalism and its eventual impact even on the "serious" newspapers. In 1917 Northcliffe called on Swaffer and showed him a proof of *The Times* with a full page of news photos – "I suppose you have won," Northcliffe said.

(10) Harold became Lord Rothermere in 1914 as a reward for supporting a Liberal measure to restrain the power of the House of Lords. Cecil Harmsworth (senior) meanwhile became a junior minister at the foreign office and was given a peerage by Chamberlain in 1939, apparently at the behest of Rothermere. Leicester Harmsworth, the fourth son, got a baronetcy in 1920 after serving as a Liberal MP. Hildebran, the fifth son, got a baronetcy in 1924, according to Cecil King simply because his son wrote "a very nice letter to Rothermere asking if he could arrange for him to have one". Rothermere himself famously commented that the advantage of being a newspaper proprietor was that, if you wanted a peerage, you did not have to buy one like other industrialists.

(11) In his memoirs, *My Life,* published in 1968, Mosley recalled: "I had known Lord Rothermere for a long time and had always been on good terms with him... A genuine patriot, he was concerned with the way things were going and had over the years discussed the situation with Lloyd George, Churchill, myself and others. He observed with growing interest the progress of the Blackshirt movement, and finally his action was characteristic. I had not seen him for some time, and he was at Monte Carlo when he suddenly sent me a telegram affirming his support. Then the headlines came pelting like a thunder storm: 'Hurrah for the Blackshirts' was the general theme." Mosley also reveals that Rothermere built an aeroplane called Britain First for the use of the Blackshirts and gave large and regular cash gifts directly to Mosley to cover some of his expenses in setting up the British Union of Fascists, although a *Daily Mirror* beauty contest for women Blackshirts was not a success.

(12) The May 30, 1929 general election result was: Labour 288 seats; Tories 260; Liberals 59. It was known as the "flapper election" because it was the first time twenty-one-year-old women had the vote. The *Mail* and the *Mirror* had campaigned against the extension of the franchise to women under 30 and on election day the *Mirror's* front page headline was: WOMEN'S DUTY TO VOTE TODAY TO KEEP SOCIALISTS OUT. The paper's post-election comment on the arrival of a Labour government included the thought: "Ought we to call this a plunge in the dark? Ought it not, after all, to be more accurately named a leap with the eyes open – to suicide?" In the previous 1924 election Rothermere's *Mail* had produced the notorious "Zinoviev letter" – forged letters from Moscow supposedly instructing British agents to organise an insurrection in the event of the Labour Party winning the election. The *Mirror* joined in the campaign: even its furry animal cartoon strip "Pip and Squeak" contained an evil Russian-looking character called Popski – an anarchist or Bolshevik with a bomb, whom they were always defeating.

(13) The phrase, written for Baldwin by Rudyard Kipling, brought the house down and later became one of the most famous political quotes of all time. But some in the audience were not quite so sure. When the applause died down Charles Cavendish, a Conservative supporter who had volunteered to canvass the Shepherd's Market part of the constituency and London's Red Light district of the time, leaned over to the Conservative election agent, tapped him on the shoulder and said: "Well... there goes the whore vote..."

(14) When Rothermere decided to cash in his *Mirror* shares he had boasted in a letter to Beaverbrook that he could take millions and yet still control the paper as tightly as if he were the sole owner. For £10,000 a year, Rothermere bragged, it was possible to hire an entire board of "trustys" who would manage the board of newspaper and do anything they were told. The "trusty" chairman Rothermere chose was John Cowley, later unflatteringly dismissed by one newspaper historian as "an uninspired accounting clerk, part of the human flotsam which washed aboard when Rothermere added

the *London Evening News* to his empire." For Cowley the job of running the *Daily Mirror* amounted to not upsetting Rothermere.

(15) Northcliffe had fathered his first child at the age of 17 at the expense of his mother's parlour maid. The story of Bart's Fitz-Northcliffe status was probably untrue, quite possibly spread by himself, or others who were jealous of his success or one of the small army of people who came to hate him, but Bart did nothing to deny it. Others said they had discovered – not from Bart – that his father had been "a Bob Cratchit-type clerk" in the city of London.

(16) Cecil Harmsworth King, the nephew of Rothermere and Northcliffe, was born on February 20, 1901. He was brought up in Dublin where his father, Sir Lucas King, was a former Indian civil servant of Irish Protestant stock who became professor of Oriental languages at Trinity College. His mother, Geraldine, was one of thirteen Harmsworth children and sister of the future Lords Northcliffe and Rothermere. King was educated as a boarder at Winchester, which he hated. He had an unhappy childhood, marked by loneliness and the indifference of his parents. One abiding memory of his infant years was of his mother disappearing to spend long hours in the British Library digging out facts for the magazine which made the Harmsworth fortune – *Answers to Correspondents*. King wrote in his autobiography that during his childhood: "I felt as if I were an orphan brought up by step-parents, a stepfather who was completely null and a stepmother who was loveless, capricious and occasionally cruel". King always said that his early years had taught him to be "attached to nothing and nobody". The misery of a loveless childhood was made worse when both his brothers were killed during the First World War – one at the front, the other torpedoed by a German submarine in the Irish Sea. When he was 15 years old, his childhood sweetheart died of brain cancer. These events may have shaped his personality. He struck most people he met throughout life as lugubrious, cold, aloof and intensely private.

(17) The irony was that *Daily News* editor Joseph Medill Patterson had copied much of the paper's style from the *Daily Mirror*, which he seen in London for the first time while serving in the US army during the First World War. At the time the *Mirror* had been going through one of its golden phases, powered by Bart's startling war photography, a populist social agenda and the punchy presentational style created by Hannen Swaffer. The *Daily News* was launched as the *New York Illustrated Daily News* in June 1919. At the time there were plenty of "yellow" tabloid-type newspapers in New York, led by William Randolph Hearst's *Evening Journal* and Joseph Pulitzer's *World*. But there had never been a "British"-type "picture paper". Patterson gave New Yorkers one and it was an immediate hit.

(18) The *Graphic*'s owner, Bernard MacFadden, like Bart began in life as a photographer. He made a fortune with titillating, multi-million-selling "true romance" and "true detective" magazines, as well as beefcake and cheesecake magazines ostensibly about bodybuilding and exercise, moving into newspapers as a way of expanding his market.

(19) Much later when he was editorial director of the *Daily Mirror* in late 1950s Cudlipp decreed that the high season in Blackpool should be sponsored by the paper as *Daily Mirror* Week as the best way to promote the paper's sales. At a meeting recounted by the paper's show-business reporter Noel Whitcomb, Cudlipp had planned to "plaster every square yard of the town with *Daily Mirror* posters. We will have banquets and balls and firework displays". Whitcomb was ordered to hire Errol Flynn, one of the biggest Hollywood stars of the day, to "sail into Blackpool on his yacht, with a flotilla of seagoing craft of every kind to meet him and sirens blaring everywhere, and then have him airlifted by helicopter and landed by rope and tackle outside the town hall to declare *Daily Mirror* week open." It did not quite work out that way.

(20) Jane was drawn by Norman Pett and the model was Christabel Leighton-Porter, a strip-tease artist and "glamour model" who continued her act as Jane until the 1960s. She also appeared in a film called *The adventures of Jane*. Jane ran from 1932 to 1959, when she was replaced by the less well-starred Patti. In the late 1980s the strip was revived for a while by Robert Maxwell.

(21) King himself was to have a long-standing relationship with British intelligence (de-classified documents at the Public Records Office showed that he was setting up secret meetings with Irish terrorists on behalf of British intelligence as late as the 1970s). At that time the former MI5 officer Peter Wright also claimed that King had been an MI5 agent for "many years". Whatever the case might have been after the MI5 vetting which followed the Cabinet's worries about a hidden Nazi (or communist) propaganda network responsible for outrages like Zec's Price of Oil cartoon, Bart and the *Mirror* were entrusted with the extremely sensitive top-secret work of producing a paper for British submarine crews. It was entitled *Good Morning*. A letter from King in the Cudlipp archive says in passing that "I think your idea of joining the intelligence service is a good one". The archive contains no reply from Cudlipp, or any further mention of secret intelligence or propaganda work.

(22) Women were banned by Bower from entering El Vino's by the front door, or from standing at or near the bar or from even walking through it – even after formal discrimination of this sort was made illegal. Female customers had to walk down a passage at the side of the pub and enter through the back door and were allowed to sit at a table in the back room "if accompanied by a gentleman".

(23) 1945 election result: Labour, 393 seats. Tories 213. Liberals 12. Others 22. Turnout 72.7 per cent.

(24) In 1943 the *Mirror* board took the corporate decision to back the Labour Party in the post-war election. Bart was not sure. He felt the party had little appeal outside the big cities – a problem for a paper like the *Mirror* which needed circulation everywhere. He also thought that support for any single party would be unpopular and that the *Mirror* might be better off appealing to the non-political majority, adopting a "plague on all your houses"

approach to the politicians. When the 1945 election came there was in effect a compromise. The paper adopted a "non-political" stance of voting against the officer class and the politicians of the 1930s who had been responsible for the war in the first place.

(25) Landmarks in the *Mirror* vs *Express* circulation battle are as follows:
    January 1934 – *Mirror* circulation 732,448; *Express* 1,709,904
    January 1941 – *Mirror* 1,685,821; *Express* 2,511,333
    March 1947 – *Mirror* 3,446,856; *Express* 3,706,669
    July 1947 – *Mirror* 3,741,971; *Express* 3,879,938
    January 1949 – *Mirror* 4,187,403; *Express* 3,985,336

(26) One example of the Bart-Bish relationship in operation concerned the *Mirror*'s legendary science writer Ronnie Bedford who suffered from the twin congenital problems of a hare-lip, blindness in one eye and short-sightedness in the other. Bart spotted Bedford in the office holding a piece of paper close to his face and squinting at it with his one good eye. "Who's that blind fucker we've got on the staff?" Bart demanded of Bolam. Bedford was summoned to Bolam's office where he was told "the Chairman wants to know why you read like that". Bedford explained about his bad eye and Bolam seemed satisfied. But within the hour Bedford was summoned again. "The chairman wants to know what you are going to do about it." There was nothing that could be done, but Bart had generously offered to pay if Bedford needed an operation. Later, Bedford met Bart in the gents at Geraldine House, becoming aware that somebody was standing on his blind side. "You're Bedford, aren't you?" Bart boomed. "I read your piece this morning – it's a load of piss. But it's not bad piss."

(27) Haigh was executed by hanging at Wandsworth prison on August 6, 1949. He bequeathed his clothing and death mask to Madame Tussaud's Chamber of Horrors, where he became a famous attraction. As part of the bequest he specified that his wax figure must always be kept in perfect condition with trousers properly creased and hair combed and parted neatly.

(28) Cecil King had established a chain of newspapers in West Africa, the first and most successful being the Nigerian *Daily Times*. They were set up at the request of "Whitehall" and were for a while run by the former MI6 officer Percy Roberts. The papers were used to test out new printing technology and they were thus always much better equipped than any British paper in Fleet Street. The titles were sold off by IPC in 1974, after Cecil King had been ousted from the chairmanship of the company.

(29) According to some people, Mr Lucas became one of the wealthiest employees of the paper because of the favour Cudlipp bestowed upon him or, possibly, as a result of share-price sensitive information he overheard in meetings or – a more remote likelihood – because he was on a retainer from other newspapers to leak details of any exclusive stories he had seen Cudlipp and others setting up. Such subterfuge was widespread in Fleet Street. Derek Jameson, for example, claimed that he used to sometimes get stories for the *Sunday Mirror* by looking through the windows of the *News of the World*

production department from a neighbouring building and reading headlines with very powerful binoculars.

(30) The cartoon – a sort of Homer Simpson of its time – was drawn by Reg Smythe, originally a postman from Hartlepool. The cartoon became a massive hit, eventually syndicated to 1,400 newspapers in 31 countries and read at its peak by an estimated 175 million people in 13 languages. Cudlipp described the character as "a work-shy, beer-swilling, rent-dodging, wife-bashing, pigeon-fancying, soccer-playing, uncouth codger".

(31) It was remembered as a golden age, later, but there was a lot of what reporters at the time called "dross" and "corn" in the paper as well: part of the Bart and Cudlipp formula had always included an appreciation of the value of cute animal picture "stories" of the "Kitten in a Wineglass" genre.

(32) During the 1955 General Election, Hugh Gaitskell told a senior journalist thinking of joining the *Mirror* that Cecil King was "a very strange man… a combination of Northcliffe and a Wykehamist… very able, but very isolated". Crossman described King as "a great big, beefy, rather silly fellow who lives in Chelsea, is a Wykehamist but is otherwise insignificant". Cudlipp had meanwhile warned the Labour leadership: "The *Mirror* might not be able to win you the next election, but if we turn against you, we can certainly lose it for you". Crossman regarded the election as lost six months before it happened. He had heard that King had wanted the *Mirror* to adopt the slogan: "We are pro-Labour but not this time," because the party was divided and needed fresh leadership and policy changes which could only come in opposition. The 1955 election result was: Tories 344; Labour 277; Liberals 6; Others 3. The *Mirror* verdict on the result was: "Labour lost because its leaders are too old, too tired, too weak".

(33) The *Mirror* political editor John Beavan remembered that Cudlipp had a mean streak that meant he could suddenly "blow his top and assault with verbal violence somebody who had said the wrong thing". But he would then indulge himself with the power and perks of office, according to Beavan: "His contrition after one of these attacks never failed, and was often expressed by a pay rise for the victim, or even promotion."

(34) The *Daily Mirror* supported Labour by name for the first time in 1951, following the discovery by the Gallup polling organisation that the working class was now more solidly behind the Labour Party than it had been in 1945. Politics had begun to shape up on tribal class lines in a way which would not really change until the 1980s and against this background there was a more comfortable association between "*Mirror* reader" and "Labour voter" than there had been even during the war. On election day the paper ran the front-page headline WHOSE FINGER ON THE TRIGGER?, which was a dig at the elderly Winston Churchill who, the paper maintained, was too old and too warlike to be in charge of Britain's new and supposedly "independent" nuclear strike force. The fear was that Churchill would start a war with the Russians. The front page was one of Bart's last acts as editorial director. He was replaced soon afterwards by King and, a few

months later, Cudlipp. The Conservatives won the election with a majority of 17. Churchill sued for libel over the slight on his character and won damages of £1,500.

(35) According to one school of thought, an out-of-control group of paranoid right-wing MI5 officers had decided that the whole of British intelligence (and perhaps most of the American CIA) had been infiltrated by the Russian KGB with the aim of steering Russian agents into, at least, 10 Downing Street and, possibly, the White House as well. Harold Wilson, according to the most extreme version of the theory, was that agent. Some of this talk among senior intelligence officers naturally found its way on to the Whitehall grapevine and, eventually, to Williams and Wilson.

(36) *Good Morning* was a fascinating daily magazine carried on board submarines in packages and released each day to help preserve something like the rhythm of the daily routine for the submariners. The venture came about because of a rare personal friendship between Harry Guy Bartholomew and A V Alexander, a Sheffield MP and First Lord of the Admiralty in Churchill's wartime coalition. The first issue was produced on April 1943 and in all 924 issues were produced. The news from home was a psychological boost, created in part by the serial nature of the cartoons including "Jane". The paper also featured plenty of pictures of girls from the chorus line of the Windmill theatre in Soho, the star attraction for off-duty servicemen during the war. There was later a harrowing tale of how one crew, thinking they were trapped on the deep ocean floor facing certain slow suffocation, had been allowed to read the whole coming week's editions so as to follow the Jane strip.

(37) Mountbatten also mentioned Air Marshall Derek Stapleton, Colonel Duncan Lewin, Beeching, Troughton of W H Smith, Wilson's cabinet rivals Roy Jenkins and Jim Callaghan, Reginald Maudling, the leader of the right wing of the Conservative party, former Tory leader Alec Douglas-Home for the Foreign Office, and William Armstrong, Michael Carey, Jim McKay from the civil service. An odd suggestion was Jimmy Carreras – "according to Mountbatten 'a great go-getter' – a film tycoon whom Dickie has met through the Variety Club".

(38) Mountbatten had his own reasons for wanting to see the back of the Labour government. He had been financially crushed by death duties imposed by Labour after the death of his wife Edwina. It had forced him to sell his grand London house and live in a relatively small flat above a garage in Kinnerton Street, Mayfair. Also, Healey had thwarted Mountbatten's ambition to become the formal head of a united command of all three services. Healey had listened to the plan, but rejected it when he found that of the forty highest-ranking military officers in the Ministry only Sir Kenneth Strong, the Director General of Intelligence – Mountbatten's closest confidant in Whitehall – was in favour of the change. "When I told Dickie of my decision not to make the appointment he slapped his thigh and roared with delight; but his eyes told a different story," Healey later wrote.

(39) A further account of the meeting was given in 2003 by Mountbatten's personal assistant William Evans, who described in his memoirs how there had been not one but two meetings between Mountbatten and King at Kinnerton Street. During the first, Evans was in the bedroom doing some packing while Mountbatten and King spoke to each other. After three or four minutes Mountbatten walked in to the bedroom and told Evans: "We've got a complete nutter in there. He wants me to throw the government over and put troops on the streets. Can you imagine it? He's bloody insane. Give me two minutes and come and get me out." Williams went in with a note and Mountbatten said to King that he had to hurry away but, strangely enough, offered to have "a proper meeting" at six o'clock the following evening. Evans continues: "This time [Cecil King] invited Hugh Cudlipp and Sir Solly Zuckermann, the chief scientific officer. They were in there for ten or twelve minutes. Then Solly came out, saying: "Dickie, get rid of the man. Have nothing to do with him." But Mountbatten went back and talked, according to Evans. Afterwards, Mountbatten consulted others, including his son-in-law Lord Brabourne, who also advised: "Have nothing to do with it, Dickie." Finally, Wilson was summoned for a chat. And that was the end of the "plot".

(40) The entry for the day of the Kinnerton meeting is unusually brief, simply recording: "At the [Bank of England]: the Governor gloomy as usual these days. Things are sometimes better, sometimes worse, but our reserves slip away all the time." Interestingly, the preceding entry in King's diary records a dinner for leading Tory MPs at which the replacement of Edward Heath as leader of the party was discussed. King also recorded the fact that he spoke to "a senior civil servant" [name blanked out] which, in the style adopted by King in his diaries, meant he was almost certainly a high-ranking intelligence officer (since hundreds of others are named without any discretion at all). In February 1968, some three months before the Kinnerton Street meeting, Cecil King happened to have lunch with the dedicated fellow-diarist Tony Benn, who recorded it thus: "I said that I thought that devaluation had been quite successful and that our prospects of a surplus in 1969 were good. [Cecil King] cited Cromer who he said shared his view; the United States Ambassador, who agreed with him that the Government was finished and others who shared the view too. He even said that Sir William Armstrong, the Permanent Secretary to the Treasury, was extremely depressed about the outlook... Did he think that coalition government was necessary? Yes, indeed he did... Wilson would be totally swept away – nobody believed a word he said and he had no future whatsoever... So I rang Harold [Wilson] and about, I suppose, half past eleven, he rang me back and I told him the gist of what I had heard. Harold was rather agitated and excited to hear this, and said that Cecil King was mad, with which I would not really dissent, and also that this was part of the explanation of why he [Wilson] had sacked Will Howie, the Whip, because apparently Will had been plotting with Jim Callaghan and others."

(41) The relationship between national newspapers and spies was close anyway. The *Express* defence correspondent claimed that he knew the names of some fifty MI5 agents working in Fleet Street – there was a contingent on every paper. Apart from anything else the status of "journalist" provided brilliant cover for spies. The most famous British spies of the twentieth century, Kim Philby and Guy Burgess, were both given journalistic "cover" by MI5 and MI6 (even though they were secretly working for the Russians) on the *Observer* and at the BBC respectively. David Walker, the *Mirror's* foreign correspondent in the 1950s, was named as an MI6 agent after a security scandal – causing much amusement among his colleagues in the office. It explained why Walker, who was regarded as a hopeless journalist, would send back reams and reams of material when he went to do a reporting job in a Soviet-bloc country like Hungary. He was regarded as a reporter of monumental incompetence and some thought that King, with his Whitehall contacts, had got him a job as a spy as some sort of favour. Another *Mirror* journalist, Stanley Bonnet, admitted working for MI5 in the 1980s, investigating the Campaign for Nuclear Disarmament, supplying reports on Russian subversion via Tom Tullet, the ex-Scotland Yard officer hired by Cudlipp who was known to have worked with or for MI5's "foot soldiers" – the police Special Branch.

(42) In an angry and indiscreet moment Cecil King's Mosley-admiring wife Ruth Railton told a member of the *Mirror's* Paris office staff that her husband had been "kicked off the board of IPC because Jewish bankers did not want him to save the pound and the British economy. Jewish financiers had paid out £2.5 million in bribes to members of the IPC board in order to get rid of him."

(43) Larry Lamb was born in 1929 in the pit village of Fitzwilliam in West Yorkshire. He left school at 16 and got a brain-numbing clerical job at the Town Hall in Brighouse. Larry's father was a committed socialist and an official of the miners' trade union. The *Daily Herald* was compulsory reading in the Lamb household and Larry himself became a trade union activist at the Town Hall, proudly accepting the nickname "Red Larry". At the age of 24 Lamb moved into journalism after editing a trade union magazine. He worked in quick succession for papers in Yorkshire and the North East, including the *Brighouse Echo*, the *Shields Gazette* and the *Newcastle Journal* before moving to the London *Evening Standard* and then the *Daily Mail*, where he became a sub-editor. In 1958, having ditched his union activism, Lamb moved to the *Mirror* – in many ways his natural home. At the time, Nener was in full flood, rising to the fierce competition for readers and advertisers unleashed by the end of newsprint rationing.

(44) The *Mirror's* Irish edition was also produced from Manchester. The Irish *Mirror* was produced using a new printing factory, the first in the UK to be equipped with advanced electronics and full-colour printing – a legacy of Cecil King's interest in all thing Irish and, possibly, a result of co-ordination or co-operation with the intelligence services he was assisting at the time.

The full-colour editions of the *Mirror* were a massive hit, and the *Mirror's* circulation increased from 55,000 weekly to 210,000 in a few years. The success continued until the plant was blown up by the provisional IRA in 1972.

(45) Waterhouse was the author of a style and writing guide for *Mirror* journalists which was later published and is still highly regarded by many journalists. Naturally there was great concern that a textbook on journalism and newspaper production should contain no errors. It did. In the first edition the page numbers were wrong and the whole run had to be pulped. After the arrival of Robert Maxwell as the *Mirror's* owner, Keith Waterhouse left and went to work for the *Daily Mail*.

(46) Robert Maxwell was born in 1923 as Jan Ludwig Hoch in Czechoslovakia. He took the name Robert Maxwell in 1940. In 1946 he became the sole UK and US distributor of scientific journals produced by the Springer group in occupied Germany. The scientific journals business was consolidated as Pergamon Press in 1949 and was the source of his fortune. He made his first million in 1951 when the big British publisher Butterworths and the Axel Springer Group itself bought stakes in Pergamon. In 1964 Maxwell was elected Labour MP for North Buckinghamshire. In 1968 he made unsuccessful bids for ownership of, first the *News of the World* and, secondly, the *Sun*. In both cases he lost out to his great rival Rupert Murdoch. In 1969 he was censured over his attempt to falsely represent the asset value of Pergamon Press during an attempted sale of the company to Leasco Data Processing. The sale went ahead anyway. In 1970 he established the fraudulent Maxwell Foundation in Liechtenstein. The foundation was the ultimate owner of Maxwell's businesses, but in fact had no funds. In 1973 a Department of Trade and Industry report declared that he was "not a person who can be relied on to exercise proper stewardship of a publicly quoted company". The following year, 1974, Maxwell bought back control of Pergamon, which began publishing scientific information obtained cheaply from Russia and eastern Europe. Pergamon profits enabled Maxwell to buy the British Printing Corporation, which he renamed the Maxwell Communications Corporation. In the following years he bought the Odhams printing plant in Watford from Reed International, owners of the Mirror Group newspapers, sparking his interest in buying the *Mirror*, which he achieved in 1984.

(47) Stott was an exact contemporary of *Sun* editor Kelvin MacKenzie. He had been born in Oxford, educated at Clifton College, Bristol, leaving school to become a reporter on the *Bucks Herald* in Aylesbury before moving into the competitive world of agency reporting with Ferrari's – the legendary East End crime-reporting syndicate where he worked for a while alongside MacKenzie. But, while the future *Sun* editor headed off for the Express – the natural home for his nationalistic, flag-waving right-wing politics – Stott went on to the *Mirror* as a reporter, where he excelled. Stott was involved in the investigations of public figures like Don Revie, which Molloy had used

as ammunition for his counter-attack against the *Sun*. He progressed to become features editor and was Molloy's deputy and anointed successor by the time Maxwell bought the paper.

(48) Richard Stott strenuously denied to the author that drinking and other aspects of the "old culture" was a problem at this time, and accuses Greenslade in effect of exaggerating or otherwise getting it wrong on this point. Stott told the author: "It would have been impossible to have senior staff drunk on the job. Maxwell lived above the shop and knew much more about what was going on in the *Mirror* than Murdoch ever knew was going on at the *Sun*." The two men simply disagree about this matter and gave the author flatly contrary accounts.

(49) This was a rare lapse in security. Maxwell was paranoid. From 1988 onwards he was secretly tape-recording all the conversations in his suite of offices, sitting room and dining room – hence the habit of keeping people waiting. He also bugged the offices of six of his directors and executives – he even bugged his own sons. The bugging was done by a former member of Scotland Yard's anti-terrorism squad taken onto Maxwell's private "security team" with the help of a former army intelligence surveillance officer with experience in Northern Ireland. At first, simple tape recorders were used, but in the end Maxwell spent £40,000 on a ramified system of sensors and wires running through a large and growing part of the building. He established an office where all the tapes would be transcribed and summarised for him. All the transcripts were then destroyed.

(50) The Mandela concert was covered on TV and in all the papers, though the *Sun*'s show-business correspondent – a certain Piers Morgan – appeared on TV to say that newspaper readers really didn't care much at all about Mandela. He would only be writing about the pop groups. Pop fans and young people were not interested in politics, he said.

(51) Montgomery's workaholic approach was clear from the start. Over the two years he edited the paper he filled huge amounts of space with fantastically hum drum reports under the by-line "Dave Montgomery" with stories under headlines such as HOW DOES A STUDENT SPEND HIS GRANT? (an attack on "the frivolous student who devotes himself to a surfeit of alcoholic pleasure"), TEETHING TROUBLES FOR RAG COMMITTEE and the all-time humdinger FIRE DESTROYS SCIENCE HUTS. The paper's most intriguing story – RUFUS IN COMBAT WITH TURD MUNCHERS – was not his work. He and his colleagues also introduced into the *Gown* a cover-girl competition, reminiscent of the *Sun*'s Page Three and featuring busty members of the student cohort.

(52) *The Observer*, London, May 20, 2001. The same story was broadcast as a documentary on BBC Radio on the same date, under the title "Richard Desmond, Naked Ambition".

CHRONOLOGY

1903: November 3: *Daily Mirror* launched by Alfred Harmsworth.

1905: Alfred Harmsworth becomes Lord Northcliffe.

1907: Alexander Kenealy becomes editor. Hannen Swaffer becomes art editor.

1908: *Daily Mirror* sales reach 500,000.

1910: World record sale of 2,013,000 copies achieved with death-bed pictures of King Edward VII. Northcliffe floats the *Daily Mirror* on the stock market.

1911: *Mirror* prints North African atrocity pictures from Turkish-Italian war.

1912: *Mirror* scoops the world with special illustrated *Titanic* sinking edition.

1914: Northcliffe sells his controlling block of *Mirror* shares to his brother Lord Rothermere (Harold Harmsworth).

1915: Launch of *Sunday Pictorial* (becomes *Sunday Mirror* in 1964).

1917: Rothermere joins the war cabinet as Air Minister.

1921: Rothermere launches Anti-Waste League.

1922: Northcliffe dies. Rothermere inherits his newspaper empire including the *Daily Mail*. Neglect of the *Mirror* means it begins to lose circulation, becoming a "genteel Tory newspaper with an ageing readership".

1924: General election dominated by *Daily Mail's* "Zinoviev letter" affair. *Daily Mirror* urges readers to vote against the Labour party by deciding if they want to be "British or Bolshie".

1926: Cecil Harmsworth King joins the *Mirror* in advertising department (becomes advertising director in 1929).

1928: New York tabloid circulation war marked by *Daily News's* printing of execution of Ruth Snyder.

1929: Rothermere and Beaverbrook launch the United Empire Party.

1931: Baldwin's "Prerogative of the Harlot" speech criticising Rothermere and Beaverbrook.

1932: Rothermere helps launch the British Union of Fascists, backed by the *Daily Mirror* and the *Daily Mail*.

1933: The "free gift" circulation war unleash by the *Daily Herald* peaks. Adolf Hitler writes to Rothermere praising his work to improve the image of his regime in Germany. *Mirror* circulation down to 800,000 and losing readers at the rate of 30,000 a year.

1934: Harry Guy Bartholomew ("Bart") becomes editorial director and embarks on the *Mirror's* "tabloid revolution".

1935: Hugh Cudlipp joins the *Daily Mirror* as deputy features editor.

1936: *Mirror* introduces several pages of cartoon strips, following the model of the New York tabloids.

1937: New-style tabloid *Mirror* described as "A daily affront to bishops, magistrates, schoolmasters, the retired élite and the combined forces of officialdom and respectable society".

1938: Hugh Cudlipp appointed editor of *Mirror*'s Sunday sister paper, *The Pictorial*.

1939: *Mirror* circulation is 1.5 million on the eve of war – up from 800,000 in 1933 when "re-launched".

1940: Rothermere dies.

1942: *Mirror* threatened with closure over Philip Zec "price of oil" cartoon. MI5 investigates the paper for possible Nazi or Communist subversion.

1944: Bart becomes chairman of the *Daily Mirror* publishing company. Education Act indicates that by the mid-1950s readers of popular newspaper readers will be better educated and highly literate.

1945: *Mirror* claimed 2.5 million sales and 11 million readers. Subtle pro-Labour party "Vote for Him" front page in general election.

1949: *Mirror* editor Silvester "Bish" Bolam sent to prison for contempt of court. Sales reach 4.1 million, making the *Mirror* the country's best-selling daily (the paper remains the number one best seller for thirty years until the late 1970s).

1948: Hugh Cudlipp sacked as editor of *Sunday Pictorial* by Bart. Goes to *Sunday Express*.

1951: Bart sacked. Cecil King becomes chairman of *Daily Mirror*.

1952: Hugh Cudlipp returns from *Sunday Express* to become editorial director of *Mirror*.

1953: Jack "F'ing" Nener becomes *Mirror* editor. June Coronation edition sells over seven million copies.

1954: Marje Proops column starts.

1955: *Mirror* backs Labour in general election. Labour loses. *Mirror* campaign against the death penalty peaks with Cassandra's influential "Fine Day for a Hanging" article.

1956: *Mirror* opposes British military action against Egypt during the Suez Crisis. Loses 70,000 readers as a result. *Mirror* libel battle with Liberace. Launch of ITV increases competition to sell advertising.

1959: Newsprint rationing ends, intensifying competition to sell advertising, forcing the *Mirror* to move "up-market" and compete more directly with the *Daily Express* and resulting in "Youth Revolution" re-launch.

1960: *Mirror* takes hard-line stance in Cold War with anti-Khruschev "Who the bloody hell do you think you are" front page.

1961: *Mirror* moves from low-rent Geraldine House to status-symbol modern Holborn Circus tower block "the House that 14,000,000 readers built". Lee Howard replaces Jack Nener as editor. *Mirror* buys Odhams magazine publishing company, merging it with other assets to create the IPC (International Publishing Corporation), the world's biggest publishing company. In the process *Mirror* newspaper acquires the (Sunday) *People* and the ailing *Daily Herald*.

1962: *Mirror* class sailing dinghy launched.

1963: Cecil King becomes chairman of IPC (and therefore in control of the *Mirror* titles).

1964: Crisis at *Daily Express* after death of Beaverbrook. Regular daily sales of the *Mirror* reach five million. *Mirror* plays vital role in bringing Harold Wilson and the Labour party to power. Hugh Cudlipp writes Wilson's party conference "White Heat of Technological Revolution" speech. *Daily Herald* re-launched as the (IPC) *Sun*.

1967: *Mirror* sales peak at 5.25 million (April).

1968: Cecil King is sacked as IPC chairman after publishing his ENOUGH IS ENOUGH attack on the Harold Wilson's Labour government and is involved in talks about a possible "coup" to replace the elected government with a national emergency committee backed by Lord Mountbatten and the armed forces.

1969: Rupert Murdoch buys the *Sun* from Mirror-IPC and re-launches it in 1969 as an aggressive competitor, based on the *Mirror's* "down-market" editorial formula of the 1950s and early 1960s.

1970: IPC merges with the paper manufacturer Reed to create Reed International. *Mirror* becomes a subsidiary of the new company.

1971: Tony Miles becomes editor.

1972: Hugh Cudlipp announces he is retiring.

1975: *Mirror* prints first "Page Three"- type nude. The feature is dropped soon after its introduction.

1978: *Sun* overtakes *Mirror* as best-selling paper in the country. *Daily Star* is launched.

1982: Falklands conflict.

1983: Clive Thornton becomes *Mirror* chief executive.

1984: Robert Maxwell buys the *Daily Mirror*.

1985: Richard Stott becomes editor of the *Mirror*.

1986: Maxwell negotiates big cuts in staffing levels and begins substantial investment in colour-printing presses.

1988: Cudlipp denounces intrusion by tabloids.

1989: Roy Greenslade becomes editor of the *Mirror*.

1990: Roy Greenslade sacked as *Mirror* editor. Richard Stott re appointed. Calcutt committee on media standards meets and reports.

1991: In May, Robert Maxwell raises £245 million by floating 49 per cent of the *Mirror*. Maxwell dies in mysterious circumstances in November.

1992: David Montgomery takes over as *Mirror* chief executive. David Banks becomes *Mirror* editor.

1993: Alastair Campbell, Paul Foot and Lord Hollick lead "exodus" of journalists unhappy with Montgomery's rule. *Mirror* prints Diana "gym" pictures. Price-cutting war started by the *Sun* sees the *Sun* and *Mirror* being sold for 5p or 10p on some days.

1994: *Mirror* returns to profitability after move to Canary Wharf. Plan to launch L!ve TV is announced with Kelvin MacKenzie as director in charge.

1995: Cudlipp castigates the *Mirror*. The paper's use of colour and garish design makes it look as if somebody has been sick all over the front page, Cudlipp says. Piers Morgan head-hunted from *News of the World* by Montgomery to be *Mirror* editor.

1996: "Achtung! Surrender!" headline during Euro '69 football championship. *Mirror* Pepsi "Blue" advert and handing back of budget leak leads to wave of criticism.

1997: Death of Diana, Princess of Wales.

1998: Hugh Cudlipp dies.

1999: Montgomery leaves the *Mirror*, allowing takeover by Trinity local newspaper chain to take place. Richard Desmond's *OK!* pays £1 million for rights to pictures of the wedding of David Beckham and Posh Spice.

2001: *Mirror* turns to new "serious" editorial agenda after September 11 terrorist attacks.

2002: Formal re-launch as a "mid-market" newspaper. Circulation drops below two million – lowest sales since the 1930s.

2003: *Mirror* sales fall below two million.

Mirror Editors 1903–2003
1903: Mary Howarth (Kennedy Jones, editorial director 1903–1913)
1904: Hamilton Fyfe
1907: Alexander Kenealy
1915: Ed Flynn
1920: Alexander Campbell
1931: Leigh Brownlee
1934: Cecil Thomas (HG Bartholomew, editorial director 1934–51)
1948: Silvester Bolam (Hugh Cudlipp, editorial director 1952–1974)
1953: Jack Nener
1961: Lee Howard
1971: Tony Miles
1974: Michael Christiansen
1975: Mike Molloy
1985: Richard Stott
1990: Roy Greenslade
1991: Richard Stott
1992: David Banks
1994: Colin Myler
1995: Piers Morgan

BIBLIOGRAPHY

Abrams, M. *The Newspaper reading Public of Tomorrow*, Odhams, 1964.

Allen, R and Frost, J. *Daily Mirror*, 1981.

Baistow, Tom. *Four-Rate Estate*, Comedia, 1985.

Barson, S and Saint, A. *A Farewell to Fleet Street*, English Heritage, 1988.

Barton, Frank. *The Press of Africa*, 1979.

Belloc, Hilaire (et al). *Press Gang*, 1937.

Benn, A. *Office Without Power, Diaries 1968–1972*, 1990.

Boston, Richard. ed *The Press We Deserve*, 1970.

Bourne, Richard. *Lords of Fleet Street: The Harmsworth Dynasty*, 1990.

Bower, T. *Maxwell: The Final Verdict*, 1995.

Boyce, G, Curran, J, and Wingate, P. *Newspaper History from the Seventeenth Century to the Present Day*, 1978.

Brendon, Piers. *The Life and Death of the Press Barons*, 1982.

Bundock, Clement. *The National Union of Journalists – a jubilee history 1907–1957*, 1957.

Catterall, P, Seymour-Ure, C and Smith, A. *Northcliffe's Legacy: Aspects of the British Popular Press 1896–1996*, 1998.

Cockett, R. *Twilight of Truth: Chamberlain, Appeasement and the Manipulation of the Press*, 1989.

Clarke, Tom. *My Northcliffe Diary*, 1931.

Cleverley, Graham. *The Fleet Street Disaster*, 1976.

Cohen, Nick. *Cruel Britannia*, 1999.

Connor, Robert. *Cassandra – Reflections in a Mirror*, 1969.

Cross, Colin. *The Fascists in Britain*, 1961.

Cudlipp, Hugh. *Publish and Be Damned!*, Andrew Dakers, 1953.

Cudlipp, Hugh. *At Your Peril*, 1962.

Cudlipp, Hugh. *Walking on the Water*, 1976.

Cudlipp, Hugh. *The Prerogative of the Harlot*, 1980.

Curran, J and Seaton, J. *Power Without Responsibility – The Press and Broadcasting in Britain*, 1982.

Daily Mirror. The Romance of the Daily Mirror 1903–1924, an illustrated record.

Davies, Nicholas. *The Unknown Maxwell*, 1992.

Donoughue, B & Jones, G.W. *Herbert Morrison: Portrait of a Politician*, 1973.

Drawbell, James. *James Drawbell: Autobiography*, 1964.

Driberg, Tom. *Swaff – The Life and Times of Hannen Swaffer*, 1974.

Dudley-Edwards, Ruth. *Newspapermen*, 2003.

Edleman, Maurice. *The Mirror: A Political History*, 1966.

Edwards, Robert. *Goodbye Fleet Street*, 1988.

Engel, Matthew. *Tickle the Public*, 1996.

Fienburgh, W. *25 Momentous Years, a 25th Anniversary of the Daily Herald*, 1955.

Fyfe, Hamilton. *Northcliffe: An Intimate Biography*, 1930.

Fyfe, Hamilton. *Press Parade*, 1936.

Fyfe, Hamilton. *My Seven Selves*, 1937.

Fyfe, Hamilton. *Sixty Years of Fleet Street*, 1949.

Gannon, Franklin. *The British Press and Germany 1936–39*, 1971.

Gray, Tony. *Fleet Street Remembered*, 1990.

Grade, Michael. *It Seemed Like A Good Idea At The Time*, 1999.

Greenslade, R. *Maxwell's Fall*, 1992.

Griffiths, Dennis. *Encyclopaedia of the British Press 1422–1992*, 1992.

Grose, Roslyn. *The Sun-Sation: The Inside Story of Britain's Best-Selling Daily Newspaper*, 1989.

Haines, Joe. *Maxwell*, 1988.

Harris, Robert. *Gotcha! The Media, the Government and the Falklands Crisis*, 1986.

Healey, Denis. *The Time of My Life*, 1989.

Herd, Harold. *Seven Editors*, 1955.

Hirsch, F and Gordon, D. *Newspaper Money, Fleet Street and the search for the affluent reader*, 1975.

HMSO, *Royal Commission on the Press 1948–49*.

HMSO, *Royal Commission on the Press 1961–1962*.

HMSO, *Royal Commission on the Press 1975–76*.

HMSO and Imperial War Museum. *Union Jack, a scrapbook of British Forces newspapers, 1939–45*, 1989.

HMSO, Department of Trade and Industry. *Mirror Group Newspapers plc, Investigations under sections 432 (2) and 442 of the companies act 1985 (report by Sir Roger Thomas and Raymond Turner)*.

Horrie, C and Chippindale, P. *Stick it Up Your Punter*, 1998.

Horrie, C and Chippindale, P. *Disaster: The Rise and Fall of News on Sunday*, 1988.

Horrie, C, and Nathan, A. *Live TV*, 2000.

Horrie, C. *Sick as a Parrot*, 1993.

Hudson, Derek. *British Journalists and Newspapers*, 1945.

Hutt, Allen. *The Changing Newspaper*, 1973.

Jameson, D. *Touched by Angels*, 1988.

Jenkins, Simon. *Newspapers: The Power and the Money*, 1979.

Jenkins, Simon. *The Market for Glory*, 1986.

Jones, Aled. "The British Press 1919–45" (in the *Encyclopaedia of British Journalism*, Griffiths, 1992).

Jones, Kennedy. *Fleet Street and Downing Street*, 1919.

Journalism Studies Review, June 1977, "How the Tabloid was Born".

King, Cecil. *The Future of the Press*, 1967.

King, Cecil. *Strictly Personal*, 1969.

King, Cecil. *With Malice Towards None*, 1970.

King, Cecil. *The Cecil King Diary 1965–1970*, 1972.

King, Cecil. *Without Fear or Favour*, 1973.

Koss, Stephen. *The Rise and Fall of the Political Press in Britain*, 1984.

Lamb, Larry. *Sunrise*, 1989.

Lansbury, G, *The Miracle of Fleet Street*, 1925.

Lee, Alan, J. *Origins of the Popular Press 1855–1914*, 1976.

Leigh, David. *The Wilson Plot: How the Spycatchers and Their American Allies Tried to Overthrow the British Government*, 1988.

Linton, David. *The Twentieth Century Press in Britain: An annotated bibliography*, 1992.

Manvell, Roger. *This Age of Communication*, 1955.

Maloney, M and Hall, W. *Flash! Splash! Crash! All At Sea with Cap'n Bob: My Astonishing Adventures with Robert Maxwell*, 1996.

Montgomery Hyde, H. *Privacy and the Press*, 1947.

Morgan, Janet (ed). *The Backbench Diaries of Richard Crossman*, 1981.

Morrison, Stanley. *The English Newspaper*, 1932.

Mosley, Nicholas. *Rules of the Game*, 1982.

Mosley, Oswald. *My Life*, 1968.

Neil, Andrew. *Full Disclosure*, 1997.

Northcliffe, Viscount Alfred. *My Journey Around the World*, 1923.

Oborne, Peter. *Alastair Campbell – New Labour and the Rise of the Media Class*, 1999.

Orwell, George. "The Art of Donald McGill" in *Collected Essays, Journalism and Letters*, 1968.

Penrose, Barrie and Courtiour, Roger. *The Pencourt File*, 1978.

Pilger, John. *Heroes*, 1993.

Porter, Henry. *Lies, Damned Lies and Some Exclusives*, 1985.

Pound, R and Harmsworth, G. *Northcliffe*, 1959.

Proctor, Ben. *William Randolph Hearst: The Early Years 1863–1910*.

Randall, Mike. *The Funny Side of the Street*, 1988.

Routledge, P. *Mandy: The Unauthorised Biography of Peter Mandelson*, 1999.

Simonis, H. *The Street of Ink*, 1917.

Smith, Anthony (ed). *The British Press Since the War*, 1974.

Snoddy, Raymond. *The Good, The Bad and the Unacceptable*, 1993.

Sparks, C & Tulloch, J (eds). *Tabloid Tales*, 1992.

Stott, Richard. *Dogs and Lamposts*, 1998.

Symon, James. *The Press and Its Story*, 1914.

Taylor, Sally. *Shock! Horror!: The Tabloids in Action*, 1991.

Taylor, Sally. *The Reluctant Press Lord*, 1999.

Thompson, P and Delano, A. *Maxwell: A Portrait of Power*, 1988.

Thurlow, Richard. *Fascism in Britain, 1918–1985*, 1987.

Tunstall, Jeremy. *Newspaper Power: The New National Press in Britain*, 1996.

Watkins, A. *A Short Walk Down Fleet Street*, 1990.

Waterhouse, Keith. *Streets Ahead: Life After the City Lights*, 1995.
Whitcomb, Noel. *A Particular Kind of Fool*, 1990.
Williams, Francis. *Dangerous Estate*, 1957.
Wilson, Peter. *The Man They Couldn't Gag*, 1977.
Wintour, Charles. *Pressures on the Press*, 1972.

INDEX